So—
You Want to Be
an Innkeeper

The Definitive Guide to Operating
a Successful Bed-and-Breakfast
or Country Inn

THIRD EDITION

Mary E. Davies
Pat Hardy
Jo Ann M. Bell
Susan Brown

Illustrations by Sally Mara Sturman

CHRONICLE BOOKS

SAN FRANCISCO

So~You Want to Be an Innkeeper

To Be an Innkeeper

THE DEFINITIVE GUIDE
TO OPERATING A SUCCESSFUL
BED-AND-BREAKFAST
OR COUNTRY INN

Mary E. Davies

Pat Hardy

Jo Ann M. Bell

Susan Brown

REVISED AND EXPANDED THIRD EDITION

Library of Congress Cataloging-in-Publication Data:
    So—you want to be an innkeeper / Mary E. Davies . . . [et al.];
    illustrations by Sally Mara Sturman ; assisted by Sharyl Duskin. —
    3rd ed.
          p.   cm.
    Includes bibliographical references and index.
    ISBN 0-8118-1226-X (pbk.)
    1. Hotel management.   2. Bed and breakfast accommodations—Management.
    I. Davies, Mary E.
TX911.3.M27S624   1996
647.94'068—dc20   95-37028
                                                                                  CIP

Printed in the United States of America.

Distributed in Canada by Raincoast Books
9050 Shaughnessy Street
Vancouver, B.C. V6P 6E5

10 9 8 7 6 5

Chronicle Books LLC
85 Second Street
San Francisco, CA 94105

www.chroniclebooks.com

ACKNOWLEDGMENTS

Mary: thanks to the gang at Ten Inverness Way for holding the fort while I wrote; the other innkeepers who teach me so much when I'm a guest at their inns; my own guests, who are so quick to enjoy every little thing we do for them; and my husband, Jon Langdon, who actually believes I'm the best innkeeper in the world.

Pat and Jo Ann: thanks to the thousands of innkeepers who have shared their dreams, their fears, and their realities—those individuals who, every day, fulfill the fantasies of millions of guests staying at bed-and-breakfast and country inns; the past guests and staff of the Glenborough Inn, who for nine years taught us lifelong lessons about ourselves; and the subscribers to innkeeping *newsletter and members of the Professional Association of Innkeepers International, who remind us daily what it's like to run an inn.*

Susan: thanks to the marvelous innkeepers who kept the Bath Street Inn going while I was writing; the workshop participants who kept asking for things I didn't have on paper, forcing me to write everything down; and the guests, who, every time I think I have them categorized, surprise me and show me a different reason for being an innkeeper.

And we all thank one another for a wonderful collaboration.

CONTENTS

Acknowledgments .... *iii*

The Spirit of Innkeeping .... *vi*

A CLOSER LOOK *1*

What Is an Inn? *3*

State of the Art *5*

Who Makes a Good Innkeeper? *12*

GETTING YOUR ACT TOGETHER *23*

Preparing for Innkeeping *25*

Getting What You Need *27*

Researching Your Market and Site Selection *29*

Evaluating Your Selection *31*

Zoning *37*

For Better, For Worse: Choosing a Legal Structure *42*

Playing Politics: Who Wants What? *50*

Butcher, Baker, Candlestick Maker: Selecting Your Support People *58*

GO OR NO GO? FINANCIAL PLANNING *63*

Your Business Plan *65*

Evaluating the Opportunities *71*

Other Financial Reports for Your Inn *88*

Getting the Money *90*

LET'S MAKE A DEAL: BUYING OR LEASING AN EXISTING INN *95*

Buying an Existing Inn *97*

Leasing an Inn *110*

GETTING INN SHAPE *115*

Ambience *117*

"Green" Rooms *119*

Renovating *122*

Accommodating the Disabled *137*

Fireplaces *141*

Choosing a Computer for Your Inn *143*

Telephone Logistics *146*

Kitchen Organization *150*

Breakfast Ideas *152*

Room Planning *160*

Laundry *161*
Shopping: Making the List, Checking It Twice *162*
Something Old, Something New: A Compendium of Decorating Ideas *164*
Amenities *171*
Sources and Suppliers *175*

SO — YOU WANT TO SERVE DINNER *177*
Types of Meal Service *180*
Personal Preparation *182*
Is Your Building Ready? *182*
Who Will Do the Extra Work? *185*
Staffing Techniques *186*
Hiring a Chef *188*
Budgeting *192*
Fine Dinner Service: *Mise en Place* *195*

MARKETING: YOU GOTTA HAVE A GIMMICK *199*
Establishing an Image *201*
Selecting a Name *202*
Designing a Logo *205*
Producing a Brochure *207*
Ongoing Marketing *216*

UP AND RUNNING *237*
Professionalism *239*
Guest-Friendly Policies and Procedures *241*
Handling Reservations *248*
Staffing *255*
The IRS and You *269*
Insurance *273*
Setting Rates *282*
Where Has All the Money Gone? Cash Flow Management *285*
The Inn Group: Innkeeper Associations *286*
Taking Care of Yourself *288*

Appendices *295*
Resources *305*
Index *310*

The Spirit of Innkeeping

We four each had different reasons for becoming innkeepers. What we left behind, what we found, and what we made of it tell the story of what innkeeping is about. For every innkeeper, the story is different. And that, in a way, is the point.

Susan Brown spent ten years as a personnel–employee relations executive, three of those years with a *Fortune 500* company for which she crisscrossed the country almost weekly. Susan snapped on the day she couldn't get the manager of the Skokie Hilton to recognize her as anything other than "Room 212."

"I'd been assigned to the room in error," Susan says. "I'd ask for the room change, and he'd say, 'You're Room 212.' I'd say, 'No, I'm Susan Brown, and I'd like a different room.' When I started yelling and stamping my foot in the lobby, I realized I'd had it. I took the 'red-eye' home to Los Angeles, sold my house, and quit my job. Hello, Bath Street Inn!

"I didn't even talk to other innkeepers about how to proceed," Susan says. "I knew what I wanted to create, because I was doing it for myself, almost in direct opposition to what I had experienced in the previous several years. For me, creating the inn was stage-managing my own fantasy."

For Pat Hardy, too, her inn represented what she wants most when she travels. "I want quiet," she says, "and a chance to choose whether to be alone or with other guests. The Glenborough Inn is equally comfortable whether you prefer to curl up in a guest room and read or come to the parlor and visit."

Pat's parents owned their own business for thirty-five years, and Pat started and operated her own employment business at age seventeen. She has been a full-time mom and wife, a Girl Scout leader, a camp director and counselor trainer, and both development officer and fill-in cook for a private school. During her four years as executive director of a nonprofit agency, Pat took it from employing two and a half employees to twenty-five, from an annual budget of $25,000 to $225,000, and from a single-community program to a countywide one. "I wanted to put the skills honed there to work in a business of my own," Pat says. "I also wanted work that would allow me to be around when my daughter Colleen, now age eighteen, got home from school. The inn met both these needs. It was also great for Colleen. Because of her experience as an assistant innkeeper, handling almost every part of the business, her confidence in the workplace brings her kudos wherever else she works."

Having developed their own inn, Pat and partner Jo Ann Bell, along with Susan and other members of the Innkeepers Guild of Santa Barbara, developed workshops to share their knowledge and experience with prospective innkeepers. People of all ages, sizes, incomes, and education levels come to the innkeeping workshops with high hopes.

"It's exciting that this entrepreneurial opportunity exists in the United States," Jo Ann says. "You don't need half a million dollars, a franchise, and somebody else's rules and concepts to make your own business. I didn't like corporate life, to put it mildly. I didn't like wearing dark suits and high heels. Santa Barbara, our home, was wide open with no inns at all. Developing the Glenborough Inn felt like a wonderful option. Which is not to say that I wasn't terrified I'd use all the money I'd ever had on an inn—and nobody would come." The proverbial farmer's daughter from upstate New York, Jo Ann might have been worried about the money, but she was fearless when it came to the work. Until the day they sold the Glenborough, whenever a faucet needed repair, Jo Ann just gathered up her tools and did the job.

Both Jo Ann and Pat are also active directors and fund-raisers for nonprofit agencies in their community, and feel strongly about the importance of this work for its own sake, as a matter of personal responsibility and as an opportunity for balance in their lives.

Mary Davies enjoyed some of the most exciting and satisfying work of her life before she decided to move to the California coast. "I was deputy director of the Employment Development Department of the State of California, doing their lobbying in Sacramento and Washington, D.C., and directing a staff of analysts. Matching that job, for challenge, support, and fun, would be impossible. But it ended, and in Inverness, with one grocery, a service station, a post office, and miles of beaches, the opportunities for corporate success weren't overwhelming, in any case.

"In 1979 my friend Stephen Kimball and I were working with our local realtor to find investment property. The realtor told us about a house and suggested we make it an inn. Stephen said he didn't have time to run an inn. Did I? Hey, I was Betty Crocker Homemaker of Tomorrow in high school—no problem! Ten Inverness Way was a dream come true before we had time to dream it!"

Eventually, reality set in. In mid-1982, Mary was discarding in disgust an unsolicited publication with a name like *Fast-Food News*, wishing there was a publication that addressed her needs as an innkeeper, when she decided to write one herself. Her monthly newsletter, *innkeeping*, has since become the basic tool for professional innkeepers across the country. In 1985, Mary had to make a choice between full-time innkeeping and full-time publishing. The inn won out and she bought out her partner. And the newsletter? She sold *innkeeping* to Pat Hardy and Jo Ann Bell!

How has innkeeping met our needs and expectations? Susan likes seeing results. "Most of us came from a business world where so much is nonproductive," she says. "As an innkeeper, everything you do counts. For the first year or two, you get direct, immediate feedback on almost everything. What *must* be done somehow *gets* done. You do it." As an executive, Susan unwound by wallpapering, slipcovering, and painting. Today, these things are "work." She also puts her background in business administration and psychology to work at conferences and training sessions at the Bath Street Inn, as well as during everyday guest encounters. "I'm immensely curious about people, and whatever else guests may experience at our inn, they definitely get treated as whole individuals," Susan says.

After eight and a half good years of innkeeping, Pat and Jo Ann launched the first inclusive association focused on the innkeeper, the Professional Association of

Innkeepers International (PAII). Shortly thereafter, they sold the Glenborough Inn. Now they have the chance to share their own and others' expertise, and to speak up for inns on an international level.

Jo Ann's delight has been the chance to utilize her training as a licensed social worker and her experience with community organizations to help innkeeper associations develop and grow. She also speaks "computer" to anyone who will listen. Pat's phone conversations with PAII members—innkeepers and aspiring innkeepers—are the highlights of her days, as she provides some new idea or resource to callers who can find answers nowhere else.

Pat and Jo Ann continue to run the world's largest professional association serving innkeepers of bed-and-breakfasts and country inns, speaking to groups around North America and, increasingly, other parts of the world. "We have a whole new view of who innkeepers are now. What we have learned about the different approaches each individual or couple takes to operating *their* businesses has been eye-opening. We were innkeepers who had to make the business work in order to eat. Many innkeepers have this as a second job in the household. Some have a retirement or investment income and have a limit on how much they want this B&B 'job' to intrude on their lives."

People often ask Pat and Jo Ann why they are not innkeepers anymore. "We could not run the inn and take on the intensity of a growing association and still do both well." But another reason came along. "While we were innkeepers we really enjoyed that, but this is another phase in our lives. We believed, as many others did, that we would own an inn forever. What we found was that, not unlike being a mother whose children are grown, that other period of life was a good one—and so is this one now."

For Mary, Ten Inverness Way is a chance to share what is important to her. "I'm always saying Ten Inverness Way is an inn for hikers—we're right on the edge of the Point Reyes National Seashore—and for readers, especially those who think inns were invented for curling up in front of a fire with a book after a walk in the rain. I love breakfast, so at our inn, breakfast is serious—Mom's home cooking. To me, the worst thing at an inn is an innkeeper who talks too much. We often fall into wonderful conversations here, but I recognize that my guests haven't trekked out here just to spend their wedding anniversary with me. I love the fact that I can make the inn be just the way I want it."

Naturally, we all make adjustments. As Pat says, you can set your own hours, just so long as it's twenty a day. Mary never did get to serve a breakfast of warm, homemade fruit pies in bowls with cream; too many people said it just wouldn't fly. For Susan, the adjustment was facing up to the reality that "wherever you go, there you are"—with both faults and assets. "I escaped the corporate world with all its nonproductive cover-yourself activities," she says, "to create my own corporation and a partnership, which requires compliance with many government regulations—hence, nonproductive work. I was a workaholic in the corporate world; I still am."

But we're our own bosses, much of our work we do for fun, and we're building something for the future. That's the spirit of innkeeping.

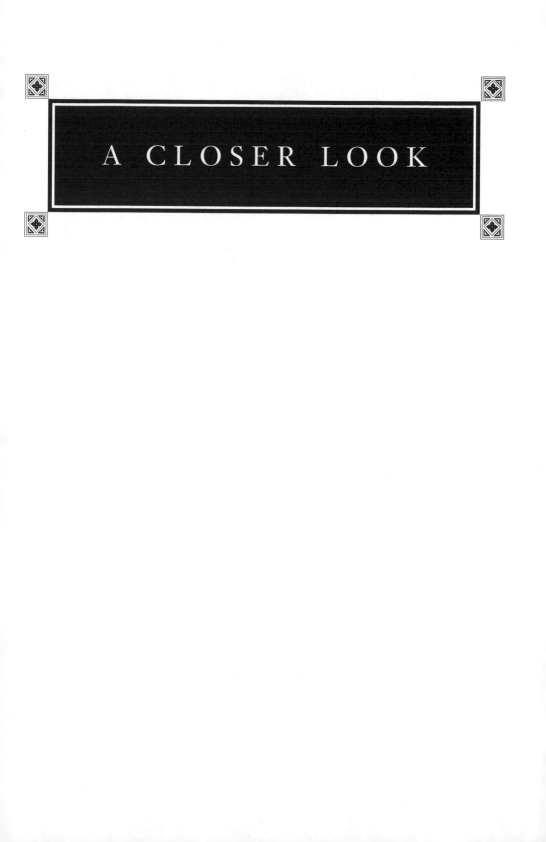

A CLOSER LOOK

✸ WHAT IS AN INN?

*C*ountry inns, bed-and-breakfasts, guest houses — it's getting down-right complicated to choose an escape to a simpler era. And with Nevada casinos advertising "bed, breakfast, and blackjack" on freeway billboards, somebody has to get serious about saying what's what. Travelers are often unclear on the concepts, and good innkeepers do a lot of listening to make sure prospective guests are booking reservations at a place that corresponds with the image in their heads. As a prospective innkeeper, you need a particularly clear vision of the nature of your future business.

The inn boom in the United States began in the late 1970s, but even now, staying at inns is an exciting new way to travel in many parts of the country. The origins of these hostelries are historic, based on the traditions of New England and Europe. Country inns, indigenous to New England, provided food and lodging to travelers and locals and were often a focal point for a community. George Washington slept there. Bed-and-breakfasts in Great Britain and tourist homes and guest houses in the United States were historically the projects of widows or wives who supplemented the family income by renting out spare rooms.

Accommodations in the United States today include both country inns and home-style bed-and-breakfasts, as well as that unique American invention, the bed-and-breakfast inn. At the same time, hotels have responded to the traveler's love for the individuality and personal attention of inns by creating concierge floors and entire properties that, although large, seek to imitate the inn experience. What exactly are the distinctions between these properties? The Professional Association of Innkeepers International uses the following definitions.

HOMESTAY OR HOST HOME   This is an owner-occupied private home where the business of accommodating a few paying guests in one to three rooms is secondary to the use of the home as a private residence. The hosts are primarily interested in meeting new people and making some additional money while continuing their present employment or retirement. Breakfast is the only meal served. Since these homes are usually located in residential areas, zoning or other government restrictions may prevent the use of signs and public advertising. These homes are often members of a reservation service organization (RSO) that inspects them, but are otherwise rarely required to be licensed or inspected by local governmental agencies.

In some cases, RSOs will book unhosted apartments or, increasingly, cottages, where a self-serve breakfast is left in the refrigerator.

BED-AND-BREAKFAST OR B&B   Once a single-family dwelling, this owner-occupied establishment with four or five guest rooms is both home and lodging. The B&B is located in a legal zone and meets all the appropriate tax, fire, building, and health requirements. The owners advertise, and may legally post a sign. Like the homestay or host home, because of its size, the profits from a B&B usually cannot support a family unit, so it is often one partner's job while the other works outside. Sometimes the property is purchased specifically to be a B&B, but many are converted family homes. Reservations may be made directly with the property.

BED-AND-BREAKFAST INN   These are generally small, owner-operated businesses providing the primary financial support of the owner, who usually lives there. The building's primary use is for business. Inns advertise, have business licenses, produce their own brochures, comply with government ordinances, pay all appropriate taxes, and post signs. Breakfast is the only meal served, to overnight guests only. The inn may host events such as weddings and small business meetings. Room numbers range from four to twenty or even, rarely but increasingly, as many as thirty. Reservations may be made directly with the property. Obviously, the distinction between a B&B and a bed-and-breakfast inn is elusive. In short, the B&B is as much home as business; the inn is primarily business.

Definitions: Chuck Ramsey and Tim Wilk, partner-owners of the Gray Goose Inn in Chester, Indiana, started out by opening two rooms to guests in the home they had owned for six years. When they were ready to expand their homestay, they discovered that the city would only grant temporary permission: if they decided to sell, the permit would not be transferable. So they found another property in a commercial area and opened a five-room B&B. For nine years they both continued to work part-time at a steel mill until they attended a PAII conference, where they were inspired to add a meeting room, private baths, Jacuzzis, and fireplaces, and to become full-time innkeepers. With eight well-equipped rooms today, their successful bed-and-breakfast inn serves business travelers who work with two steel companies in the area.

COUNTRY INN   This type of inn is a business offering overnight lodging and meals, where the owner is actively involved in daily operations, often living on-site. These establishments are, in fact, bed-and-breakfast inns with from six to thirty rooms that serve at least one meal in addition to breakfast and operate as restaurants as well as lodging. Modified American Plan (MAP) country inns serve dinner to overnight guests only, and the cost of dinner and breakfast is generally included in the room rate. A country inn with a full-service restaurant serves meals to the general public. Some lodges and dude ranches fall into this category, as do some city properties. To be a country inn, an establishment doesn't have to be in the country.

Note: Cottages are also found as adjuncts to bed-and-breakfast and country inns, located on inn property or at an independent location.

To understand bed-and-breakfast and country inns in the context of other properties with which they are confused, consider also the boutique inn or small luxury hotel. These properties are expensive and elaborately decorated, emphasizing hotel services with a personal touch from employees. The size ranges from fifteen to fifty or even one hundred rooms. The owner may be involved in daily operations, but generally a manager is responsible to a corporation. Meal service is usually breakfast only, but in some instances high-quality dinner and/or lunch service and room service are also available on the premises.

BED-AND-BREAKFAST HOTEL   And finally, the bed-and-breakfast hotel is a thirty-plus-room historic hotel offering breakfast. Only the historic structure, and perhaps some decorating components and the included breakfast, provide the B&B feel.

STATE OF THE ART

The entrepreneurial spirit is burgeoning in the United States, and bed-and-breakfast and country inns are among the brightest blossoms. People are reevaluating their goals, values, and lifestyles, and opening their own businesses in a reach for freedom and a greater sense of control over their destinies.

As author John Naisbett predicted so accurately in *Megatrends*, people are returning to smaller businesses, face-to-face contact, and a sense of connectedness, and moving away from anonymity and isolation. In many ways, prospective innkeepers are seeking, as are inn guests, a way out of the plastic, sterile, mass-market hotel environment into something personal and welcoming.

Innkeeping is a dream business that many today are choosing to make a reality. It's an entrepreneurial opportunity people can tackle . . . and make a success.

What constitutes success in the inn business today? Guests often ask innkeepers how they can possibly make a living. The answer, of course, depends entirely on how you define "living." A surprisingly high number of innkeepers say that if they can afford the travel, the antiques, the books, or the wines they want, they feel successful. Part of the reason financial success is so ambiguous is that inns must have live-in innkeepers, most of whom are owners. As a result, the business often provides shelter, food, and sometimes even clothing, if the inn's image requires you to look more or less like George and Martha Washington. All you need — and often all you get — is an allowance.

Beyond the concrete indicators, like an ability to pay the bills, success also means that innkeeping works for you. It's a lifestyle as much as a business.

Country Inn: *"Peter threatened me with opening a restaurant for twenty-five years," Marged Higginson of the Under Mountain Inn in Salisbury, Connecticut, tells her guests. "I finally said, if we're going to be married to a business, I want to live in it." They researched their decision for a year, traveling to country inns, looking at ways to mesh the food service with the lodging, and taking a course from inn consultant Bill Oates. Bill helped them find a neglected seven-room inn owned by an older couple in poor health, and they turned it into a respected, comfortable getaway. They have discovered that, while Peter is regularly featured as an accomplished chef in articles and reviews of the inn, the food is actually considered just an adjunct to the lodging. Since help is hard to find in this area, these ten-year innkeepers have chosen to maintain their country inn at seven rooms, even though they know it would be easier financially with ten. "If the help doesn't show," says Marged, "we know we can clean the inn ourselves and still pleasantly greet and feed the guests."*

URBAN OR RURAL?

Where are inns located? We expect them on Cape Cod and in California's Napa Valley, but inns can also be found today in Hannibal, Missouri, Tallahassee, Florida, and five minutes from Disneyland.

Where does it make sense to locate a new inn?

Small-town or rural bed-and-breakfasts provide an invaluable service to communities where there is either no place at all to stay or no place other than the budget motel. And these B&Bs are making money, often functioning as a focal point for bridge groups, teas, traveling salespeople, and special occasions. Many innkeepers find that they provide the touch of class for a small town.

Urban and suburban inns are coming into their own as a serious option within the bed-and-breakfast and country inn market for business travelers, providing amenities specifically aimed at them: telephones in guest rooms, a television lounge, earlier breakfast hours, and facilities for small meetings. Destination cities like San Francisco attract weekend getaway travelers as well, and vacationers who love inns and like the idea of staying in, for example, one of the characteristic Victorians there.

Marketing Urban Inns

A new marketing organization, Urban Inns, has been formed by a group of Midwest innkeepers in response to the needs of business travelers. To belong, an inn must meet the following requirements:

Pass the third level of inspection by American Bed & Breakfast Association (AB&BA), American Automobile Association (AAA), or Mobil, or be a member of Independent Innkeepers' Association (IIA).
Be located in an urban area, as defined by the individual innkeeper
Be owner-operated, year-round, and the primary business of the owner
Have flexible cancellation policies
Have a fax machine on-site
Accept all major credit cards

Provide:
Unlimited access to staff twenty-four hours a day
In-room television, well-lit writing surface, phone, clock radio, and bath
Ice and twenty-four-hour beverage service
Flexible check-in and checkout
Wake-up call
Full breakfast at flexible hours

The group encourages these additional services: national newspaper available daily, light breakfast option, airport transportation available or can be arranged, tray available for breakfast in the room, light supper available, meal delivery list, iron and board in the room, access to a copier either on-site or nearby, taxi service nearby, exercise facility nearby, information on evening events, restaurant menus, snack foods available on-site, express check-in, modem, word processor or typewriter access, stationery, office supplies on hand, and laundry service.

From an occupancy perspective, one of the best locations for an inn is a destination resort area where people expect inns. New innkeepers often are afraid to consider an area with lots of inns, but the advantages include the opportunity to buy existing inns that are not reaching their full potential because of tired or out-of-touch owners. Areas with high property values usually mean high occupancy, but it's expensive to buy in. Seasonal locations where inns are filled every night from "twig to twig" (the first blooming to the last leaf) provide good opportunities for owners who are willing to work hard for part of the year in exchange for taking several months off to travel. If your financial projections in such a location require you to stay open and struggle during the off-season, you may be taking on more than you'll want to handle.

Locating in an area with no inns may be a great opportunity or a disaster. Maybe you're just the first to tap a rich vein, inn-wise, or maybe it's a ghost town. Keep in mind that there must be attractions or activities for guests at or near the inn. Few people will travel simply to stay in a nice inn if there is no other reason to go to the area.

GUEST EXPECTATIONS INCREASE COMPETITION

Inn guests are sophisticated creatures, and to a great extent innkeepers foster that sophistication. The B&B tradition may have begun in the simple, private homes of Britons who needed a bit of extra income, but in the United States the bed-and-breakfast and country inn guest wants more. Inns compete for guests with furnishings, hot tubs, and Godiva chocolates.

Once optional, private baths are now de rigueur. But if the inn next door puts in a swimming pool, it won't necessarily diminish your business. If you provide high-quality, caring, professional accommodations, if your inn, while retaining its uniqueness, is comparable in quality and services to other establishments in the area, and if your guests appear to depart satisfied and send their friends to you, you've no doubt met and probably exceeded their expectations.

Basically, the inn guest has come to appreciate a different mode of travel, the "inn experience." Once hooked, inn guests consider themselves part of a travel elite, discoverers of a cherished place, a secret unknown to the mainstream. Fostering this feeling is important.

The longer an inn is in business, the more likely the innkeepers will hire staff, take vacations, and even move off the premises. This is important for the innkeepers, but guests often don't like it; they tend to want to see the owner. It's a real challenge to establish an ambience that can be maintained to the satisfaction of the guests without the innkeeper doing the impossible: being everywhere, all the time.

TRENDS

Where is the inn industry going? The answer depends on whom you ask, what you read, and where you look. It's still a new industry in many ways, but one clear thing is the public interest in inns, reflected in their prominent coverage in national media from *Newsweek* and the *Wall Street Journal* to *Vogue*.

But the kind of coverage is changing, reflecting the maturity of the industry. In addition to glowing articles describing dropout New Yorkers who have found happiness at last at their Maine inns, you'll also read stories of disillusionment by travel writers who were disappointed that the famous chef was out the night they stayed at the inn. There's even a national consumer publication that prefers Motel 6 to B&Bs for value, which makes you wonder about their sample of inns!

Perhaps the issue of value results from confusion about the nature of inns. They are no longer just an economy option for travelers. In fact, room prices for some inns are in the luxury range, as are the features provided. If, however, basic value for you includes an in-room television and telephone and lots of space, you may find that you've paid over $100 for an inn that doesn't provide them—but it will have antique furnishings, homemade chocolate chip cookies, and an inviting common room with a warm fire on the hearth. And, of course, it's possible today to pay $250 for a room at an inn that will include every modern comfort as well as the traditional ones.

Innkeepers provide many extras to guests at no extra cost. These may include refrigerator use; sitting room, porch, or patio for social interaction; fresh flowers; puzzles and games; and even bicycles. Inns routinely offer complimentary wine, fruit, candy, cookies, hors d'oeuvres, social hours, or afternoon tea. In fact, large hotels have responded to these typical inn services by providing their own concierge floors with social hours, breakfast, and evening desserts, special greeters who welcome guests at the door, training programs that encourage all staff who see guests to talk with them, all-suite hotels providing elaborate breakfast buffets, and stocked refrigerators.

Do inns take business away from hotels? Probably not, because the total number of inn rooms is small. Although more and more people try inns and

PAII 1994 Amenities Survey

Amenities	Percentage of inns providing
Breakfast Items	
Baked Goods	97%
Cereal	72%
Cheese, Eggs, Meat	88%
Fruit	98%
Juice	99%
Pancakes, Waffles	83%
Regional Dishes	31%
Yogurt	47%
Other: Granola, Grits, etc.	19%
Afternoon Tea	43%
Bicycles	27%
Candy Dish	76%
Cookies	56%
Fax	51%
Flowers	64%
Games	77%
Hors d'oeuvres	19%
Hot and Cold Beverages	80%
Liquor	7%
Notions	43%
Pool	10%
Refrigerator twenty-four hours	82%
Sauna	3%
Social Hour	27%
Take-home Gift	11%
Telephone, Guest Use	97%
Telephone In Room	44%
Television On-Site	57%
Television In Room	52%
Turndown	24%
Wine or Sherry	40%
Whirlpool	22%

then continue to use them, the majority of travelers do not. The number of inngoers continues to increase, with innkeepers now reporting that one-fourth of their guests are first-time "B&Bers." These newcomers to the inn travel population see inns as another option, not the only place where they will stay. While the primary inn traveler is an upper-middle-class couple in search of a memorable experience, inngoers also include former guests who now have children with whom they want to share this experience. Many inns are creating special suites to accommodate these families, while protecting the quiet and privacy of other parents who use inns as an escape from their own children.

Finding the perfect inn is not always simple for inngoers. Travel agents are still rarely used; less than 5 percent of inn reservations come from them. For most inns, the airline reservation systems don't work. Purchased inn guidebooks are still a major referral source for inns, along with word of mouth. But traditional mainstream travel guides, including the *AAA TourBook*, *Mobil Travel Guide*, *Official Hotel Guide*, and Fodor's and Frommer's many guidebooks, now actively seek and include bed-and-breakfast and country inns.

Inns and bed-and-breakfasts are here to stay. The traveler, travel industry, researchers, and writers may all define them somewhat differently, but the confusion is understandable when you look at the variety of lodging opportunities the industry provides. More important than the definition is the guest experience. Inngoers can, and do, enjoy the log cabin located at a dairy farm where you can cross-country ski and milk a cow, the upscale Victorian with a true English tea and candlelight breakfasts, the family home redecorated and made guest-friendly, and the traditional country inn where dinner is prepared by a superbly trained chef.

When asked why they choose inns, travelers say the inns are located where they want to go, and they can get to know the area while sharing good food with friendly people. Travelers choose inns because they are looking for a special getaway rather than just a bed for the night.

Bed-and-breakfast travel is steadily growing, but the exponential growth of the industry happened in the 1980s. Most areas of the country still see new inns opening, but the inn business has finally reached a level of maturity where inns change hands. Like other small businesses, approximately 30 percent of inns are on the market at any one time. Aspiring innkeepers now tend to buy existing inns, where they may add rooms, upgrade, and add services.

The longer you own an inn, the greater its chance of success. As the mortgage payment decreases in relation to the room rate, longtime innkeepers find they can go on vacations, hire staff, and send their children to college. Smaller seasonal properties have a tough time; inns need more rooms to capitalize on short seasons. Yet many innkeepers make the decision to remain small and manageable and take on other interests outside the inn.

Nowhere are there any signs that running inns will become less work. It is a time- and energy-consuming business, but the rewards are many, and customer demand is still growing. Innkeepers tend to see a bright future for the industry.

SUPPORT SERVICES

A number of innkeeper support industries and service providers also expect a bright future. It is possible today, for example, to buy commercial insurance packages developed exclusively for bed-and-breakfast inns, from brokers who make insuring inns and answering their insurance questions a full-time career.

Two-thirds of the states in the United States and a third of the Canadian provinces now have regional innkeeper associations. The industry also has its own trade newsletter, *innkeeping* (first published in 1982); a national consumer organization and an international trade association for innkeepers based in the United States; a national association in Australia; a glossy magazine for travelers and some two hundred guidebooks published specifically on bed-and-breakfast and country inns; local and state legislation; inn realtors and consultants; an international biennial conference; and hundreds of vendors regularly serving and catering to the small-lodging-property marketplace. Seminars for aspiring innkeepers are widely available in areas where inns are found.

The state of the art? Based on sheer growth, variety, and vigor, the prognosis is excellent.

WHO MAKES A GOOD INNKEEPER?

You like to cook, you're great with people, you start tingling when you're a block away from an antiques shop, and you slipcover all your own furniture. Putting all that to work is part of the reason you want to have an inn. Every one of those skills will come in handy, along with a number of others. To be successful in today's market, it's crucial to delight in helping other people have a good time. In the rest of the travel industry, they call it a service mentality.

Innkeeping is serious business, requiring energy, responsibility, and leadership for success. It's a lifestyle change for anyone. For some, the change fits like a glove; for others, it's like a mitten: warm, toasty—and clumsy.

LIFESTYLE CHANGES

There is a timeless quality to innkeeping. The work never seems to be done, you are plagued by phone interruptions, sporadic eating patterns, late-night arrivals, a water heater that burns out when the inn is full, a travel writer who arrives unannounced when the septic tank is being pumped.

On the other hand, there are opportunities to sit down and enjoy pieces of the day most nine-to-fivers don't have: a late breakfast in the garden on a slow weekday, an early afternoon nap, the bargain matinee, evening wine with interesting guests.

Your whole idea of how to use time is changed. When you have a moment of peace and quiet, should you grab a needed nap or skim the newspaper for a crash course in current events? Time off tends to be in snatches: the concept of a "weekend" grows increasingly foreign; "quitting time" disappears.

Then there's the financial side. No more regular paychecks. Buying a car or a boat becomes a different kind of decision when you depend on the inclinations of the public for your income. Can-we-pay-the-mortgage panic can become a monthly event, along with juggling creditor priorities. In the meantime, you'll be describing to wealthy guests the charms of nearby expensive restaurants.

In some situations you may be able to try those restaurants, with the inn picking up the tab, because making restaurant recommendations is part of the innkeeper's job. (Consult with your accountant on this.) You also need to "shop" the competition to keep up with changes in the inn business, so your business pays for inn visits or you exchange nights with other innkeepers. If you live on the premises—and someone must—the expense of a separate home is eliminated. A warm resident innkeeper is expected by guests. Your presence isn't your gift to the business. The business pays by providing housing and some meals.

All the usual employee benefits can be yours: perhaps health and life insurance; car mileage allowance or repairs and gasoline; car leasing; wages for your children who perform inn tasks. Business expenses like these are not taxable profit. So, instead of a large paycheck, you will more likely receive a small allowance to supplement the essentials of life that the inn provides.

Single Innkeeper

Susan Sinclair, owner of the Maples Inn in Bar Harbor, Maine, was vice president of a large California bank. She truly enjoyed her work there as corporate training manager, but knew she didn't want to do it the rest of her life. "I always loved to have dinner parties for friends and had stayed at so many inns, I just knew innkeeping was for me, especially after an apprenticeship with another innkeeper. I bought my inn in 1991.

"I love being my own boss and not having to consult anyone else for an opinion. With six rooms, I can afford to hire an assistant and a housekeeper during our busy season. The rest of the year is much slower, and I do everything myself.

"Guests often ask how I do it all. Running up and down three flights of stairs every day takes lots of energy, as does making beds and cleaning bathrooms. Innkeeping is very demanding physically. It's also important to be extremely organized and to hire a staff that reflects your personality. Since I can't be here every minute, my staff must be not only well trained but also capable of making decisions in my absence.

"There are some negative aspects to owning an inn by myself. If I wake up feeling unwell, I still have to look after the guests. To run out to the store, I have to rely on an answering machine for short periods in the off-season. But I can't think of any other occupation that could provide more personal fulfillment. Every day I get to hear that something is wonderful—wonderful breakfast, wonderful room, wonderful hike. What other job provides such great feedback?"

IF YOU'RE NEW IN TOWN

It takes almost anybody a year or two to establish a new social base and to make close friends. Meanwhile, you'll be more or less lonely during the years when you'll most need moral support. Complicating this is the intensity of the involvement and the unorthodox hours the inn will demand, making meeting and getting to know people even more difficult than normal.

STATUS

Carol Beazley of the Beazley House in Napa, California, says this query used to drive her crazy: "Is this all you do?" Any businessperson operating out of the home experiences this to some degree, and the British B&B model of renting a spare bedroom is the mental image some guests still have of the bed-and-breakfast inn. Today, however, innkeepers wrestle less and less with the need to prove that they are professionals. Innkeeping is now recognized as a profession with professional seminars and conferences, inn inspections, local government involvement, state and national innkeeper associations linking with others in the tourism industry, and resources like research on typical guest profiles and the inn's impact on a community.

Will You Make a Good Innkeeper?

To test for yourself whether the innkeeping profession is for you, fill out the following inventory as honestly as you can, checking the answer that best reflects your reaction. Have your partners fill it out, too, for themselves and for you. Use it as a tool to evaluate how well you'll succeed as innkeepers, individually and as a team.

How do you feel about people?
____ I like people. I enjoy talking with a variety of people and can get along with just about anybody.
____ I enjoy people in general but don't consider myself primarily a "social animal." I need private time.
____ Generally, I prefer my own company to that of most others.

What was your parents' and/or your own childhood entrepreneurial experience?
____ One or both of my parents or a close relative ran his or her own business, and I helped.
____ I ran my own business before I was eighteen years old.
____ I've been running a business now for five years or more.
____ My parents and/or I have usually worked for someone else.

How persistent are you?
____ I can name five projects I've worked on where I was most tenacious in getting the job done.
____ I stick to things for a while, but when I've had it, that's it. I usually finish what I start, if it goes well.
____ I'm not sure persistence is the answer. If I start something and then discover it doesn't appear possible, I'll give it up. Why beat your brains out?

How well do you face facts?
____ I enjoy the decision-making process of learning from an event and changing my behavior accordingly.

___ I believe that the way I have decided to do things is generally right, and I need to be shown a better way before I change.

___ My experience has taught me that the way I do things is right, and I shouldn't question that.

How well do you minimize your risks?

___ Although I see myself as a risk taker, I always have a backup plan if I fail. I'm open to new ideas but cautiously plan when to stop risking.

___ I have an optimistic streak that leads me to play hunches. Planning usually just slows me down. I can make a budget, but usually I don't plan enough for expenses.

___ I thrive on risk taking. If you listen to the naysayers, you'll never get anywhere.

What is your hands-on quotient?

___ I enjoy learning by doing. I have no difficulty cleaning toilets, repairing things, and doing what needs to be done.

___ I don't mind doing the everyday things, but it's really not valuable for me as a business owner to get involved in room cleaning or doing the books.

___ It is not my plan to do this kind of physical work. My skills will be better utilized elsewhere.

How do you feel about business?

___ I love the challenge of long-range planning, endless daily decisions, and organizing to keep a step ahead of the other guy.

___ I do get bored with the repetitive problems, demands, and struggles of a business.

___ Innkeeping is my escape from business.

Do you have the energy?

___ I have worked in a setting demanding eighteen-hour days, seven days a week, and I thrived on it. I do, however, enjoy time off if I can arrange it.

___ I have worked in a setting demanding eighteen-hour days, seven days a week. I did fine as long as I got regularly scheduled time off.

___ I really need my weekend time to rejuvenate when I work forty to sixty hours a week.

___ I have no interest in working more than forty hours a week.

How do you feel about providing service to others?

___ I'm excited about providing my guests with a wonderful experience and look forward to going out of my way to make that possible.

___ I believe that what we'll have to offer is plenty, and we'll deal as best we can with guest demands.

___ I do not intend to serve anyone. A nice room and breakfast is better than our guests get elsewhere, and I think they'll be pleased with it.

What is your level of acceptance of people?

___ I enjoy giving people of all kinds (including those with different moral standards, religion, lifestyle, politics, race, ethnicity, and so on) a wonderful experience. Everyone has a right to a pleasant time.

___ My basic philosophy is "live and let live," and I can accept people of all kinds.

___ I have some difficulty with people different from myself, and would feel uncomfortable having them in my home.

How do you handle pressure?

___ I perform well under pressure. When time demands seem impossible, I enjoy the challenge.

___ If I have reassurance and assistance from someone else, I do well under pressure.

___ I dislike working under pressure and usually organize my life so that I'm not faced with undue stress.

Your sense of humor?

___ Even when things are not going well, I can always find something to laugh about.

___ I tend to be somewhat serious about life, but try to laugh when things are tough.

___ What's to laugh about? Joking only complicates an already bad situation.

Flexibility?

___ I can move smoothly from one task to another without complete "closure" and not feel bothered.

___ I prefer to complete one task before moving to another.

___ Interruptions drive me crazy.

How do you handle conflict?

___ I can usually find a way to talk to someone with whom I have a conflict without alienating that person.

___ Though I dislike conflict and my stomach gets nervous, I go ahead and sometimes disagree with another person even when it's very difficult; I work hard to find a solution that works for us both.

___ I hit head-on and let the chips fall where they may, even if it makes the other person unhappy.

___ I avoid conflict.

Like marriage and parenting, innkeeping has to be experienced: It can't be adequately described. But if you're willing to attend to the experience of innkeepers who are old hands and evaluate honestly your own feelings about the behavior the job demands, you'll minimize the surprises when you hang out your own sign. Consider the comments below as you review your completed worksheet.

PEOPLE

Successful innkeepers like people. There is no quality more important. The innkeeper's appreciation and enjoyment of every guest is what keeps visitors coming back.

Innkeepers tend to begin with a feeling of "I like people night and day," and gradually become protective of their private and family time and space the longer they're in business.

ENTREPRENEURIAL BACKGROUND

Michael Phillips and Salli Rasberry, authors of *Honest Business*, point out that most people who successfully start and run small businesses either had parents or close relatives with a business, or had significant business experience themselves before the age of eighteen. "The children of taxi drivers, greasy-spoon restaurateurs, and dentists have a very good chance of succeeding in business," they say. "Children of teachers, bureaucrats, and soldiers don't. A child who worked in her father's drugstore selling sodas, or in his mother's bookkeeping office doing ledgers, has a good grasp of how business works and can respond, intuitively, to business advice. All the unspoken, invisible issues of business are subtly communicated to children, and no amount of schooling can fully take the place of that process."

PERSISTENCE

This quality will be important in every area of your life as an innkeeper. As Phillips and Rasberry put it, it's "being willing to keep trying something long after your energy is used up, long after your enthusiasm has waned, and certainly long after other people have lost interest in helping you. The people who can't make it in business are the ones who give up easily or divert their attention from the long, hard parts to do the easier, more glamorous parts." Persistence means facing life with an awareness that change comes slowly and wisdom is gained in the process.

FACING THE FACTS

Innkeepers cannot be shifting with the breeze; it takes too much energy to change your mind and your policies every day of the week. On the other hand, you must be open enough to examine the consequences of your decisions and directions, willing to learn from the evidence, and able to change in response to it. Sometimes the necessary changes will go deep; some dear principle on which you based your inn image may not work.

One innkeeper, for example, had decided that clocks in guest rooms and televisions anywhere were an insult to her historic Victorian. When guests kept asking what time it was, showing up late for breakfast, and searching for the television, she swallowed her pride in her inn's historical accuracy. Now clock radios are at every guest bedside, and a television is available upon request.

MINIMIZING THE RISKS

We all hear stories about the businessperson who takes a gamble and reaps millions; it's enough to make you believe success requires the abandon of a gambler. But studies of successful businesspeople usually reveal not a gambler, but a cautious casino owner who minimizes risks in several ways.

Developing backup plans and alternative solutions is a common strategy of successful people. Innkeepers need to be open to and seek new ideas, but they must plan carefully for their implementation, setting benchmarks for pulling back from risks too great.

HANDS-ON QUOTIENT

Innkeeping requires many and varied skills, from plumbing and cooking to bookkeeping and gardening. Using all these skills is, for many innkeepers, a highlight of the business. Actually doing a task forces you to understand the ins and outs of it. If you've cleaned rooms for a year and then hire staff, you know how long the job should take and you notice the details. You have an advantage over the innkeeper who starts right out with a staff to clean rooms.

On the other hand, having and imposing your firm idea of the "right" way to do things may slow you down on delegating tasks to others and taking hold of new important areas. Your hands-on skill may conflict with your management skill.

BUSINESS ATTITUDE

Prospective innkeepers frequently explain their interest in the career change as a way to escape to a quiet country life, avoid the competitive rat race of business, and get back to the earth. In fact, owning this kind of small business brings a deluge of mundane problems and repetitive tasks such as preparing breakfasts, doing dishes, painting, and repairing. After the first year, some aspects of innkeeping get boring. You'll be tempted to make unnecessary changes for excitement's sake.

Enjoying the challenge of providing a quality stay for every guest is crucial. You must delight in a smooth operation—accurate confirmations, prompt follow-up on mail, regular maintenance. You must thrive on a near-total commitment to the needs of your business. Persisting through the trials and tribulations is easier when you enjoy the business side of innkeeping.

ENERGY

Even people who consider themselves dynamos get winded operating an inn. It's not only the quantity of energy necessary, it's also a restructuring of when it must be expended. Weekends and evenings are no longer time off; weekdays and afternoons more likely are. At the same time, those spare moments when guests don't demand your attention are the times you'll fill with repairs, inventory, advertising, promotion, and taking and confirming reservations. The less your start-up capital, the more you'll do yourself, and the less leisure you'll experience.

SERVICE

The importance of being enthusiastic about ferreting out ways to make guests happy cannot be overemphasized. The truly happy and successful innkeepers revel in delighting their guests with little surprises. Phillips and Rasberry define service as "the conscious act of offering our talents, resources, and support to other people." This is innkeeping, and you can tell how well it's done almost the moment you enter an inn. It doesn't mean you have to become a bellhop or offer room service. It's an attitude that puts a special stay for a guest at the top of the priority list.

ACCEPTING PEOPLE

All kinds of people visit inns, and almost all of them probably offend someone. Unmarried couples, mixed-race couples, gay couples, single women or men traveling alone, older men with younger women and vice versa, the unsociable and the gossips, drinkers, smokers, Jews, Arabs, born-again Christians, Buddhists, bratty kids, macho males. In some areas, such as smoking and drinking, you can set limits at your inn. In others you cannot. Beware of opening an inn if you are uncomfortable with people different from yourself.

PRESSURE

The idyllic image of unhurried, pastoral calm is for the guests, not the innkeepers. There is always some deadline to meet: breakfast at nine, rooms cleaned by two, tea at five.

The greatest pressure is often financial: how to pay too many bills, increase income, renegotiate swing loans or credit lines, make refunds, pay staff, and pay for necessary repairs and a new washing machine. An innkeeper makes a supermom look like a duffer.

SENSE OF HUMOR

Being an innkeeper is fun—and you'll make it fun. The longer you're in business, the less the disasters feel like *your* fault, and the more humorous the problems seem. Laughing at problems removes them from that anxious area in your stomach to a warmer place in the heart.

A healthy sense of humor helps avoid burnout. At the same time, when situations you could once have laughed off start looking serious and like just more bad news, a red light should go on: time for a day off. Make it a habit to ask yourself, "What's funny here?"

FLEXIBILITY

If being in the center of everything happening at once sounds like fun to you, so will innkeeping. If wearing many hats is your style, innkeeping is too. If you can shift gears quickly without stripping them, innkeeping is the career vehicle you've yearned for. And if you can break briefly from a heated argument to book a room with grace, you've got what it takes.

CONFLICT

You will have to handle disagreements with staff and guests, and it's disillusioning. Someday, some couple will take one look at the room they've reserved and ask for their money back. Some staff person will rearrange your carefully planned parlor. Unfortunately, perfection, like beauty, is in the eye of the beholder. Here's where your sense of humor and flexibility receive a good workout.

GETTING YOUR ACT TOGETHER

PREPARING FOR INNKEEPING

*H*ere's the next step in evaluating your innkeeping potential: review the following checklist of skills with comments on how they're likely to be applied in a bed-and-breakfast inn. Some skills you already have, some you've always wanted to learn, and others you wouldn't touch with a tenfoot pole. Give the skills you already have a star, the ones you want to learn a plus, and the others a zero. Your partner should do the same. Then evaluate your combined inventory.

SKILLS CHECKLIST

FINANCIAL

* **Bookkeeping and accounting:** Balancing a checkbook is just the beginning. You'll also need to balance your books—and know when they're balanced. You must understand how to track the deposits you receive and the checks you write and how to set up your books so that they'll yield the information you want and need.

* **Developing and monitoring a budget:** You must know how to predict the future, so you'll know when you can expand your business or hire additional staff. The plan must be reviewed frequently, and changes must be made when the projections aren't panning out.

* **Understanding financial statements:** Good financial statements provide information on the equity you've built up, your return on investment, depreciation, cash flow, and problem areas. They need to be set up so that they'll tell you what you want to know, and you need to know how to read them.

* **Tax benefits and planning:** Understanding the tax structure and what it means in your particular situation is critical. How does your tax bracket affect decisions about whether your spouse should continue present employment for a while? What are the benefits of holding the inn as one spouse's separate property? Are the cash benefits of renovating a historical structure sufficient to offset the expense of it?

MARKETING

In an area like accounting, novices tend to recognize their need for help and gladly pay for it. In the marketing field, however, beginners more often feel they can do it themselves. Be careful; you may need more help than you realize. Getting your inn off to a slow start can be expensive in lost revenues.

* **Graphic design and layout:** You'll want brochures and stationery, and possibly advertisements, postcards, confirmation forms, gift certificates, and so on. The necessary skills range from an eye for design to the ability to create a functional reservation form that only you and your staff will see.

* **Copywriting:** Maybe you'll want to write your own brochure and regular media releases.

* **Promotion methods:** What kinds of things do people do to promote businesses? How will you promote your inn?

* **Telephone skills:** Are you comfortable talking on the phone, and is your voice pleasant and warm? Turning calls for booked Saturday nights into midweek reservations depends a lot on phone skills.

* **Media relations:** How do you get profiled in the kinds of stories about great inns you frequently see in magazines and newspapers and on television?

* **Photography:** Good photographs are a must for courting the media. Sometimes writers send their own photographers, but your good shots enable you to present your inn in the best light. This is especially helpful if there's a tornado in progress when the writer's photographer arrives.

* **Organization of special events:** When hosting your first open house or fund-raisers that benefit a favorite charity and your inn simultaneously, confidence in your ability to carry off a lulu of a party is a real asset.

PROPERTY

You may be a crack decorator, but can you fix a toilet? Read on.

* **Understanding basic building terminology and process:** You will need to work with contractors and subcontractors; you may even end up being an owner-builder.

* **Basic maintenance skills:** From changing a washer to touching up enamel, these skills will save you a lot of money.

* **Landscaping, both planting and design:** Which plants stay alive in your area? What lasts in a bouquet? What landscape design will lure passersby to your door?

* **Decorating:** Do you know how inviting a cool blue-and-white color scheme is in a snowstorm? (Not very.) Can you make a silk purse out of a sow's ear? You'll probably need to.

FOOD SERVICES

* **Menu creation:** Color, temperature, and taste combinations must be more than the sum of the parts.

* **Health department standards:** Also known as Botulism 101. Protecting the public health and safety is your responsibility.

* **Serving food to a group:** There are techniques for getting it all on the table, hot or cold. Do you have them mastered?

* **Kitchen setup and organization:** If you do this wrong, you'll be annoyed by it every time you make a pot of coffee.

STAFF

Innkeepers often start out convinced they will do all the work themselves. Still others believe that because they ran a corporation, they have managerial skills. Supervising a small corps of people involved in physical labor and customer relations is different from having a personnel director and secretary, or just telling your children what to do.

* **Employing others:** Do you understand the basics of hiring, training, supervising, and terminating staff?
* **Motivating and keeping staff:** What motivates housekeepers to keep doing routine jobs perfectly? How do you keep a chef and wait staff happy through a full season, so they won't leave you high and dry two weeks before it's over?
* **Pay:** What are the going rates of pay in this market? The benefit packages?
* **Paperwork:** What forms do you need to complete? What taxes should you pay?

GETTING WHAT YOU NEED

Now that you know the skills you want to acquire, start soon. There are numerous resources available.

PROFESSIONAL RESOURCES

The Professional Association of Innkeepers International has compiled beginning resource and ongoing reference materials on staffing, marketing, and financial matters. Their information and referral service, available to members, can provide assistance on property and food service skills as well.

CLASSES

Check the community college catalogs and adult education flyers for professional organization workshops, lectures, classes, and seminars in your interest areas.

COMPUTER SKILLS

If you don't have any, take a class, hire a consultant, read a book, or ask your kids for help. You'll want to be able to write checks and keep your books electronically, establish a guest database, or computerize inn reservations.

FRIENDS

Some of your friends are undoubtedly pros in areas where you need help. Contact them for advice or even instruction. This can be sticky, since you won't want to take advantage of the friendship to get for free something they make a business of selling; you might consider hiring them as consultants. If you're careful and courteous about how you handle the situation, working with friends can be fun.

CONSULTANTS

If you have a good general grasp of a skill area, but need specific answers to important questions, consider working with a professional consultant. A good consultant can help you design systems you'll live with for a long time. Working with someone on this short-term basis can be a good way to test whether you would work well together for the long term. If your consultant talks slowly and you talk fast, work sessions will be uncomfortable and probably not very productive.

LIBRARIES AND BOOKSTORES

People in many other businesses need much of the same information prospective innkeepers need. Books written especially for the small business can help a great deal. See Resources for specific suggestions.

PRACTICE

Maybe you could do great layouts and write fine media releases with a little practice. Give it a shot, if it interests you. Ask friends to look over your product and give you frank feedback. To check how clearly your effort communicates, ask a friend to review it and then explain to you what it says.

OBSERVATION

Keep your eyes open for the ways others handle tasks and problems with which you'll need to deal. For example, keep a file of inn brochures and advertisements. Observe a wider field, too. How do other businesses promote? What kinds of signs attract attention and still retain a "feel" you like? What can you learn about selling by analyzing television commercials?

VOLUNTEERING

Get some on-the-job experience in budgeting, say, by working with a nonprofit group. Volunteer to organize the Boy Scouts fund-raiser or to do the publicity for the women's center calendar.

WORK EXPERIENCE

While you're planning your inn, you may be able to work at a job that will help you reach your ultimate objective. If you're a retail clerk, maybe you can work in a decorator's shop. If you're a graphic designer, maybe you can take on some design work for a local inn.

APPRENTICESHIP OR INTERNSHIP INNKEEPING

All the research in the world can't fully prepare you for the actual experience of innkeeping. Some workshops arrange for the participants to take over an inn for a weekend, and some innkeepers take interns for varying periods. To be sure your experience serves your needs, consider the following:

✳ Be sure you understand the innkeeper's expectations of your time and tasks. Usually the innkeeper does not expect you to continue to carry on your other life while working at the inn, so, for example, your personal or business telephone calls may be a problem.

✳ Consider the inn's style, so that your experience can mesh with your future plans. If you want to serve dinner, try to find a country inn, rather than a bed-and-breakfast, for a full taste of the extra complications dinner introduces.

✳ Try to get a sense of how the innkeeper functions; does it fit you? Personalities are important in learning. You ought to enjoy your mentor.

✳ If you plan to own your inn with a partner, spouse, or friend, participate in the internship together to get an idea of how each of you functions in this setting.

✳ Appreciate that, even though you may be donating your time, the innkeeper is giving, too. Training is hard work on both sides.

✳ Approach the opportunity with an open and curious mind. Evaluate your experience in relation to your own plans *later*, when you're back home. Of course you have your own plans and your own ways of doing things, and your unique style is important, but an apprenticeship is not the time to exercise it. You're not there to show the innkeeper how to improve, but to try out a lifestyle for yourself.

RESEARCHING YOUR MARKET AND SITE SELECTION

If you've bought the inn concept but not the inn, this section will help you make a good choice. If you've already found the perfect inn or place to create one, this information will help you review its pros and cons, which you'll want to include in your business plan, explained in the chapter on financial planning.

RESEARCHING YOUR MARKET

To understand the milieu in which your inn will function, you need to research the travel field in general, as well as the bed-and-breakfast industry. Use the following questions as a guide.

* What are the trends?
* What is the profile (economic position, family status, interests) of the bed-and-breakfast traveler?
* Why do people travel?
* What is the overall economic health of the travel industry in general and of the bed-and-breakfast business in particular?
* What kinds of competitive influences are there in the travel accommodations market?
* Do people travel to some areas more than to others?
* How do the policies, laws, and codes of state and national governments affect local travel?
* How do people make travel arrangements?

Be creative in finding the answers. Try these avenues.

* Watch for sales trends as you travel. Are travelers being offered unusual services or bargain prices?
* Subscribe to travel magazines and read travel ads. You can get a sense of the health of an industry and a destination by evaluating the desperation of the ads and the number and kinds of special deals.
* Attend industry meetings, seminars, and training sessions.
* Interview industry people as you travel. Ask innkeepers, hotel managers, and travel agents the market questions given here.
* Talk to your librarian. Find out what's new on the shelves.
* Subscribe to hospitality industry publications.

MEETING YOUR PERSONAL NEEDS

Like everyone else, people considering new careers as innkeepers have distinct likes and dislikes about where to live. Many are city-bred and intend to stay that way; for others, heaven is the desert, or the mountains, or the sea. Don't get so excited about a particular property that you ignore these personal parameters. The first criterion for selecting your site is that the environment meets the needs of you, your family, and your innkeeping partners.

Look next at recreational, social, educational, and employment needs. Does one of you intend to continue working while another runs the inn?

This naturally limits your site to areas with desirable employment opportunities. What about schools for your children? You may dream of living in the desert, but if your child is training for Olympic ice-skating events, your options will be severely limited. Whether your favorite pastime is miniature golf or amateur theater, be sure you choose a place where you can pursue it.

You can save time and money by establishing and agreeing on some basic search guidelines with the other members of the new inn family or families. The guidelines could read something like this:

✳ Ten to fifteen miles from the ocean, for cool climate and love of the sea.

✳ A city population of forty thousand to seventy thousand, to satisfy needs for community involvement, good educational system, and cultural events.

✳ Not more than a day's drive to parents and grandparents.

✳ Employment opportunities in the computer field.

Starting from a framework like this—and it can have many more selection criteria—use a map to begin choosing possible locations. You can gather a tremendous amount of information even before you leave home, by contacting the local chambers of commerce, subscribing to area newspapers, and doing library research.

Then the fun begins. Vacation trips become business trips. (Ask your accountant about tax write-offs for these exploratory forays.) Areas you may simply have passed through on the way to somewhere else will become important stopping places. Towns, cities, historical monuments, and scenery suddenly look different.

Not many people can start from scratch to decide where to live. Enjoy it!

Evaluating Your Selection

Now that you've found a place that meets *your* needs, you need to decide whether anyone else would like to spend time there. If not, you won't have any customers.

Who Will Be Your Customers?

The type of customer you attract is an important factor in the image and size of your inn, what the best location is, the room prices, and the amenities offered. So naturally your first task is to discover which type of visitor comes to your area: tourist, traveler, or businessperson. A tourist considers the area as a destination and normally stays at least two or three days. A traveler stops in the area on the way to somewhere else. A businessperson comes on a specific mission, perhaps to sell a product or attend a meeting.

Most major cities attract all three kinds of visitors. Seaside villages attract chiefly tourists. Towns along freeways attract travelers. Different sets of features tend to attract each category of prospective guests, so review the following questions carefully.

Karol Brown and her mother, Nancy, had traveled a great deal and knew what they wanted in an inn by the time they fell in love with the building that is now the Walnut Street Inn in their hometown, Springfield, Missouri. The location seemed ideal. Their historic building is one of two dozen saved in the "heartbeat of the downtown" area. Located right across from the new performing arts center, the inn became the fund-raising hub for the symphony. Located as well in the shadow of several skyscrapers and near a twenty-five-thousand-student campus, the inn is a mecca for business travelers. Karol is the primary innkeeper, with Nancy a staunch partner, supporter, and assistant. Their location also allowed for expansion. Starting with seven rooms, they went to six when they added private baths, and then, using the carriage house and cottage on the property, expanded to fourteen rooms.

TOURISTS

✳ Are you close to a large city? Americans enjoy minivacations three or four times a year. In general they drive no more than three hours each way for a two- or three-day vacation.

✳ Are there enough tourist attractions to encourage people to stay more than a day? Are there good restaurants, historical sites, museums, zoos, gardens, amusement parks, unique shopping areas, cultural events, or beautiful scenery?

✳ Is there a high season, and if so, is it long enough to support the property? If snow sports are the main tourist attraction, are there also visitors in the spring, summer, and fall?

✳ Is there good public transportation into the area, by airplane, bus, or train?

✳ Is your location near a highway or freeway? Are the on- and off-ramps convenient to drivers who hate to lose even ten minutes' driving time? Will your location be visible from the freeway?

✳ Is your area a logical overnight stopping point? Portland, for example, is a good stop between San Francisco and Seattle.

✳ Are there already signs on the freeway encouraging travelers to stop and eat, buy gasoline, or sleep?

BUSINESSPEOPLE

✳ Is there a significant, large industry in the area?

✳ Is your location a state capital or county seat, which attracts government agencies?

✳ Is your location a central shopping area for the surrounding population? Such locations tend to attract salespeople and distributors, who can be regular customers.

In most areas you will deal with some guests from all three groups, but there may be many more from one category than from another. Consider your personal preferences about the type of guest that would be most interesting. If you've spent much of your life in the corporate world, you may prefer to play host to businesspeople—or you may strongly prefer not to! If you're most comfortable with casual encounters, travelers would be best. If you enjoy knowing people on a more intimate, one-to-one level, tourists who stay awhile and return often would be good guests. Your daily life as an innkeeper will be significantly affected by the guests you choose to attract.

RESEARCHING YOUR SPECIFIC LOCATION

This is where you apply your general field research to the specific area you are considering for your inn. This information will help you in big and little decisions about ambience, breakfast, pricing, promotion, amenities, location, specific property, and so on. Don't skip this research step. Questions to ask include the following.

✳ What is the nature of the overnight guest in the area? Consider age, economic status, children, interests and activities, purpose of visit.

✳ What is the occupancy level of nonconference hotels, motels, and inns?

✳ What is special about the inns in the area?

✳ What is lacking in existing inns? How would you make your inn unique?

✳ When is the season? Are there off-season prices?

* Where do guests come from?
* What hostelries have opened and/or have gone out of business in the last two or three years?
* How many inns are there in the area? How long have they been in existence?
* What role does the government or chamber of commerce take in supporting tourism?
* What kind of recreational and cultural activities are there in the area?
* What is the restaurant scene like?
* What new commercial or recreational developments are planned?
* What special events bring travelers to the area?

How to Find Out the Answers: A Resource List

The sources below will have answers to the above questions. The more sources you consult, the broader and more accurate the perspective you'll have on a location.
* Chamber of commerce or visitor bureau. Ask for tourist materials and research materials on the area; have an in-depth discussion with the tourism director.
* Brochures and rate sheets of lodging establishments.
* Local reference librarian.
* Local elected officials.
* Local Service Corps of Retired Executives (SCORE) consultant of the Small Business Administration (SBA).

Other Suggestions
* Stay in local lodgings, especially inns or the most obvious competition.
* Subscribe to a local newspaper. Read the ads to see what the best hotels stress and when they offer specials. Take a business or travel reporter to lunch and talk about the general health of the economy and the prospects for a new inn.
* Talk to experienced innkeepers in adjacent areas. They may be more willing to speak candidly about what works in your area than innkeepers located right there.
* Talk to new and longtime innkeepers in the immediate neighborhood.

EVALUATING EXISTING INNS

How do you determine whether the inns in an area are prosperous? Some innkeepers don't keep good records and won't be able to answer questions concretely; others are naturally hesitant about sharing such information. Here are clues to look for.

* Do they require minimum stays? This often indicates that an establishment is successful enough to be selective.

* Have existing inns expanded? When, how much, and in what way: more rooms, additional services, more baths?

* Are price ranges at the area's inns similar? If they are uniformly high, innkeepers may be prospering; if low, competition may be intense.

* How do special deals and amenities affect prices? Do prices vary based on midweek stays, fireplaces, private baths, bed sizes?

* When did prices last increase?

* Does the inn support the innkeepers financially? Is one partner working outside? Are there other apparent sources of income, such as retirement pensions?

* Is there a supportive innkeeper association in the area?

* What do innkeepers see as trends?

* What kind of media coverage have area inns received?

* What are the impressions of inn staff?

HOW TO TALK TO INNKEEPERS

Most innkeepers are helpful and will be happy to talk with you, but they're also busy, and your questions aren't the only ones they get. To make your time together most productive, plan to book a room and stay at the inn on a weekday or during the off-season, when the innkeeper will not be too busy. Identify yourself as a prospective innkeeper and make an appointment to talk. Offer to pay a consulting fee.

Don't ask directly about occupancy rates. For some innkeepers, this is as touchy as inquiring about their salary level. Other innkeepers will offer the information. If not, ask what a new innkeeper could expect in occupancy for the first year or how long it takes for area inns to become financially successful. Another approach would be to ask what kind of occupancy other inns in the area are experiencing.

Treat the innkeeper as an expert consultant, even if you don't like the inn or the way business is done there. Innkeepers don't owe you time and information just because they've succeeded or just because you've booked a room.

Be willing to share your plans and ideas with innkeepers in the area. Don't be secretive; remember, you're getting a great deal of help from them, and you may want to join the local association.

After you've done the research, sit down and put it all together: the industry, your personal needs, the realities of the area. If people come to your area to hike or ski, capitalize on it; don't proselytize about the joys of fly-fishing. Build on the mood, energy, environment, neighborhood, and facilities that exist. Create a great inn that fits.

INN LOCATION

As bed-and-breakfast inns become increasingly popular, you can more often find an established one for sale. The following location guidelines for buying a building to convert to an inn apply also to buying an existing inn. Even with an established property, it is important to look ahead to when you may wish to expand. Consider these factors.

LOCATION WITHIN THE COMMUNITY
* Close, but not too close, to restaurants, shops, and similar businesses.
* A safe area, with a low crime rate.
* Falls within the service area for police and fire departments, emergency vehicle services, and hospital facilities.
* Convenient to highways.
* Roads and utilities are developed.

THE LOT
* Large enough for off-street parking for guests and owners.
* Room to expand.
* Outdoor living area for guests that includes a variety of amenities, such as a garden, croquet field, barbecue, swimming pool, spa; a separate outdoor area for the innkeepers.
* Acceptable adjoining properties, with privacy, fences, landscaping, sound insulation, animals, children, and air pollution all well considered.

THE BUILDING
* Charm, character, curb appeal, historical significance.
* Structural soundness.
* Resale value.
* Size and number of bedrooms; features of dining room, parlor, and kitchen areas.
* Number of bathrooms or convertible closets.

* Private innkeeper quarters and storage.
* Inn storage areas and laundry facilities.
* Utilities, water, and sewage systems.
* Ventilation, natural light, protection from sun, wind, snow.
* Cost and future availability of energy: gas, electricity, water, solar.

Of course, no one can say you should consider only properties that meet certain very specific standards, like closets for every guest room or certifiable historic status. Your decisions will relate to many other factors, including the type of inn you wish to have, the community you've chosen, and your budget. The guidelines above are designed to help you compare your first-, second-, and third-choice inn locations. Appendix 1 is a sample worksheet on which you can record impressions.

ZONING

By their nature, bed-and-breakfast and country inns feel like home, and naturally tend to appear in areas with a residential character. As a result, as the industry has grown, communities have felt the need to recognize these new lodging options and limit them appropriately.

The Professional Association of Innkeepers International produced a report in late 1993 based on a survey of fifty-two communities, including a review of present regulations, interviews with innkeepers and planners, and a traffic analysis. Of the thirty-four enacted ordinances received, only five were at the state level; most occurred at local county and city levels.

Two recent planning trends indicate greater acceptance of bed-and-breakfast inns. First, planners are seriously researching the state of the industry and developing regulations where none existed before. Increasingly rare are the days when eager innkeepers-to-be appear at town meetings with plans in hand, only to be confronted by a row of blank-faced folks who never heard of a bed-and-breakfast!

Second, existing regulations are being refined and even relaxed, reflecting the maturity of the industry and its successful incorporation into the community. For example, inns are being allowed more resident managers, more rooms, and multiple buildings.

However, the problem with much zoning regulation is that it occurs as a response to one particular prospective B&B owner and a few affected residents, rather than as the result of a look at the industry as a whole and how it will function within a community in five or ten years. So, for example, definitions vary greatly from area to area. Not only are terms like guest house, homestay, lodging and rooming house, inn, and so on used by different jurisdictions to mean the same thing, but also they can be used to mean opposite things! One jurisdiction defines an inn as having fifteen or more guest rooms while another describes a hotel as a lodging facility with twelve or more guest rooms!

A very few jurisdictions include requirements beyond the usual zoning scope: that registration cards be retained for a period of three years; that soap, clean sheets, and towels be provided to guests; and that insurance coverage meet a prescribed standard. Interestingly, not even hotel ordinances include such requirements.

The following findings on how communities regulate inns are presented as a guide while reviewing and responding to your own community's approach.

WHERE DO YOU FIT?

Zoning codes generally allow homestays and small B&Bs in single-family residential zones, and commercial B&Bs, bed-and-breakfast inns, and country inns in multiple-family, commercial, historic, or tourist zones. Communities not specifically identifying B&Bs in the zoning code may allow them as rooming or boarding houses.

Inns that serve meals to the public fall under community restaurant regulations even if you are serving dinner only to your overnight guests. This introduces additional issues such as adequate parking for outside diners or wedding guests and liquor license requirements.

WHAT DO THEY WANT OF YOU?

SIGNS   In communities where existing regulations forbid signs in your neighborhood, some provision needs to be made to reduce the confusion of guests looking for their reserved lodging. Placing the sign *on* the building is sometimes the compromise. In any case, the very nature of the small inn is offended by a large neon sign. Small, discreet signs placed on the front lawn with a tasteful light and single post are the overwhelming pattern. The sign should be in keeping with the inn structure and the neighborhood.

When an inn is located on a major roadway, a sign does help to bring in business, and there will generally be a sign ordinance.

PARKING   Off-street parking is frequently required, though in some neighborhoods this is not possible or necessary. In urban areas, parking is a major issue; in suburban and rural areas, less so. Recent codes require one space per guest room, plus the spaces required for a single-family dwelling.

Adjacent parking or satellite parking is often permitted in communities where parking is at a premium, as is parking shared with businesses that have different peak parking hours, like banks and offices. The parking requirement is often the limiting factor that discourages the inappropriate locating of a B&B.

OWNER RESIDENCE   Zoning regulations often make specifications about who lives on the premises. In single-family zones, the owner-operator is required to live on the premises. In some cases, this can be a part-owner. For bed-and-breakfast inns and country inns located in commercial or multiple-family zones, this requirement is not common, though most states require someone to be on the premises of lodging properties in the evenings, depending on the number of rooms.

LENGTH OF STAY   To assure that guests do not become renters, many zoning codes add regulations limiting the length of stay from seven to fourteen days, for example, or up to fourteen consecutive days in a single thirty-day period.

FOOD SERVICE   Bed-and-breakfast, by definition, automatically includes the service of breakfast. However, some codes add further limitations: a continental breakfast only, for example, or breakfast served only to guests, or no other meal service allowed. Should the innkeepers wish to serve outsiders, they face the possibility of parking problems and the requirements applicable to restaurants.

Problems have occurred when innkeepers expand their business to include weddings, events, or meetings, which cause parking, noise, and traffic congestion problems. This kind of activity is not allowed or is limited in many communities' regulations.

Cooking facilities in guest rooms are generally prohibited and rarely desired, except for in a few bed-and-breakfast inns and country inns with cabins, or urban inns where guests' business stays may be lengthy.

SIZE   Restrictions on the number of rooms allowed is the most common problem aspiring innkeepers face when selecting a location. In general, the more residential the neighborhood, the fewer rooms allowed. You may feel that, with a small B&B, the character of your operation will be clearly residential, but in an area where townspeople prefer that businesses—no matter how small—be in commercial areas and homes in residential areas, changing these rulings by taking on the community and the bureaucracy will waste your valuable money and time. Be sure that you understand the requirements and attitude of the community before you buy. Generally, rural areas do not seem as concerned about this issue.

PERMITS   Some jurisdictions require a special permit to open a B&B. This could be a bed-and-breakfast permit or a conditional-use permit. The latter is designed to permit a particular use in a specified zone, but not simply as a matter of right. It recognizes that while the basic use is compatible with other permitted uses, some aspects of your proposed use could cause problems. Often, conditional use is the only course open to new bed-and-breakfasts in a community; however, be aware that use permits often run with the premises and the owner named on the permit. If ownership changes, the new owner needs a new permit.

MAKING THE CASE FOR INNS

Almost always, despite occasional community concerns before opening day, inns are good neighbors. Experience has shown them to play important and beneficial roles in numerous ways. Don't be shy about pointing this out.

Inns strengthen the economic base of a community by introducing a new type of nonpolluting business, deriving income from otherwise non-income-producing property, and thus strengthening the economic viability of the neighborhood without reducing its residential character. Unlike large corporations that are likely to bring in nonlocal management and labor and use outside suppliers for construction, small inns use local contractors, sub-contractors, architects, attorneys, and accountants as well as local manage-ment, cleaning, and gardening personnel. Though one inn may not hire many employees, a community that encourages inn growth will find that ten inns with ten rooms each will actually hire more staff—and not just manual labor—than a hundred-room hotel. The staff-to-guest ratio in a B&B inn is closer to that of a fine resort than to that of a budget hotel.

Inns also help stabilize a community's tourism industry by increasing the choice of lodging, providing lodging at tourism sites where commercial hotels and motels are out of place, and by relieving any lodging shortage during seasonal high-occupancy periods and major events.

Inn guests are big spenders. At the 1994 PAII conference, Gregg Sallee of the *Yellow Brick Road* newsletter presented a session on "Bed and Breakfast Frequent Guests: A Study in Contrasts," which showed that guests spent $110 per person per night on meals, shopping, admissions, and incidentals. That's a whopping $220 a room per night. This is triple the national average. Thus at forty percent occupancy, one bed-and-breakfast-inn or country-inn guest room brings $63,000 a year to town, not counting the income on the room and the room tax.

Inn guests are also nice folks. They're quiet, and theft is almost unknown. (With residential owner-operators in a neighborhood inn, secu-rity is actually improved as compared to neighborhoods where most residents go off to work each day.) According to industry studies, inn guests are generally married, upper-middle-class, well-educated professionals, managers, or white-collar workers seeking a quiet getaway or comfortable security on a business trip. Once a B&B has opened and the neighborhood is aware of its presence, complaints about guest noise and traffic are extremely rare. Drive-by traffic is very low, compared to other lodging, because most guests at inns make reservations before leaving home. A recent survey of traffic flow for a Washington bed-and-breakfast inn found that traffic is actually less for the rural five-room property than for a family of four using a similar house. The typically low midweek occupancy, the elimination of the owners' commute to work, and the need to organize one's trips away from the business tend to lessen the neighborhood traffic.

Inns revitalize and conserve neighborhoods. They require the kind of large, older dwelling whose original use as a home for one family is obsolete. More than 90 percent of publicly operating B&Bs are in buildings over seventy-five years old. Innkeepers are committed to their communities and personally invested in the health of the town. Not only do B&B owners do spectacular restoration jobs on their properties, but they also often start and actively support other historic preservation efforts in their previously run-down neighborhoods, projects local agencies can rarely afford to tackle. Conversion to a B&B not only offers the opportunity to restore historic structures and provide ongoing maintenance, but it can also bring life back into neighborhoods by attracting overnight guests who will support shops, restaurants, and museums.

Finally, innkeepers are collectors and disseminators of historical information about neighborhoods and whole communities. Old pictures, stories about past generations, and furnishings from other eras are often returned to their original home—now the B&B—and used in guest rooms or as part of the lore of the inn.

YOUR ACTION PLAN

Jim Goff, once director of planning for the city of San Diego, California, and now innkeeper of the nine-room Strawberry Creek Inn Bed and Breakfast in Idyllwild, California, makes these recommendations.

* Recognize that folks who don't comply with laws and regulations cause suspicion of the industry, which can result in more stringent or even prohibitive regulations as violations become apparent.

* Be a good neighbor. Get involved with community and neighborhood councils to gain their support and show them how you can help make the neighborhood more vital.

✳ Don't be confrontational with neighbors and local zoning officials; it can backfire, causing more restrictions and prohibitions. Instead, work closely with local zoning officials in an education program before buying or attempting to start a B&B in a residential neighborhood.

✳ When dealing with legislation or regulation affecting your personal situation, take the long view for the industry as a whole. Guests are interested in all types of inns and should be able to make a choice of lodging, from small homestays to larger inns. The wider the range, the more likely you are to find guests that are happy at your kind of place.

FOR BETTER, FOR WORSE: CHOOSING A LEGAL STRUCTURE

Exploring the question of legal structure is a mental giant step for anyone who has been mostly an employee, especially of a large corporation or organization. These institutions are so complex that most of us don't even think about their legal structures, let alone understand them. But for the entrepreneur, choosing a legal structure is one of the most important decisions.

There is a strong temptation to seal your business agreements with partners or investors with simple handshakes. Don't do it. It rarely makes good sense and can lead to legal, financial, and emotional chaos. The best of friends can and do part ways, leaving in their wake angry words, depleted bank accounts, and ruined businesses. Treat the planning of your business structure with the same care, respect, and professionalism you'll bring to your guests.

Your first step should be getting acquainted with the options. In addition to the information in this chapter, you might also explore the resources of your local library or consult Small Business Administration publications. Then you'll want to evaluate your own personal situation in light of the options and, finally, consult an attorney who specializes in property law. The more you know before you see a lawyer, the briefer your meeting and less expensive your legal fees will be. You'll also want to involve a certified public accountant (CPA).

Legal language and descriptions tend to be too complicated for laypersons to navigate alone. The information that follows has been written for simplicity, so not every possible situation is mentioned and explained. The idea is to get you thinking of things you'll need to discuss with your attorney and potential partners, and to give you some idea of the complexities involved.

There are four principal business structures that can be used for operating an inn: the sole proprietorship, the partnership, the limited liability company (approved in some states), and the corporation. Each has certain general advantages and disadvantages, but each must also be weighed in the light of your specific situation, plans for the future, and personal needs.

THE SOLE PROPRIETORSHIP

The sole proprietorship is, basically, a business owned and operated by one person or a married couple. To establish a sole proprietorship, you need only obtain necessary licenses and hang up your sign. Because it's simple, it's the most widespread form of small-business organization.

ADVANTAGES OF THE SOLE PROPRIETORSHIP
* Little or no governmental approval needed, and usually less expensive to set up than a partnership or corporation.
* Sole ownership of profits.
* Control of the operation and decision making, which makes for greater flexibility.
* Relative freedom from special taxation.

DISADVANTAGES OF THE SOLE PROPRIETORSHIP
* Responsibility for the full amount of business debts, even exceeding your total investment and extending to all your assets, including your house and car.
* A potentially unstable business, which may be crippled or terminated upon your illness or death; more difficulty in selling the business.
* Less available capital, ordinarily, than other business structures.
* Relative difficulty in obtaining loans.
* Viewpoint and experience of management limited to your own instincts.
* Personally liable in the event of accidents or injuries.

THE PARTNERSHIP

The Uniform Partnership Act, adopted by many states, defines a partnership as "an association of two or more persons to carry on as co-owners of a business for profit." Though not specifically required by the act, written articles of partnership are usually drawn up, outlining the contributions of the partners to the business, whether material or managerial, and generally delineating their roles in management and sharing of profits and losses. Partnership agreements typically contain the following articles.

* Name, purpose, domicile.
* Duration of agreement.
* Performance by partners (job descriptions of active partners).
* Kind of partners, whether general, limited, etc.
* Contributions of partners, both up front and later on.
* Business expenses: specifically, how they are handled.
* Authority and rights (who's responsible for what and what rights they have).
* Separate debts (a clarification of individual debts of partners as opposed to partnership debts).
* Method of general record keeping and accounting.
* Division of profits and losses.
* Draws and/or salaries.
* Procedure for dissolution following the death of a partner.
* Release of debts.
* Sale of partnership interests.
* Arbitration.
* Additions, alterations, or modifications of agreement.
* Settlement of disputes.
* Required and prohibited acts.
* Absence and disability.

Partnerships have specified characteristics that distinguish them from other forms of business organizations: limited life span; unlimited liability of at least one partner; co-ownership of assets; mutual agency, in which either partner can act for the business; share in management; and share in partnership profits or losses.

KINDS OF PARTNERS

Partners can be "ostensible" or secret or several variations in between. The kind of partnership arrangement most inns have includes an active partner and a limited partner. To the extent the law allows, limited partners risk only an agreed-upon investment, so long as they do not participate in the management and control of the business. In essence, limited partners are investors without a vote on how you do business.

ADVANTAGES OF THE PARTNERSHIP

* Fewer legal formalities and expenses than for corporations.
* Direct sharing of profits and losses motivates partners.
* More capital and a better range of skills available than in a sole proprietorship.

* More flexibility in the decision-making process than in a corporation.
* Less government control and special taxation than in a corporation.

DISADVANTAGES OF THE PARTNERSHIP
* Less flexibility than in a sole proprietorship.
* Unlimited liability of at least one partner.
* Elimination of any partner dissolves the partnership, though you can create a new one.
* Long-term financing harder to get than for a corporation, but easier than for a proprietorship.
* Inn is bound by the acts of just one partner who acts as the agent.
* Difficulty in buying out a partner, unless that possibility has been specifically arranged for in the written agreement.
* Limits set on losses for "passive" limited partners by the Tax Reform Act of 1986. Consult your CPA.

THE CORPORATION

The corporation is by far the most complex of the three business structures, so only its general characteristics will be discussed here.

As defined by Chief Justice Marshall in 1819, a corporation is "an artificial being, invisible, intangible, and existing only in contemplation of the law." In other words, a corporation is a distinct legal entity, separate from the individual who owns it.

FORMING A CORPORATION
The two corporate structures an inn might select are usually formed by the authority of some state government agency. The procedure is, first, that subscriptions to capital stock must be taken (in other words, investors must buy shares), and then a tentative organization is created. Finally, approval must be obtained from the secretary of state, in the form of a charter for the corporation that states its powers and limitations.

ADVANTAGES OF THE CORPORATION
* Limits a stockholder's liability to a fixed amount, usually the amount of investment.
* Ownership is readily transferable.
* Stability and relative permanence, since it is a legal entity. For example, in case of illness or death of a principal (officer), the corporation goes on.

* Relative ease of securing capital in large amounts and from many investors.

* Acquisition of capital by issuing stocks and long-term bonds.

* Ease of getting financing from lending institutions, since you can take advantage of corporate assets and, often, personal assets of stockholders and principals as guarantors. (Personal guarantees are often required by lenders.)

* Centralized control through owners' delegation of authority to hired managers, who are often also owners.

* The expertise and skill of more than one or two individuals (vs. partnership).

* Less interest on the part of IRS in the division of personal living space and expenses compared with sole proprietorship or partnership.

DISADVANTAGES OF THE CORPORATION

* More legal requirements and limitations than in proprietorships or partnerships.

* Exploitation of minority stockholders.

* Extensive government regulations and burdensome local, state, and federal reports.

* Indirect reward (less incentive) if manager does not share in profits.

* Considerable expense in formation of corporation.

* Numerous and sometimes excessive taxes: the corporation itself is taxed, and profits are taxed again as income to shareholders.

SUBCHAPTER S CORPORATIONS

The shareholders of a corporation may elect to make it a subchapter S corporation. This form is increasingly used by inns for the business, with innkeepers owning the property separately outside the corporation. The property is then leased to the corporation. For tax purposes, this structure is more like a partnership, but shareholders retain the "corporate shield" with respect to liability. Profits and losses pass through to shareholders in direct proportion to ownership; consult your attorney for current details.

THE LIMITED LIABILITY COMPANY

The Limited Liability Company (LLC) is a new hybrid legal structure available in three out of every four states. Think of the LLC as a partnership whose partners enjoy freedom from personal liability, like shareholders of a corporation. It is different from a limited partnership in that this liability protection allows all owners to play an active part in managing the business. Unlike the subchapter S corporation, profit and loss can be allocated differently from ownership interest, making it more attractive to investors. Consult your attorney for details.

APPLYING THE OPTIONS TO YOUR OWN SITUATION

Now that you have some general sense of structural opportunities, these questions should help you narrow your choice. (Note that these questions are framed in terms of "I," but apply as well to couples and partners.)

* Do I want anyone else involved in owning this inn? For many, the inn is home. Owning it with someone else may not feel right.

* Do I have significant assets that will not be part of this venture that I need to protect? If you're putting all your life savings and assets into the inn, you won't have to worry about this. On the other hand, if you or your working partner have other substantial assets, you would be wise to choose a legal structure that offers protection for them.

* Do I want to share the management of the inn with someone else? Many prospective innkeepers have come from large, formal organizations. An important goal for them is being their own boss, with no one to tell them what to do. Even if you are the "boss," having several partners or shareholders will infringe to varying degrees on your freedom to do things your way. On the other hand, some prospective innkeepers feel strong in one area but weak in another, and consider a partner with complementary skills and experience an essential part of the new venture.

* Do I have enough assets and cash to do it alone? The down payment is just the beginning. Do you have enough to pay for remodeling, furnishing, stocking, and staffing the inn until it is open and revenue covers basic expenses? Can you qualify for loans on your own?

* Do I want full responsibility for start-up, day-to-day operations, and management of the inn? Partners and shareholders can provide a wealth of skills, but that may not matter much to you if you prefer to operate alone.

* Will I be a full-time innkeeper, or will innkeeping be secondary to my full-time employment? Naturally, if you plan to keep working outside the inn, someone else will have to cook breakfast and make beds, as well as supervise remodeling, building, decorating, and general start-up. That someone else may work harder for less money if he or she owns a piece of the action.

* Do I need a tax loss, or will the potential tax benefits of the inn be wasted on me? The restoration of older buildings, plus the normal depreci-

ation factors of buildings and furnishings used for income, will usually result in tax losses during the first years of operation. They may be applied against current or future income. The loss can be considerable and very attractive to potential investors.

∗ Will I be selling my personal residence or income property to get cash for the new inn? If you sell a personal residence and want to defer the gain (profit made on the sale) in order to avoid paying a tax, this may affect your choice of legal structure. If you sell income property, there are rigid IRS rulings for tax-free exchange from one type of income property to another. Either of these transactions requires the counsel of a CPA or tax attorney, preferably before you sell existing property.

∗ Is the inn your final goal or a stepping-stone? If your inn project is a way to make money so that you can move on to another career or a work-free retirement, the legal ramifications of the eventual sale of the business will vary according to its structure. Plan now for your particular situation.

In general, as you can see, the major considerations for your legal structure are personal net worth, need for capital, personal lifestyle and skills, and goals and estate plans. These all involve personal decisions for you to make before you see an attorney or CPA who can help you accommodate and implement them wisely.

GETTING DOWN TO CASES

Prospective innkeepers range from housewives and do-it-yourself folks to corporate types who hire their attorneys to check out the options first. The real-life examples that follow illustrate the way different factors interact to affect people's decisions about inn business structure.

THE COUPLE PREPARING FOR RETIREMENT

Mary and Harry Smith wish to sell the family home in Los Angeles and move to a quiet seaside town in northern California to run a small bed-and-breakfast inn. Mary and Harry are in their late fifties, have raised three children, and now have four grandchildren. Harry was in the restaurant business; Mary was a teacher. Their basic assets are their home, Harry's small restaurant, Mary's pension, and $22,000 in cash, stocks, and bonds. Harry knows the ins and outs of running a small business and is a skilled handyman. Mary is looking forward to cooking, running a large household, and entertaining guests.

Using the four general considerations just outlined, let's see if we can determine which legal structure is best for the Smiths.

PERSONAL NET WORTH   Their home, purchased twenty years ago, has appreciated from $40,000 to $175,000, a profit of $135,000. For sellers under fifty-five years of age, this profit would be taxable as capital gains. However, there is a one-time exclusion of gain on personal residences if you are over fifty-five, so Harry and Mary have, as a start, $135,000 tax free. In addition, Harry plans to sell his small restaurant (an income-producing property) for $65,000, which *may* qualify for a tax-free exchange if handled properly. Mary and Harry have roughly $220,000 in cash as seed money for the new venture.

NEED FOR CAPITAL   Assuming they buy a property for $200,000 or less, in reasonably good shape, put 20 percent down ($40,000), and spend no more than $100,000 on remodeling, furnishing, and start-up costs, they could have $80,000 to cover the first several years' negative income flow with no further investment necessary.

PERSONAL LIFESTYLE AND SKILLS   The Smiths believe that together they have the necessary skills to run their own business. Mary and Harry recognize their need to hire competent professional help in bookkeeping, accounting, legal matters, and such. They have a large family and will wish to close the inn during holidays for family visits. They enjoy traveling, so they may not want to run the inn themselves twelve months a year. Outside investors might infringe on these plans.

ESTATE PLANNING AND GOALS   Owning and running the inn is their ultimate goal, so we do not need to consider the long-range effects of selling in several years. The major consideration here appears to be estate planning. Mary and Harry will not need outside investors, will not have extensive outside assets to protect, do have the necessary management skills to go it alone, and want the freedom to run the inn as they please and when they please. Any of the three legal entities would accommodate them, assuming that they would choose a partnership or corporation that would be closely held and family centered. One form, however, may be more advantageous than another from an inheritance standpoint.

THE COLLEAGUES OR FRIENDS

Two young women, Lynn and Yvonne, have worked together for several years in a manufacturing business. They have spent many happy vacations at bed-and-breakfast inns and want to pursue innkeeping as a possible career change. Neither owns a home, but each has saved $25,000. Various wealthy family members have expressed interest in investing in an inn as a tax shelter.

We know immediately that Lynn and Yvonne's personal net worths will not be adequate, and they will need capital. Their capital sources want tax shelters, so their legal structure would probably best be a limited partnership or a subchapter S corporation.

In a limited partnership agreement, the general partners' liability is limited to the amount of their investment, as long as they do not participate in the management and control of the enterprise or in the conduct of the business. The rules are quite rigid, so the limited partners must be willing to let the general partner(s) run the show without interference.

In addition, there must be at least one working partner who has the financial reserves and the willingness to assume unlimited liability for business debts. If all these points can be worked out, the tax shelter advantages of this form of ownership can be very attractive, particularly because the losses can be distributed unevenly. For example, in the first year 90 percent of the losses can go to 10 percent of the investors, as agreed upon in advance.

In a subchapter S corporation, the stockholders have limited liability, usually equal to the amount of their investment, but the tax losses are directly proportional to the percentages of shares owned. For example, if Lynn owns 50 percent of the stock, she will get 50 percent of the tax loss. She may not give it to other stockholders.

Lynn and Yvonne have some basic decisions to make. In addition to capital needs, they may also need a partner or stockholder who knows how to run a small business. It may be that one or both must keep their jobs for a while, for financial reasons.

You can see that it's complicated. Planning and professional help are very important here for the future of the new enterprise. And innkeepers choose all kinds of variations of the options: some lease their inns instead of buying; some form limited partnerships for the first several years, then change to subchapter S corporations; some join with investors to buy and remodel property, then lease it back to a separate legal entity for management purposes.

There are many different ways to approach the structural end of your inn business, but all of them require good counsel and careful decision making.

PLAYING POLITICS: WHO WANTS WHAT?

One of your first jobs in dealing with government is to discover which of the various levels will have a hand in your business, and then to find out what each of these wants of you. The local chamber of commerce or a citizen's service office at city hall or the civic center usually provides materials describing the federal, state, and local rules and regulations that apply.

Here are lists of the basic requirements at various levels. There may be more—the list seems to grow continually—or there may be fewer, depending on the area.

FEDERAL REGULATIONS

IDENTIFICATION NUMBER, IRS FORM SS.4

You'll be required to identify yourself on tax forms and licenses. All employers, partnerships, and corporations must have a federal employer tax identification number. If you are a sole proprietor without employees, you can simply use your own social security number. Whichever number you use, it will go on the payroll tax return forms the IRS automatically mails quarterly and at year-end, which you must complete even if you have no employees.

SELF-EMPLOYMENT TAX

For employees, social security is deducted from paychecks. When you're self-employed, you must pay the government directly. This involves a separate form and is a tax in addition to federal income tax. You may owe no income tax, but still be liable for self-employment tax. When employers and employees share the cost of social security, each pays about half the total. Since no employer will supplement your contribution, it will amount to somewhat more than the half you would have contributed as an employee. Check with your accountant and the local IRS office for details.

STATE REGULATIONS

SALES TAX PERMITS

In states that require sales tax, almost all businesses need to obtain a sales-tax permit from the state. Sales taxes may be collected on the breakfast portion of room charges, gift items, books, and so on. The taxes are collected from guests and remitted to the tax collector, usually on a monthly or quarterly basis. Some local governments also require sales taxes.

STATE EMPLOYER TAX IDENTIFICATION NUMBER

If you have employees, you will need to pay unemployment insurance taxes, which are collected by your state employment service office. You'll be issued a state employer number that you'll need to complete the required quarterly and year-end payroll tax–reporting forms. The forms will be sent to you automatically.

ALCOHOLIC BEVERAGE CONTROL

Most states require you to have a license if you serve alcohol. Even if you give it away, the authorities view it as included in the room rate, and therefore a sale. Some states have special bed-and-breakfast licenses; others have reasonably priced beer and wine licenses. If you serve alcohol, you are also required to pay the United States Bureau of Alcohol, Tobacco, and Firearms (BATF) an annual $250 fee, regardless of whether you are licensed by the state. If you do have a state license, the state will automatically inform the BATF.

CITY AND COUNTY REQUIREMENTS

FICTITIOUS BUSINESS NAME

When a business operates with any name other than the operator's own, the so-called fictitious name must be filed with the county clerk and published in a public newspaper for a required period of time. (Corporations, which are registered with the state, are exempt from this requirement.) There's a small fee for the fictitious business name statement, as well as a small fee to the newspaper for publishing it. This procedure also involves a check against the names of existing businesses in your area to avoid duplication. Name publication also informs the public of your business intentions. Banks require a copy of this statement before opening a business checking account for you.

BUILDING AND ZONING DEPARTMENT

This department, called the building and safety department in some areas, protects the community from haphazard growth and from inferior, unsafe buildings. Its functions are as follows.

✳ Enforces city or county regulations and permitted uses of property in specific areas. Would you want a bar or gas station next to your home?

✳ Approves structures for safety and for compliance with local building codes. Some allowances may be made for historic buildings in areas where meeting codes would endanger the building's historic value.

✳ Approves remodeling plans to meet local setback requirements, height limitations, landscape design requirements, and building codes. This involves initial plan check and sign-off by inspectors at different stages of construction, such as framing, rough electrical, rough plumbing, drywall, finish, and roofing (See also Zoning in "Getting Your Act Together," page 37).

Department of Public Works

A good name for this department would be the street and sidewalks department. It enforces regulations that affect traffic patterns, safety for pedestrians, and flow of bicycles and vehicles. Following are some of their concerns.

✳ Off-street parking. For example, this department may require one space per guest room, plus two for owners. Some jurisdictions require that parking areas be paved, striped, and have bumper guards. A rule of thumb on space requirements is that a car should be able to exit after one back-up motion. In general, diagonal parking is allowed only if the driveway is one-way.

✳ Width of driveway, curb cut (many cities use remodeling as an opportunity to modernize curbs), and condition of sidewalk.

Fire Department

Fire department requirements vary from community to community, but are becoming increasingly stringent.

✳ Exits: Requirements are more rigid for buildings with more than two stories. These may, for example, include two legal exits, steel door jambs, and one-hour fire doors.

✳ Smoke detectors: Some building codes will accept battery-operated detectors, but hard-wired ones attached to a central alarm are becoming a common requirement. Ask where they should be located.

✳ All structures on property must be accessible by fire hose.

✳ Commercial fire extinguishers: Must be located on each floor and in kitchen.

✳ Sprinklers: though not required for many existing inns, these may be required when the building changes hands or if you renovate or build a new structure. By the year 2000, the National Fire Protection Association would like sprinklers to be required in every home. Seriously consider including the new misting sprinklers in your renovation budget.

Planning Commission

This commission approves or disapproves requests for modifications, special-use permits, variances, conditional-use permits, and rezoning. Any of these exceptions to the rule may be applied for if your project does not meet zoning or building codes.

Review Boards

✳ Architectural review: Many communities have standards, color schemes, or themes with which all new projects or exterior remodels must be consistent.

✳ Sign reviews: Height, size, colors, and lighting may be subject to review.

✳ Landmark review: If you would like your inn to be classified as a historic landmark, this review board must approve remodeling plans.

✳ Environmental review: This process requires you to prove that your project will not damage the environment. It can be expensive and involve questions of drainage, air quality, and even visual damage. Find out early if you're subject to it.

BOARD OF HEALTH

This is an inspecting and licensing board charged with protecting the public. License is renewable for an annual fee when standards, which usually relate to the following, are met.

✳ Kitchen and bathrooms: The board considers the general condition and cleanliness of the kitchen, including such features as washable wall and floor surfaces and absence of cracks around cupboards that would allow rodents and bugs to enter. Facilities are needed for either high-heat or chemical sterilization of dishes, including either a commercial dishwasher or three-bin commercial sink with drain boards. Adequate ventilation and exhaust over stove are required. One option may be a commercial convection oven (exhaust self-contained). Stove approval may not be necessary if only continental breakfast service is to be offered. Employee bathroom must be equipped with liquid soap, paper towels, and automatic door closure.

✳ Spas and swimming pools: There are specific requirements for tub and deck materials, grab bars, water-depth markers, and chemicals. Filter, heaters, and other mechanical and electrical equipment must meet commercial-use standards.

✳ Many states require a food handlers permit. This can usually be obtained by attending a special class.

BUSINESS LICENSE

Most cities require a license and fee to do business. The fee is usually annual and is based on projected gross income. This agency may also collect local bed taxes, which are added to room prices.

ASSESSOR'S OFFICE

Local property taxes are based on purchase price and reassessment of improvements. In addition, there may be an annual business tax on furniture and equipment, and some local governments also have a sales tax ordinance separate from the state one.

Good intentions are not enough. The first step toward being a law-abiding business owner is discovering the laws.

"Button, button, who's got the button?" Few things are as frustrating as making the fourth trip to the building and zoning department to retrieve signed preliminary plans and building permits, only to discover that public works hasn't signed off yet on the parking, or the fire department took your plans last week and won't have them back until tomorrow. Meanwhile, your crew is waiting another week to get started.

Aggravating? Yes. Exaggerated? No. Few wheels turn as slowly as those of government, or of any bureaucracy, for that matter. The people and systems that hold the future of your business in their hands have flaws, foibles, and limitations. On the other hand, you may run into individuals and even entire departments that will go out of their way to be helpful and downright expeditious.

Bed-and-breakfasts are still so new that few communities know what to do with them. Existing zoning categories don't seem appropriate, and health regulations don't quite fit. As a result, innkeepers inadvertently create a lot of work and brand-new problems, even for people with a great deal of experience. Some bureaucrats enjoy the challenge, others do not, and the effect individuals have on the process is enormous. No department treats two different innkeepers the same, and no bureaucrat responds, interprets, and implements policy exactly the same as another.

Every business faces this situation, but many of us innkeepers expect a warmer greeting than we get. We think we improve our neighborhoods, encourage tourist dollars, increase tax revenues, and provide unquestionably outstanding quality. Apparently, every new business person feels this way.

Prospective innkeepers also need to be aware of the social and political ramifications of their plans. In many towns, for example, there's a critical shortage of affordable housing. Therefore, when some well-meaning entrepreneur seeks approval to renovate a run-down Victorian presently housing six families, numerous legitimate concerns are raised. Such a situation immediately puts the prospective innkeeper in an adversarial position, at odds with the community and its governing bodies, before plans are even submitted.

You can often avoid this unfortunate position. Spend some time to become familiar with and to understand the needs of the community, especially if you are a newcomer. Newcomers start out on the defensive. People tend to be territorial and protective, and often resent outsiders "coming in and taking over." You need someone on your side who knows the ropes.

Respected architects and contractors representing you with governing agencies can smooth the way simply because they have proven themselves with quality past performances.

In addition, any contacts you may have with longtime residents can be very beneficial. A phone call from such an ally to the mayor or city councilor can smooth the way for permit approvals. In any corporation, school district, or other bureaucracy, some people accomplish their goals with ease. You need these people on your side.

Here are some tips on the positive way to deal with codes, regulations, and inspections:

* Avoid adversarial positions.
* Sit down and talk.
* Get the experts involved to talk with each other.
* Know the regulations yourself, but listen carefully to the ones that most interest your inspector.
* Believe that modifications can happen.
* Expect everything to take time.
* Provide all the information you can, but *only when it's requested.*
* Don't try to get away with things.
* Go to the top, gently, when problems seem insurmountable.

Finally, be there for the inspections; accompany the inspector around the site.

PREVENTIVE MAINTENANCE IN THE POLITICAL REALM

In many areas, bed-and-breakfast inns are operating under little or no legal authority, somewhere in the definitional crack between boarding-houses and hotels. How long this will be allowed to continue is anybody's guess. Even inns that meet all current requirements are constantly subject to political changes that affect them: sprinkler-system requirements, earthquake-safety modifications, handicapped-access ordinances, and off-street-parking proposals, for example.

For political problems, as for forest fires, prevention is the best cure. These problems often occur because somebody is angry with somebody else. On the other hand, they are often avoided because people don't want to cause their friends trouble. You can prevent problems by making friends.

At the most basic level, be a good neighbor. Be alert to problems your inn may cause the residents in the neighborhood and try to solve them. Figure out ways your inn can benefit your community. Hold neighborhood meetings there, initiate a neighborhood crime-watch program, or work together on disaster-preparedness planning. Share some cuttings from your geraniums. Have a coffee klatch. Be a friend.

On the larger community level, be visibly involved in issues of concern in your town or city. Donate accommodations for the public television station fund-raiser auction, hold benefit teas for a local charity, or cook the Shrove Tuesday pancake supper for the parish. Try to position yourself in the best light in the eyes of your community and the media—before you have reason to need public support on a political issue. You'll not only be building goodwill, you may also get some helpful free publicity.

KNOW YOUR OFFICIALS

Make a point of getting to know the people who represent you on the city council, on the county board of supervisors, in the state legislature, maybe even in the United States Congress. And be sure they know who you are. Invite them to an open house. Ask them to speak briefly at an innkeepers association meeting, then follow up their remarks with a question-and-answer session. This will give you a chance to demonstrate your political interest and awareness and to present yourself to political figures—who are always running for office—as part of a constituency to be reckoned with. Do some research before you become directly involved with an elected official, so that you will know the issues of prime interest to him or her. Take a look at where the official's support is weak and try to figure out ways you can benefit him or her by providing some good publicity or by helping polish an image.

Find out your officials' positions on issues likely to affect you: development, economic growth, local control of local issues, historic preservation, and conservation, for example. Get involved in issues they care about, whether they affect you directly or not: If you're available to help your officials on their issues, you're in a good position to ask them for help on your issues.

WHAT ARE THE CANDIDATES' NEEDS?

Every elected official is a candidate all the time. No matter how idealistic and dedicated officials may be, they can't be effective unless they can get elected. Election is the bottom line, and in all your dealings with political people, don't forget it. You need to understand and be able to communicate how your issues can make political mileage.

For example, let's say Councilor Doe is a staunch supporter of preserving coastal access and has been taking a beating as a result: The development community is scaring the voters with stories about economic decline. If you want support in opposing an ordinance that threatens to put your inn out of business, you might approach Doe armed with data on the positive economic impact the inns have had in your area, not only on your own businesses, but also on the local restaurants and merchants. You might suggest organizing a press conference at one of the inns to give Doe a showcase for presenting her version of economic development: using existing buildings to bring in tourism, thus avoiding the additional strain on taxpayers of paying for the new streets and educational and fire-fighting facilities that new construction usually requires.

Never approach a legislator for assistance without having a good case to make on how helping you will help him or her.

SAY THANKS LOUD

When you get help from an official, be noisy about it. Write a letter of thanks and send copies to your local newspapers. If your local chamber of commerce has a newsletter, write an article about the help you got and send copies of it to the legislator's office for constituents to see when they drop in. The help you receive may merit an award. This gives you the chance to stage a media event, presenting your legislator with something like an over-sized key to the inns of your area or a handmade quilted wall hanging naming him or her the *"Inn*sightful Legislator of the Year." Do something that will make clear to the official who helped you out, and to others who might, that helping you pays off. The publicity opportunities here are limitless, for the legislator and for you and your inn.

The political game is complicated, but you neglect it at your own risk. Plan a preventive maintenance strategy now. If you need political solutions to problems, do your homework and get help from the friends you've made. Never, ever forget that all officials are candidates and that you get the most earnest assistance from people who stand to gain from being helpful.

BUTCHER, BAKER, CANDLESTICK MAKER: SELECTING YOUR SUPPORT PEOPLE

There are so many "professionals" in the marketplace today, it is difficult to know *if* you need them, *when* you need them, and *how* to choose them.

Naturally, you'll want to work with people who are competent in their fields. Ask friends and other professionals for recommendations, and consult local business publications. You can begin to evaluate competence on the basis of the professionalism with which initial contacts are handled. Are they on time for appointments? Do they provide reports on the outcome of meetings? Are the documents they prepare clear and attractive? Can you get in touch with them conveniently?

Once you've narrowed your choices, ask your candidates for references from local businesses; then check them out. Before you make your final decision, there's one last aspect to consider, and it's one of the most important.

Take an honest look at how you feel about your candidates. Comfort and trust must characterize your relationship with all the people you hire. Don't allow yourself to feel inferior to them because they know something you don't. Remember, they all work for you; you pay them to provide services to you and your inn. Of course you don't understand the intricacies of accounting; that's exactly why you hire an accountant. Good professionals won't encourage your feelings of inadequacy. They'll work with you, spend enough time with you to meet your needs, and give reasonable answers to your questions, no matter how naive they may sound to them. Choose support people with whose pace you are comfortable. You shouldn't feel like you're racing your engines or struggling to keep up during your meetings.

What are reasonable fees? You can find out by shopping. Ask about prevailing rates in the field. The range can be very wide, and the highest-priced professionals may not necessarily be the best. Make your choice based on the balance of comfort, trust, expertise, and price that feels right to you. If you find you have chosen the wrong person, don't hesitate to end the relationship.

ACCOUNTANT AND BOOKKEEPER

Tales are told of the business owner who hauls three shoe boxes to the accountant every year on April 14. Accountants worth their salt would probably smile politely and hand the boxes right back. Your inn is a business. Whether it's a corporation, a partnership, or a sole proprietorship, well-organized financial records are imperative. The Glenborough Inn's accountant was chosen long before the doors opened, because, as Jo Ann puts it, "we were spending a lot of money, and I had no idea where or how to account for it.

"We started out with a very basic accounting system and chart of accounts. My fantasy was that I could do the bookkeeping, and it turned out to be a real fantasy. Early in our second year of business, our accountant suggested very gently that I might consider the services of a reliable bookkeeper she could recommend. I got the hint: My bookkeeping skills are nil, and the money I had hoped to save by doing my own bookkeeping was being spent to correct my poor efforts."

At most inns, it's unlikely that the innkeeper will be able to avoid every financial task. With the wide availability of simple computer programs for home and small business, many innkeepers are finding they can capably handle bookkeeping tasks like posting to general ledger and reconciling bank statements, leaving more complicated jobs, such as preparing quarterly returns, to the professionals. The financial accounting jobs are often shared like this:

INNKEEPER
* Writes all checks, including payroll.
* Assigns expenses to appropriate ledger categories, e.g., utilities, advertising, and laundry.
* Receives and records income.
* Makes all bank deposits.
* Prepares monthly bed-tax return.
* Reconciles bank statements.

BOOKKEEPER
* Prepares quarterly sales-tax return.
* Prepares quarterly payroll-tax returns.
* Readies all information for business income taxes for the accountant.
* Prepares financial reports, such as profit and loss statements and balance sheets.

CERTIFIED PUBLIC ACCOUNTANT
* Prepares the business income tax return.
* Prepares any other necessary tax-related information.
* Consults with innkeeper or bookkeeper as necessary.

ATTORNEYS

An attorney's skill is invaluable, and the fees reflect it! But buying a few hours' consultation at the right time can help prevent real heartache and grave financial repercussions. Negotiating contracts, deeds, and leases, or choosing the appropriate legal entity for your inn, are examples of areas where you probably need legal advice.

In any case, do your homework before you call. With a little research, you may be able to answer some legal questions yourself. At the very least, you can clarify your problem so that it's easier, faster, and therefore cheaper to resolve. Find out whether your attorney bills for every minute or will answer occasional telephone questions for free. Many attorneys are very cooperative in responding to telephone queries about whether a particular situation genuinely warrants their attention. It's something like calling your doctor to find out if an aspirin will do the job, instead of paying for an office visit to get the same advice.

INSURANCE

Surely one of the most difficult expenditures to make is one that does not apparently pay off at all unless some minor or major catastrophe strikes. If that loss occurs, you will want and need the immediate, caring attention of an efficient, prompt, and fair claims service.

Choosing the right insurance agent, whatever the details of the policy, requires the same kind of analysis you use in choosing other support people. (Getting the right coverage is a complex subject that's dealt with in-depth later in this book; see Insurance in "Up and Running," page 273.)

Insurance is complicated; agents should not only be willing and able to answer your questions about policies, they should also spend time outlining your coverage and clarifying what it will mean in case of a loss.

As your business grows and changes, your policy should, too. Even if nothing else changes, inflation can erode your coverage. Your provider should maintain a regular schedule of contact with you, probably annual, to make necessary updates.

Insurance agents make money on insurance renewals, so keeping you happy is important to them. If you're not pleased with the service you get, take your business elsewhere.

BANKERS

"Know more about your business than anyone else does," a banker will tell you. No matter how large or small your operation, bankers don't like to be told you'll have to check with your accountant when they ask a question. They want to know you're in charge. They'll expect you to understand your cash flow and be able to discuss financial projections intelligently. (And if you've chosen your other support people with care, you'll be prepared for your banker!)

Just like anybody else, bankers lend money in situations where they feel comfortable. So choose your bank and your banker wisely. Find someone interested in small business, and build a relationship based on professionalism. Don't hesitate to ask about special services: a business credit card, a line of credit, payroll services, and so on. The more banking needs you handle through one bank, the more valuable a customer you are. As a result, it can pay to concentrate your banking business instead of giving it in pieces to the least-expensive provider of each banking service.

Is it possible to go it alone? You can operate your business without a bookkeeper, accountant, or attorney, and without real relationships with an insurance agent or banker. But that approach will require a great deal of time and a high degree of skill. Except in a few areas where you are undeniably a pro, you're wisest to put your talents to work choosing terrific support people and using them well.

GO OR NO GO?
FINANCIAL
PLANNING

Which comes first, the chicken or the egg? The inn structure or the business plan? In other words, do you develop a business plan and base your inn search on it, or do you find a promising inn and then develop a business plan?

It's a dilemma. You'll find that material already covered on inn location, image, marketing, and so on will be required for your business plan. At the same time, other financial material, which the plan also requires, will be developed as you move through this section. There is an inevitable moving back and forth.

In addition, until you are ready to compare possible inn properties and make detailed budget projections, this section may be heavy going. It's okay to speed through the first time; you'll be back, and you'll find the detailed explanations and charts extremely useful when you get down to specifics.

One final word of caution: Attorneys and CPAs make full-time careers in matters of finance with good reason because reporting, taxation, and financing questions are complex and continually changing. The information that follows is accurate and current but prepared by innkeepers, not financial professionals. Use it as a guide to issues and an introduction to questions you'll be handling with professional assistance.

YOUR BUSINESS PLAN

At the beginning, getting the inn building in shape seems like the primary hurdle. But just as you wouldn't renovate an inn structure without a full set of plans and cost estimates, you shouldn't move ahead on your business without a comprehensive plan for its construction.

The Small Business Administration indicates that businesses with plans have a far higher success rate. If you've been working your way through this book, you've already developed much of the information for your business plan, in your head, your lists, and your files. Writing the plan will make all those pieces fall into place. It's also a check to see if you've considered everything and whether your plans can be made clear and compelling to others.

In addition, your business plan has other beneficial uses.

* **Financing:** Your plan is crucial in approaching banks, friends, and prospective partners for money. It's your "application."

* **Communication tool:** The plan is an efficient, effective summary of your business concept to share with your attorney, insurance agent, accountant, partners, and directors. They'll understand your ideas for the future better when you present them in such an organized format.

* **Organization medium:** Writing and developing the plan gives you practice in thinking and making decisions based on a business approach, not just a dream.

* **Focus:** A business plan can be the inn's bible to which you turn when nothing seems to be going right; it acts as a reminder of why you're in this business anyway. It can help keep you on track when another great idea — making quilts on the side, maybe, or adding a restaurant — threatens to sidetrack you.

* **Base from which to flex:** It's not a hard-and-fast rule book; it's a framework. "Rolling with the punches" is different from reeling from one crisis to another, and a plan helps to keep everything, including change, in perspective.

A plan that can do this much for you should be done well. It will represent your inn, so make it look professional: typed, reproduced on high-quality paper, and kept in a neat folder or binding. Copies should be numbered and dated. Keep a log of those who have the plan; it's privileged information.

Developing a plan requires time to think, and think creatively. Getting away from interruptions and routine daily pressures to work on it can be the start of a good management practice. Managers need perspective. In innkeeping, it's difficult but crucial to be far enough away to gain that perspective. Start here.

WHAT GOES INTO THE PLAN?

Naturally, plans differ in outline as well as in content, but here's a good model.

INTRODUCTION
* Title page with date, writer's name, inn name.
* Table of contents.
* Overview or summary of what the plan will cover.

DESCRIPTION OF THE BUSINESS
* The type of inn you will provide.
* Auxiliary services offered, if any.
* Description of physical structure.
* Location.
* Legal structure, i.e., partnership, corporation, sole proprietorship.
* History of business if it is an existing inn.

MARKETING

DETERMINING SALES POTENTIAL   Include the information you've gathered about site selection, market research, and so on, including, specifically:

* Who will be your customers (age, family, occupation)?
* Who is your competition (inns, hotels, B&B services)?
* What are the visitors statistics and accommodations occupancy rates in the area?
* What makes your inn competitive in that market?

HOW WILL YOU ATTRACT GUESTS?   Include here information on inn ambience, initial and ongoing marketing, plus pricing structure and policies and procedures.

PERSONNEL

Your own résumé(s) and business histories/accomplishments. The bank and others will want to know what qualifies you to be an innkeeper. If you have little business experience or no hotel or inn experience, you may want to include the background(s) of your outside consultants.

* Names and histories/résumé(s) of your board of directors, if you have one.
* How will work be arranged? Will you do it all or hire staff? When? How many? To do what? It may be helpful to include a simple chart of responsibilities describing who will deal with the bookkeeper, supervise cleaning staff, and so on, to clarify roles and structure.

CONSULTANTS AND OUTSIDE RESOURCES

Successful businesses are not opened all alone, and the resources you have can help you get others. Include here all the people you can think of who have helped or will help you in your business: architect, attorney, contractor, accountant, promotion professional, consultants, insurance agent, decorator, and innkeepers and innkeeper associations.

COMMITMENTS

These are arrangements already made: building in escrow or leased, furniture already available or promised, arrangements made with antique dealers, innkeeping class scheduled to be taken, and inn association promise of referrals.

FINANCIAL INFORMATION

Many of your readers will turn to the financial figures first. For them and for your own peace of mind, develop this section carefully and honestly.

Try to follow these guidelines. First, estimate expenses high and income low. This is no time for optimism. Be as pessimistic as you can bear to be, so you build in contingency plans. You will feel much better about a low December if you've planned for it than if you unexpectedly need $2,000 you haven't set aside. If you've allocated $2,000 for the expected deficit, you'll have the satisfaction of knowing you're at least good at planning!

Second, go over your figures in detail with someone who will ask hard questions, like why you expect your gas bills to be identical in summer and winter. Talk to more than one knowledgeable person, and preferably someone familiar with hotel or inn operations.

These figures might be developed with an accountant, but there are very substantial advantages to doing them yourself. You'll be making presentations to bankers and investors as well as making decisions based on these numbers. If you develop them, you'll know them. If your financial situation is a mystery at this stage, you'll be totally lost once you're in operation.

Try not to let sensitivity about finances get in your way. Like most people, innkeepers tend to take on the good old American value of secrecy about money. This can not only make it difficult to disclose finances but also to develop them honestly. Remember, the inn is not *you*. It's created by you, but it is not you. If it should need repairs or overhaul, it won't mean you're a loser.

WHAT TO INCLUDE IN THE FINANCIAL SECTION

In brief, the financial section should be divided into seven pieces: a summary of financial needs and your plan to meet them, your personal financial statement, the projected personal benefit income, projected occupancy rate, a cash-flow projection month by month, a balance sheet (if buying an existing inn) and a pro forma (estimated or projected profit/loss statement), and an itemization of start-up costs.

SUMMARY OF FINANCIAL NEEDS

This section summarizes the financial plan that will be developed in the pages that follow. Don't get stuck here trying to figure out the source of the figures. That will become clear as you read on. The summary is based on a hypothetical turn-of-the-century residence. It is in good condition, has two bathrooms, and costs $250,000. It could provide five guest rooms in addition to innkeeper quarters. The summary for this property begins with a list of financial needs and dollar amounts, followed by a list of financial resources.

PROJECTED FINANCIAL NEEDS

Five-Room Inn, Tourist Town, USA

Start-up costs		**$236,000**
Renovation/furnishings	150,000	
Down payment	50,000	
Working capital*	30,000	
Closing costs	3,000	
Moving costs	3,000	
First three years' deficit projection		46,436
First trust deed on building		
Purchase price $250,000, less down payment		200,000
Total projected financial needs		$482,436

* Includes office supplies, legal and professional fees, utility deposits, licenses and permits, advertising and promotional materials, owner's draw and expenses during renovation, and petty cash.

Plan to Meet Financial Needs

Capital supplied by partners		256,436
Cash from sale of present home	150,176	
Savings and stock	47,250	
Partner No. 2 continues present employment 18 months	59,010	
Capital needs from bank or investors		216,000
Mortgage on building	200,000	
Loan from Mom (deferred interest)	16,000	
Additional financial needs from bank		
Cash flow credit line collateralized on money-market account for 1 year, then uncollateralized		10,000
		$482,436

The following section includes descriptions of other financial reports that most business plans contain. Two other pieces, your personal financial statement and personal benefit income, are described here.

YOUR PERSONAL FINANCIAL STATEMENT

Readers of your business plan who might provide loans or business support are interested in your ability to repay a loan or your collateral assets as represented by your financial situation. Potential investors will also want to evaluate your stake in the business.

The sample financial statement in Appendix 2 includes categories specifically relevant to the inn business. It's an excellent information tool for you, whether or not you plan to seek outside funding. If you do need a bank loan, a form like this will be required, along with your last three years' personal tax returns. Financial statements include a current listing of assets and liabilities, including all real estate, stocks, bonds, insurance, loans, pension funds, personal property, and fixed expenses (child's college, alimony). You can also include here assets like the value of antique furnishings you'll use in the inn.

PERSONAL BENEFIT INCOME

Owners who live on the inn premises and are involved in daily inn operations receive related benefits of significant value. A projected breakdown of this information can help explain to bankers why you'll be able to pay back a requested loan even without a large salary.

In the Past Experience column enter your previous year's personal costs. Under In an Inn, project these costs, which will be covered in the

	Past Experience	In an Inn
Housing		
Utilities		
Gardening service		
Food		
Insurance		
Auto expenses		
Travel and entertainment		
Home repairs		
Cleaning service		
Miscellaneous supplies (toilet paper roll ends, used soap, etc.)		
Total		

inn's budget. In some areas, the inn will cover your personal costs completely; in others, partially. For example, travel to other inns to keep up with the market is a justifiable expense, but a Caribbean cruise isn't. Eating breakfast breads with the guests is a justifiable expense, but a filet mignon dinner for twelve at a bed-and-breakfast inn is not.

With additional financial pieces that you'll develop as you go through the next chapters, you'll have a complete business plan. The plan is an important step in organizing your intentions and your finances. Done well, it will be a valuable resource that you and your potential investors and assistants will use for planning, evaluation, and decision making.

EVALUATING THE OPPORTUNITIES

You've found a lovely, turn-of-the-century residence that hasn't seen a coat of paint for thirty years, but the lines are good and you know a Queen Anne when you see one. How do you evaluate whether it will pay for itself as an inn? And if you've found more than one attractive property, how do you choose among them?

There are four areas of projections to compare: start-up costs, including purchase and renovation financing; operating expenses; income, based on room rates and occupancy levels; and cash flow. In the following pages we'll look at each in detail, then put them all together for comparison in a property evaluation worksheet.

START-UP COSTS

Let's begin with the question of cash up front. This is divided into several major categories: building acquisition, renovation and decorating, and the typical start-up costs for any business. Remember to estimate high.

BUILDING ACQUISITION COSTS

How you account for building acquisition costs varies with how you plan to acquire the inn. If you already own it, list it in the asset section of your business plan. If you plan to lease, the costs of first and last months' rent and security deposits must be included, as well as any fees involved in negotiating the arrangement. If you plan to buy, the down payment, closing costs, points, and so on need to be included.

Typical acquisition costs of houses to convert to inns will depend on property values in your selected town. They could range from $15,000 to $50,000 per usable guest room. Generally speaking, wherever you go, property values are likely to be higher in cosmopolitan and tourist areas than in rural or small town areas.

Say you can buy an attractive structure with six bedrooms and two baths for $250,000. Typical renovation and furnishings costs are $20,000 to $40,000 per guest room. Acquisition and renovation costs are keyed to number of guest rooms, but the figures are guides to total acquisition and renovation costs, inclusive of common room, kitchen, and the like. After reserving one bedroom and one bath for innkeeper quarters, there are five guest rooms left. The acquisition cost of each, therefore, is $50,000.

RENOVATING AND FURNISHING

Since the acquisition costs are high on the scale, which should indicate that the house is in reasonable condition, let's estimate renovation and furnishing costs in the middle at $30,000 per room, or $150,000 for the hypothetical five guest rooms. The $150,000 will break down into costs for bathrooms (created out of closet space, with no additional square footage), furnishings, painting, landscaping, and so on. To cross-check your estimate, figure $7,000 per room for furnishings, small equipment, linens, wall coverings, drapes, carpeting, and so on for guest rooms and common areas. This estimate will be lower if you already have a houseful of antiques, linens, and crystal.

If your detailed breakdown is higher than your renovation/furnishings estimate using the $20,000 to $40,000 guide, use the detailed total for planning purposes.

RENOVATION AND FURNISHINGS

Cost Estimate

Parlor/living room	$ 7,000
Dining room	7,000
Kitchen	7,000
5 guest rooms at $7,000 each	35,000
Add 4 bathrooms ($5,000 to $10,000 each)	30,000
Paving/landscaping	15,000
Exterior painting	10,000
Electrical work	10,000
General plumbing (i.e., new sewer, gas, and water lines)	5,000
Carpentry, drywall, etc.	24,000
Total	$150,000

You can see that it's easy to spend $150,000 renovating and furnishing a house, even if it is apparently in good condition. Your inn now has five guest rooms, five baths, and innkeeper quarters and has cost you $400,000, which includes the acquisition cost plus the renovations.

START-UP WORKING CAPITAL

Working capital covers living costs during the renovation period, in this case an estimated six months, when the inn will generate no income, and during the first few months of operation. It also includes:

* Office supplies (letterhead paper, envelopes, typewriter, etc.).
* Deposits for utilities, and utility costs during renovation.
* Legal and professional fees (for drawing up incorporation papers or partnership agreement, setting up books, etc.).
* Licenses and permits.
* Advertising for opening, including ads, brochures, logo, business cards.
* Mortgage or lease on building during renovation, prior to opening to guests.
* Owner's draw during renovation, prior to opening.
* Operating cash (also called petty cash, probably not to exceed $100).

Your realtor can figure your mortgage payments, or you can buy a comprehensive mortgage payment table at an office supply if you want to experiment with different mortgage rates and years of payback. (The longer the mortgage, the lower the monthly payment.)

In our example, financing $200,000 ($250,000 purchase price less $50,000 down payment) for twenty-five years at 10 percent fixed will cost about $1,818 a month. For six months' estimated renovation time, the mortgage alone will cost $10,908 and other start-up costs $19,092.

SAMPLE START-UP COST PROJECTIONS*

Down payment	$ 50,000
Closing costs	3,000
Moving costs	3,000
Renovation/furnishings	150,000
Working capital	30,000
Initial costs	$236,000

*Assumes the down payment is 20 percent of $250,000, or $50,000.

These initial costs are high, but remember, they include a home *and* a business opportunity. We'll look next at projecting operating income and expenses, i.e., developing a budget.

PROJECTING EXPENSES—DEVELOPING A BUDGET

Your budget is a listing of all projected expenses and income; it's what you expect to happen financially. You can develop it initially based on the figures and percentages presented here, but after six months to a year of operation, you can use your own real figures and project them into the next year. Comparing actual expenditures with your projections, you can discover expenses to cut, expansion possibilities, slow times that need to be promoted, and problem areas.

The related income and expense statement includes the same categories of income and expense, but describes at the end of a period, such as year-end, what actually happened. It also includes noncash transactions, depreciations, and amortization, and becomes your official financial statement for tax purposes.

In 1988 coauthors Pat Hardy and Jo Ann Bell, as editor and publisher of *innkeeping* newsletter, sponsored the first comprehensive survey and analysis of income, expense, and return on investment for bed-and-breakfast and country inns throughout the United States. Since 1988 they have conducted three more studies, as the Professional Association of Innkeepers International, and the studies have become widely used by innkeepers, brokers, and lending institutions. The following expense categories are consistent with their study. They are recommended for all innkeepers, so in the years to come we will always be comparing apples and apples.

In order to establish a consistent standard of comparison (as is currently available in the rest of the lodging industry), innkeepers are encouraged to set up their accounts as listed here.

Using these categories, we will do a sample budget for hypothetical five-, seven-, and ten-room inns.

SAMPLE CHART OF ACCOUNTS

Revenue Accounts

Room revenue	Room rental with breakfast, excluding sales and bed taxes
Food revenues	Restaurant, MAP
Beverage revenue	Liquor and other beverages sold separately

continued on next page

Gift shop revenue	Revenue from sales of products
Specialty food service revenue	Teas, picnic baskets, etc.
Weddings	Revenues from weddings, not including room rental
Meetings	Revenues from meetings, not including room rental
Service charges	All revenue from service charges not directly distributed to staff as tips
Rental of equipment	Rental fees for skis, boats, bikes, etc.
Other revenue	

Operating Expense Accounts

Food and beverage payroll (hourly employees)	All wages/payroll taxes and worker's compensation for hourly food and beverage employees
Food and beverage payroll (salaried employees)	All wages/payroll taxes and worker's compensation for full-time food and beverage employees, not owners
Non–food and beverage payroll (hourly employees)	All wages/payroll taxes and worker's compensation for hourly employees not related to food and beverage
Non–food and beverage payroll (salaried employees)	All wages/payroll taxes and worker's compensation for full-time employees not related to food and beverage, not owners
Auto	Gasoline, repairs, and maintenance, car leasing
Bank fees	Including check charges, merchant credit card services
Business taxes and fees	Property taxes and business fees. Exclude sales, bed, and income taxes

continued on next page

SAMPLE CHART OF ACCOUNTS

Commissions	Agent commissions, referral services, etc.
Dues and subscriptions	Dues to associations and subscriptions to services, magazines, newspapers
Food	All food and liquor for the inn
Insurance	Nonpayroll insurance such as fire, theft, auto liability
Interest	On any inn mortgages and other business-related loans
Legal and accounting fees	Fees for legal and accounting services
Maintenance, repairs, and fixtures	Materials and purchases under $300 for appliances/fixtures
Marketing—advertising and promotion	Brochures, magazines/newspaper ads, printing, direct mail
Miscellaneous	All expense items that do not belong to another account
Office supplies	Paper, tape, pens, letterhead, office equipment rental, postage
Outside services	For services such as gardening, maintenance, laundry
Owner(s) wages or draw	Money actually taken out of business by the owner(s)
Room and housekeeping supplies	All soaps, toilet paper, light bulbs, cleaning supplies, notions, toiletries, etc.
Telephone	Telephone and related expenses
Towels and linens	Purchase price of all towels, linens, blankets, pillows, bathrobes, that are not capitalized
Training	Fees and related expenses for workshops/seminars
Travel and entertainment	Travel-related expenses and business entertainment
Utilities	Including trash, gas, electric, water, etc.

Of course, not every chart of accounts category is included in every budget or income and expense statement; only the categories that are useful to your particular situation should be included. Most prospective innkeepers underestimate expenses other than mortgages. The percentages shown in our sample budget are based on the 1994 PAII industry survey of 346 inns in the United States. Use them as a guideline.

PROJECTING INCOME

In order to begin a budget we must first project income.

Income includes all revenues from the operation of the business, plus other revenue such as interest earned on bank accounts. Typical operations income includes room rents, food sales, gift and book sales, and other services such as rental of the inn for weddings, meetings, and so on. It is wise to keep revenue sources separate so that you can evaluate their profitability. For inns, income is primarily the product of room rate multiplied by the number of rooms rented.

ROOM RENTS   Most bed-and-breakfast inns include breakfast in the room rate. As a rule of thumb, innkeepers set their standard room rate higher than an inexpensive motel; comparable to a good full-service hotel or motel; and lower than the local resort with golf course. Rate reductions may be made off-season, midweek (if this is a slow period), or for commercial customers who stay frequently and for several days at a time, or, in some cases, innkeepers are likely to offer special packages that add value during slower seasons. Tourist towns tend to be slower midweek; city inns see little difference weekdays to weekends. See the Setting Rates section in "Up and Running," page 282.

OCCUPANCY   Occupancy means percentage of available rooms actually rented. For example, a ten-room inn during a thirty-day month has three hundred available rooms, or ten rooms multiplied by thirty days. If half the rooms are rented each day of the month, the occupancy rate is 50 percent. The following formula may be used to compute the occupancy rate:

Occupancy rate (%) =
# of rooms rented annually ÷ (# of rooms available x # of days in the period)

Using this formula, you can project occupancy rates. By combining projected occupancy and projected room rates, you can project income.

To see this formula at work, we will use the example of a property in a weekend and summer tourist town. The research indicates that the inn should be full weekends year-round and all week during June, July, and August. The going room rate for weekends/summer is $85 per night for rooms with private bath.

Standard Expense Breakdown

Percentage of Income	Expense Category
7	Food and nonfood hourly employees
3	Food and nonfood salaried employees
1	Auto
2	Bank fees
4	Business taxes and fees
1	Commissions
1	Dues and subscriptions
8	Food and beverage
3	Insurance
1	Legal and accounting fees
6	Maintenance, repairs, and fixtures
8	Marketing, advertising, and promotion
1	Office supplies and postage
2	Outside services
3	Room and housekeeping supplies
2	Telephone
1	Towels and linens
1	Training
1	Travel and entertainment
6	Utilities
62%	Total operating and labor expenses, not including owner's salary/draw or interest expenses (mortgage)

Five-room inn
# of rooms rented winter weekends: 5 rooms x 80 days = 400
# of rooms rented summer weeks: 5 rooms x 92 days = 460
Total: 860 rooms rented annually
# of rooms available: 5 rooms x 365 days = 1,825
860 ÷ 1,825 = 47% (rounded) annual occupancy rate

To project annual income:
# of rooms x # days x room rate = maximum income at 100% occupancy
5 x 365 x $85 = $155,125 (maximum income at 100%)
47% of $155,125 = $72,909
or
860 rooms @ $85 = $73,100 (difference due to rounding)

10-room inn
# of rooms rented winter weekends: 10 rooms x 80 days = 800
# of rooms rented summer weeks: 10 rooms x 92 days = 920

Total: 1720 rooms rented annually
# of rooms available: 10 rooms x 365 days = 3,650 room nights
1720 ÷ 3,650 = 47% (rounded) annual occupancy rate

To project annual income:
# of rooms x # days x room rate = maximum income at 100% occupancy
10 x 365 x $95 = $346,750 (maximum income at 100%)
47% of $346,750 = $162,973
   or
1720 rooms @ $95 = $163,400 (difference due to rounding)

Local chambers of commerce or tourist bureaus can sometimes give you annual occupancy figures for existing hotels, motels, and inns. Large hotels that do convention business should be taken out of the sample, if possible. A prudent projection is 50 percent of the area occupancy rate for a new inn in its first year of business. The longer you're in business, the closer you'll come to the area rate.

Let's calculate income for our proposed 5-room inn:

_5_ rooms x 365 days x average room rate _$85_ = income 100% occupancy = _$155,125_
Projections: 1st year: 50% of area rate _60%_ = _30%_ : 100% occupancy = _46,538_
            2nd year: 1st year _30%_ + 10% = _40%_ x 100% occupancy = _62,050_
            3rd year: 2nd year _40%_ + 10% = _50%_ x 100% occupancy = _77,563_

Use the suggested guideline of half the area occupancy rate for first-year inn operation and assume an increase of 10 percent per year until area standard occupancy is reached. (An exceptional advertising program or terrific referral system with existing hotels or inns could make this low, but it's not likely.)

PROJECTING EXPENSES

The PAII industry survey shows the following total annual expenses per guest room (without salary for owner[s], capital purchases, depreciation, or mortgage/interest) for 1994:

5 rooms — $7,674/expenses/room/year
7 rooms — $6,801
9 rooms — $8,166

Adjust these figures for your number of rooms and locale. It would be very helpful to obtain expense percentages from established inns in your area. Geography, climate, mortgage interest rate, and type of food service all affect the percentages.

Projecting Expenses for the Start-up B&B Inn—5 Rooms

Detailed Expenses

Standard % of Income	Expense Category	(1) Annual Expenses Using Standard Percentages	(2) Adjustments For Reality	Comments
7	Food & nonfood hourly employees	$4,332	$7,200	Needs help so one partner can work part-time
3	Food & nonfood salaried employees	1,857	1,857	
1	Auto expense	619	619	
2	Bank fees	1,238	1,238	
4	Business taxes and fees	2,475	3,500	Property taxes higher here
1	Commissions	619	619	
1	Dues and subscriptions	619	619	
8	Food and beverage	4,951	4,951	
3	Insurance	1,857	1,857	
1	Legal and accounting fees	619	619	
6	Maintenance, repairs, and fixtures	3,712	3,712	
8	Marketing, advertising, and promotion	4,951	4,951	
1	Office supplies and postage	619	619	
2	Outside services	1,238	1,238	
3	Room and housekeeping supplies	1,857	1,857	
2	Telephone	1,238	2,400	Need 800# — approx. $100/month
1	Towels and linens	619	619	
1	Training	619	619	
1	Travel and entertainment	619	619	
6	Utilities	3,712	6,000	Utilities will run $500/month
62%	Total operating and labor expenses not including owner's salary/draw or interest expenses	$38,370 (T)	$45,713	
38%	Mortgage		21,816	
	Salary	23,517 (M+S)	10,000	
100%	Grand Total operating & labor expenses, including owner's salary/draw and interest/lease expenses	$61,887 (GT)	$77,529	

To find Total Expenses as percentage of income

Step 1: _____5_____ x _____7,674_____ =$_____38,370_____(T)

       # of rooms   C from Worksheet

         (Expenses/room for labor and operations)

           Insert (1) in column 1 Total above.

Step 2: (T)___38,370___ divided by .62 = $_____61,887_____(GT)
Insert in Column 1 Grand Total expenses including mortgage, owner draw, and adjustment for reality (Col. 2).

Step 3: Take each individual % and multiply by (GT) to figure Column 1 percentages of income.

Step 4: Reality Test: Correct the individual expense items to reflect your situation.

Step 5: Subtract Col. 1 (T) from Col. 2 (T); enter difference in C. Adjustment for reality.

Back to our calculation. The expenses for our five-room inn should be about $38,370 (5 rooms at $7,674 each). Plug this number into the "total expenses" slot on the worksheets that follow. Take your various percentages, and then apply a reality test to them. In other words, look at each item and see if it's reasonable in your particular circumstances. Make adjustments where necessary. And remember, always project expenses high and income low. The percentages will not be accurate in every instance. The following chart is in Appendix 3 as a worksheet.

In the early years of developing your inn, it is difficult to use percentage of income/revenue to project your expenses because you will probably be running in the red. To keep our percentages in line with the actual operating expenses of inns surveyed by PAII, we are assuming a break-even situation—that your expenses exactly equal your income. Column (1) shows this ideal situation; column (2) shows the actual reality after you have adjusted for your own situation.

Back to our calculation. The operating expenses (without mortgage or your salary/draw) for our five-room inn should be about $38,370 (five rooms at $7,674—taken from survey), or 62 percent of your total revenue.

Step 1: Plug this number into Total Operating and Labor Expenses under Column (1).

Step 2: Divide the $38,370 by 62 percent to find your Total Expenses, including mortgage and salary—$61,887—and put this number in the grand total slot, Column (1). The difference between the $38,370 and $61,887 is $23,517, or what is left in the money pot for mortgage and your salary.

Step 3: Take each individual percentage, e.g., 7 percent for food, and multiply it by the total operating and labor expense figure of $61,887 and put in Food, Column (1); continue this process until you have all the blanks in Column (1) filled; they should total the $38,370 figure. You now have a picture of what the expenses for your inn would look like if you were breaking even. This can all be easily done on a computer spreadsheet program.

Now comes the hard part. Look at each of these numbers and see if they make sense in your particular situation. Make any changes in Column (2), add it up, and you now have your own expenses based on what you know about your situation. Add in the actual mortgage payment calculation and your salary needs. This is your total expense figure.

It's important to try to be as exact as possible in your expense projections. The PAII study gives some average costs per room that may be helpful. For example, the survey gives an overall average food and beverage cost per rented room of $7.37 for this price room. If you take the total number of rooms you will rent in a year and multiply by $7.37 for food and beverage, you will be able to cross-check the above percentages. This kind of information will help you check your amounts in your Reality column.

Also, you will note we have held the room rate and the expenses constant for three years for simplicity, but you will want to fully develop each of those years, making adjustments for increased occupancy.

CASH FLOW ANALYSIS

Now that we have the income and expense projections, we can do a cash flow analysis. For our sample inn, with five rooms with baths, we'll compile the budget information developed so far into a simple cash flow analysis.

	CASH FLOW ANALYSIS		
Area Occupancy: 60%			
	Year 1	**Year 2**	**Year 3**
	30%	40%	50%
Income	$46,538	$62,050	$77,563
Expense	(77,529)	(77,529)	(77,529)
Cash Flow	(30,991)	(15,479)	34

For simplicity's sake, we have held both room prices and expenses constant, even though both would rise. As you can see, there is a considerable negative cash flow for the first two years. Any banker will want to know where the cash to make it up is coming from. Let's recap our financial needs.

	Start-up	Year 1	Year 2	Year 3
Down payment	$50,000			
Closing costs	3,000			
Moving costs	3,000			
Renovation/furnishing	150,000			
Working capital	30,000			
Negative cash flow		(30,991)	(15,479)	$34
Total needs ($282,436)	$(236,000)	$(30,991)	$(15,479)	$34

Now we'll combine all this financial information in a property evaluation form (see Appendix 3 for a blank form).

WORKSHEET: PROPERTY EVALUATION

Address: *5-Room Inn*
Tourist Town, U.S.A.

All amounts and percentages are estimates.

Area occupancy rate: **60%**

Number of guest rooms:
  original house: **5**
  proposed addition: ____

Area room rate:
  private bath: **$85**

Number of guest bathrooms:
  original house: **1**
  proposed addition: **4**

A. FINANCIAL NEEDS: PURCHASE/RENOVATION PHASE

Purchase:	Total price:	**250,000**	GUIDE
	Mortgage:	**200,000**	1st, 10% fixed, 25 yrs
			$15,000–50,000 per guest room
Down payment: _____		**50,000**	Usual is 20–30% of price
Closing costs, loan fees, etc.		**3,000**	Get realtor or banker estimate
Moving costs		**3,000**	
Working capital		**30,000**	Expenses from purchase period
			(**6** month renovation)
Renovation and furnishings		**150,000**	Estimate $20,000 (good condition) to
inc. bathrooms			$40,000 per guest room in original house
Additional guest rooms:			Estimate new construction at $90–$200 per sq. ft.
construction		**n/a**	(room with bath–250 sq. ft.)
Additional bathrooms:			
construction		**n/a**	Estimate $5,000–10,000 each
Additional guest rooms:			
furnishings		**n/a**	Estimate $7,000 per room
Other _____			
Total		**$236,000**	

B. INCOME

5 rooms x 365 days x average room rate: **$85.00** = income @ 100% occupancy	=	**$155,125**
1ST YEAR PROJECTION:		
50% of area rate **60% = 30%** x 100% occupancy	=	**$46,538**
2ND YEAR PROJECTION:		
1st year **30%** + 10% = **40%** x 100% occupancy	=	**$62,050**
3RD YEAR PROJECTION:		
2nd year **40%** + 10% = **50%** x 100% occupancy	=	**$77,563**

C. PER ROOM EXPENSES–PAII INDUSTRY STUDY

5 rooms	$7,674	7 rooms	$6,801	9 rooms	$8,166
Survey Expenses (# of rooms: **5 x 7,674** [survey])				=	**$38,370**
Mortgage, lease payment				=	**21,816**
Adjustment for reality (See E–Detailed Exp., Col. 2)				=	**7,343**
Owner's salary/draw				=	**10,000**
TOTAL				=	**$77,529**

D. CASH FLOW PROJECTION / BREAK-EVEN ANALYSIS

	1st Year	2nd Year	3rd Year
Income (B)	**$46,538**	**62,050**	**77,563**
Per room expenses (C)	**(77,529)**	**(77,529)**	**(77,529)**
+ or – Cash flow	**(30,991)**	**(15,479)**	**34**

To break even:
Expenses = **$77,529** = **50%** occupancy needed
Income @ 100%   **$155,125**

The break-even percentage at the bottom of the property evaluation worksheet is the figure important to the question of cash flow. If you do not break even, you must continue to put cash into the business. If your break-even occupancy level is too high, you will have a constant cash struggle. In this example, the 50 percent occupancy needed to break even is a difficult goal, since the area rate is 60 percent.

The five-room inn property is relatively expensive at $250,000, and it has room for just five guest rooms and bathrooms, and the owner's quarters. Let's say, for example, that in addition to the five-room property, you're also looking at a turn-of-the-century residence in good condition that could provide seven guest rooms in addition to innkeeper quarters. The cost is $275,000, $25,000 more than our first example house, but this property has potential for several more expensive rooms with balconies. Here is a second example, using the larger property.

The partners have put into the projected five-room inn $282,436 from the sale of a home, their savings, and the income from one partner continuing to work outside the inn for a year and a half. Let's take a look at how much more cash would be needed to invest in the seven-room inn.

PROJECTED FINANCIAL NEEDS—SEVEN-ROOM INN

Down payment	$ 55,000
Closing costs	3,500
Moving costs	3,000
Renovation/furnishings	210,000
Working capital	30,000
Total immediate cash outlay	$301,500
less	
Positive cash flow at end of third year	8,640
Investment at end of third year	$292,860

For a larger initial investment of approximately $65,000 (the difference between $236,000 cash outlay for the five-room inn and $301,500 for the seven-room inn), the buyer now has a more luxurious seven-room inn with much more potential return and a break-even point of 39 percent.

WORKSHEET: PROPERTY EVALUATION

Address: *7-Room Inn*
Tourist Town, U.S.A.

Area occupancy rate: *60%*

Area room rate:
  private bath: *$95*

All amounts and percentages are estimates.
Number of guest rooms:
  original house: *7*
  proposed addition: ____
Number of guest bathrooms:
  original house: *3*
  proposed addition: *4 Back to Back*

A. FINANCIAL NEEDS: PURCHASE/RENOVATION PHASE

Purchase:	Total price:	*275,000*	GUIDE
	Mortgage:	*220,000*	1st, 10% fixed, 25 yrs

2nd for additional down payment and part of renovation cost

$15,000–50,000 per guest room
Usual is 20–30% of price

Down payment:____	*55,000*
Closing costs, loan fees, etc.	*3,500*
Moving costs	*3,000*
Working capital	*30,000*

Get realtor or banker estimate *$43,000 @ 11% for 10 years*

Expenses from purchase period
    (___6___ month renovation)

Renovation and furnishings *210,000*
  inc. bathrooms

Estimate $20,000 (good condition) *7 @ $30,000*
  to $40,000 per guest room in original house

Additional guest rooms:
  construction *n/a*

Estimate new construction at $90–$200 per sq. ft.
  (room with bath–250 sq. ft.)

Additional bathrooms:
  construction *n/a*

Estimate $5,000–10,000 each

Additional guest rooms:
  furnishings *n/a*

Estimate $7,000 per room

Other ____

Total *$301,500*

B. INCOME

7 rooms x 365 days x average room rate: *$95.00* = income @ 100% occupancy = *$242,725*

1ST YEAR PROJECTION:
  50% of area rate *60%* = *30%* x 100% occupancy = *$72,818*
2ND YEAR PROJECTION:
  1st year *30%* + 10% = *40%* x 100% occupancy = *$97,090*
3RD YEAR PROJECTION:
  2nd year *40%* + 10% = *50%* x 100% occupancy = *$121,362*

C. PER ROOM EXPENSES–PAII INDUSTRY STUDY

5 rooms $7,674   7 rooms $6,801   9 rooms $8,166

Survey Expenses (# of rooms: *7* x *$6,801* [survey])	=	*$47,607*
Mortgage, lease payment	=	*31,092*
Adjustment for reality (See E–Detailed Exp., Col. 2)	=	*5,511*
Owner's salary/draw	=	*10,000*
TOTAL	=	*$94,210*

D. CASH FLOW PROJECTION / BREAK-EVEN ANALYSIS

	1st Year	2nd Year	3rd Year
Income (B)	*72,818*	*97,090*	*121,362*
Per room expenses (C)	*(94,210)*	*(94,210)*	*(94,210)*
+ or – Cash flow	*(21,392)*	*2,880*	*27,152*

To break even:

$$\frac{\text{Expenses}}{\text{Income @ 100\%}} = \frac{\$94,210}{\$242,725} = 39\% \text{ occupancy needed}$$

E. DETAILED EXPENSES

Standard % of Income	Expense Category	(1) Annual Expenses Using Standard Percentages	(2) Adjustments for Reality	Comments
7	Food & nonfood hourly employees	$ 5,375	$ 7,200	Same as 5-room
3	Food & nonfood salaried employees	2,303	2,303	
1	Auto expense	768	768	
2	Bank fees	1,536	1,536	
4	Business taxes and fees	3,071	4,000	Higher purchase and
1	Commissions	768	768	renovation costs
1	Dues and subscriptions	768	768	
8	Food and beverages	6,143	6,143	Additional $ covers
3	Insurance	2,303	2,303	
1	Legal and accounting fees	768	768	
6	Maintenance, repairs, and fixtures	4,607	4,607	
8	Marketing, advertising, and promotion	6,143	6,143	
1	Office supplies and postage	768	768	
2	Outside services	1,536	1,536	
3	Room and housekeeping supplies	2,303	2,303	
2	Telephone	1,536	2,400	800#
1	Towels and linens	768	768	
1	Training	768	768	
1	Travel and entertainment	768	768	
6	Utilities	4,607	6,500	
62%	Total operating and labor expenses not including owner's salary/draw or interest expenses	$47,607 (T)	$53,118	
38%	Mortgage		31,092	
	Salary	29,178 (M+S)	10,000	
100%	Grand Total operating & labor expenses, including owner's salary/draw and interest/lease expenses	$76,785 (GT)	$94,210	

To find Total Expenses as percentage of income

Step 1: ___7___ x ___6,801___ = $___47,607___ (T)
      # of rooms   C from Worksheeet

      (Expenses/room for labor and operations)

      Insert (1) in column 1 Total above.

Step 2: (T) ___47,607___ divided by .62 = ___76,785___ (GT)
      Insert in Column 1 Grand Total expenses including mortgage, owner draw, and adjustment for reality (Col. 2).

Step 3: Take each individual % and multiply by (GT) to figure Column 1 percentages of income.

Step 4: Reality Test: Correct the individual expense items to reflect your situation.

Step 5: Subtract Col. 1 (T) from Col. 2 (T); enter difference in C. Adjustment for reality.

And now let's look at what a difference just a few more rooms can make in your bottom line. In a nine-room example, the detailed expenses are not included, since you already have two examples.

WORKSHEET: PROPERTY EVALUATION

Address: *9-Room Inn*
Tourist Town, U.S.A.

Area occupancy rate: *60%*

Area room rate:
  private bath: *$95*

All amounts and percentages are estimates.
Number of guest rooms:
  original house: *9*
  proposed addition: _____
Number of guest bathrooms:
  original house: *2*
  proposed addition: *7*

A. FINANCIAL NEEDS: PURCHASE/RENOVATION PHASE

Purchase:	Total price:	*395,000*	GUIDE
	Mortgage:	*296,250*	1st, 10% fixed, 25 yrs

$15,000–50,000 per guest room

Down payment:_____   *98,750*   Usual is 20–30% of price
Closing costs, loan fees, etc.   *3,500*   Get realtor or banker estimate
Moving costs   *3,000*
Working capital   *31,000*   Expenses from purchase period
  (___*6*___ month renovation)

Renovation and furnishings   *270,000*   Estimate $20,000 (good condition)   *9 x $30,000*
  4 bathrooms inc.   to $40,000 per guest room in original house
Additional guest rooms: Estimate new construction at $90–$200 per sq. ft.
  construction   *n/a*   (room with bath–250 sq. ft.)
Additional bathrooms:
  construction   *21,000*   Estimate $5,000–10,000 each *3 @ $7,000*
Additional guest rooms:
  furnishings   *n/a*   Estimate $7,000 per room
Other _____   _____
Total   *$427,250*

B. INCOME

9 rooms x 365 days x average room rate: *$95.00* = income @ 100% occupancy   =   *$312,075*
1ST YEAR PROJECTION:
  50% of area rate *30%* = *30%* x 100% occupancy   =   *$93,622*
2ND YEAR PROJECTION:
  1st year *30%* + 10% = *40%* x 100% occupancy   =   *$124,830*
3RD YEAR PROJECTION:
  2nd year *40%* + 10% = *50%* x 100% occupancy   =   *$156,037*

C. PER ROOM EXPENSES–PAII INDUSTRY STUDY

5 rooms $7,674   7 rooms $6,801   9 rooms $8,166
Survey Expenses (# of rooms: *9* x *$8,166* [survey])   –   *$73,494*
Mortgage, lease payment   =   *32,577*
Adjustment for reality (See E–Detailed Exp., Col. 2)   =   *9990*
Owner's salary/draw   =   *10,000*
  TOTAL   =   *$116,071*

D. CASH FLOW PROJECTION / BREAK-EVEN ANALYSIS

	1st Year	2nd Year	3rd Year
Income (B)	*$93,622*	*124,830*	*156,037*
Per room expenses (C)	*(116,071)*	*(116,071)*	*(116,071)*
+ or – Cash flow	*(22,449)*	*8,759*	*39,966*

To break even:
Expenses _____ = *$116,071* = *37%* occupancy needed
Income @ 100%   *$312,075*

The following three-year investment analysis will show the net results for the three properties, at the end of the third year—and the very dramatic effect of beginning to have a positive cash flow in the early years. This can be even greater when you purchase an existing inn.

THREE-YEAR INVESTMENT ANALYSIS

	Initial Investment	3-Year Cash Flow	Net Investment after Three Years
Five rooms at $85	$236,000	($46,436)	$282,436
Seven rooms at $95	301,500	8,640	292,860
Nine rooms at $95	427,250	26,276	400,974

Further insight is provided when you look at the annual profit for these same inns at 60 percent occupancy.

Five rooms	$15,546
Seven rooms	$51,425
Nine rooms	$71,174

Big is economically better, but with more guest rooms, you'll spend more of your time dealing with staff and organizational matters than dealing with guests. Financial projections before you buy help you make comparisons, understand all the options, and then make an educated decision.

OTHER FINANCIAL REPORTS FOR YOUR INN

Balance sheets show the relationship of current assets and liabilities; income and expense statements show the profitability—the bottom line—

of your operations. Your accountant prepares these financial statements based on your general ledger records of all income and expenses of the year.

The balance sheet reflects what you own and owe at a moment in time: "at December 31, 19__" or at "June 30, 19__." It consists of a listing of all your assets and all your liabilities. The difference between assets and liabilities is the owner's share of the business, which is added as "equity" and balances the totals. The income and expense statement, also called a profit and loss statement, is your formal financial statement for tax purposes. It is particularly important if you are looking for a personal tax shelter for investors. Like your budget, this document will cover a period of time: "twelve months ending December 31, 19__," or "three months ending _____," or "the month of _____."

In addition to the actual expenses and income reported in the budget or cash flow analysis, it also includes the noncash expense of depreciation. Depreciation is the "using up" of a building, automobile, furniture, equipment, dishes, linen, and so on. It recognizes the life expectancy of these things and their declining usefulness over the years.

If you buy an older house for an inn, you are buying both land and structure. Property tax bills break out the assessed values of each; you can generally find the ratio on an old tax bill. (Your CPA may not accept the ratio, but will need to justify any new one.) In California coastal cities where land costs are high, the ratio may run as high as two to one, land to buildings. In rural areas or in the East, it may run two to one, buildings to land. You want the building portion to be high, because land is never depreciated: it doesn't wear out. Depreciation may put your business in a loss position for tax purposes even when you break even.

In addition to buildings, all other assets such as furniture and equipment are depreciated each year on a schedule followed by your CPA. IRS depreciation rules change often; ask your CPA about them.

Other major changes in the budget to make it a profit and loss statement include moving capital purchases from expenses to assets, which are then depreciated, and moving out of the budget the portion of your mortgage payments that is principal.

The government grants tax credits that can be even more important than tax losses in restoring old buildings, since they come directly off the taxes you owe. Check with your CPA for current legislation on tax credits.

Financial statements are management tools. When you understand them you will be better able to recognize and respond to business problems, and you'll be able to discuss the money side of your business intelligently with anyone.

What? You say you don't *have* a couple of hundred thousand dollars to start an inn? Don't despair. Just because our examples call these enormous sums "cash needs" doesn't mean you need cash in your pocket to get started.

WHERE TO LOOK FOR MONEY

If you presently own the building you wish to turn into a bed-and-breakfast inn, you have the best of all worlds. You have residential financing which is usually at a lower interest rate, often fixed, for a longer amortization period—up to thirty years. The longer the loan is amortized, the lower the monthly payments. These loans are obtainable because you have adequate income from other employment to convince the lender the loan will be paid off.

If you are buying a building in a town distant from your home for the purpose of converting it to an inn, you will probably not be able to get residential financing unless you have income from other continuing employment or plan to work at a new job in the new location. Some people who are doing long-range planning will buy a home suitable for inn conversion and work at salary-paying jobs for years to finance the project.

Friends and family are possible sources for loans. A caution here: Since you know you will be in a negative cash flow situation for the first few years, delay repayment until a period when your projections show you'll have adequate cash flow. Extend out your projections as long as necessary to reach this point, possibly as many as five or ten years.

Include in a formal promissory note the agreement to defer all interest and principal payments for the first three years, say, when monthly payments of a specified amount will begin, the total to be repaid in full by a specific date.

If you are applying to a financial institution for funds, they are interested in the "five Cs" of credit.

1. **Character:** This is by far the most important of these. If you are not someone to be trusted, then the lender doesn't want anything to do with you, no matter how good the deal is.

2. **Capacity:** What is your track record in this business or in previous businesses? What is your financial strength?

3. **Capital:** How much of your own (and/or investors') money is in the project? If you are not willing to invest your own money, no lender will, either.

4. **Collateral:** What is available to support the primary source of repayment on the total amount of the loan?

5. **Conditions:** What is the economy doing, and how will it affect your business and the loan it is seeking?

If you have substantial other property, retirement funds, and stocks and bonds that you can pledge for collateral, you may obtain financing from a local lender.

Your loan proposal should contain the following items presented in a clear, clean, concise format:

LOAN REQUEST
Use or purpose(s) of the proceeds of the loan
Amount required
Source(s) of repayment
Collateral offered
Terms desired

HISTORY AND NATURE OF THE BUSINESS
A description of your potential business and the history of the bed-and-
breakfast industry (one to two pages)
A short- and a long-term marketing plan
Description of your planned facilities

PROJECTED OCCUPANCY AND GROSS REVENUES (with substantiation and/or explanation)

BUSINESS FINANCIAL STATEMENTS
Pro forma (after the loan projections) balance sheet for one year and
pro forma income statements for three years prepared by your CPA
(with explanations and substantiation as necessary)
Some lenders will also want you to include a cash budget

MANAGEMENT
Current résumés of all principal owners and managers
Current personal financial statements on all owners (within ninety days)

Some lenders want three years' worth of personal tax returns from the owners

A listing of key advisors, such as the CPA, attorney, consultant(s), insurance agent, real estate agent, broker, etc.

OTHER

Anything else that may be pertinent, such as partnership agreement, incorporation papers, title insurance, photographs, etc.

Remember the old saying that "banks only lend to people who don't need the money"? This is very true when you try to borrow money for an inn. Banks are trained to require two sources of repayment. The primary source, cash flow for short-term loans and earnings for long-term loans, should be backed up by some form of collateral, such as accounts receivable, inventory, or a mortgage on fixed assets. Then if something goes wrong with the original plan, the lender always has at least one fallback position.

They will also usually require a personal guarantee from the owner(s) of the business, because they want your psychological commitment to the success of the business. Your lender does not necessarily expect to gain a great deal of financial security from your personal signature, but he wants your total dedication to making the business successful.

If you are buying an existing inn, a lender will require the business profit and loss statements, the balance sheets, and tax returns for the past three years. Again, your ability to pledge other assets as collateral will be most important.

Many inns sold today carry Small Business Administration guaranteed loans. Check with the local banks and find several that do business with the SBA. SBA loans require a commercial appraisal (usually at a cost of $3,000 to $10,000), a loan origination fee, a business plan, a personal guarantee from the owner(s), detailed monthly projections for the first year, personal financial information of borrower(s), and all available collateral, preferably equity in owned real estate.

Offices of the Service Corps of Retired Executives throughout the country can direct you to retired professionals who donate their time to the SBA to help entrepreneurs; they can help you through the notoriously precise, detailed, cumbersome, and lengthy application procedure.

As a rule of thumb, it's unwise to finance short-term needs like working capital with long-term financing (financing for more than a year). The reverse of the maxim is that you *should* finance furniture or building improvements—long-term fixed assets—with long-term loans or liabilities.

Your ability to arrange for a new mortgage will be based on your income at the time, which must be high enough to support the monthly payments. If at the end of three years you are breaking even and have a three-year track record of income, refinancing should not be too difficult.

Financial institutions will ask you two questions: How much money do you need? How are you going to repay it? The more thorough your preparation for the project, documented with a business plan and financial projections, the more impressed a lender will be with your seriousness and your dependability.

Some of the problems faced by would-be borrowers who desire to start up a business or need to borrow for a newly established business are:

Most lenders require a minimum loan of $100,000—some will be willing to lend as little as $50,000.

If all goes well, loan payout may occur as much as twenty-four months after application. If there are problems, payout will begin even later.

Lenders invariably prefer that the borrower has at least 30 percent of the total required to start a business from sources other than the loan.

Besides all of the above, lenders are difficult to convince that new businesses will succeed. A recognized franchise applicant has a better chance of securing a loan. A business successfully established for over three years, needing at least $50,000 for expansion, has a much better chance of securing a loan. The lender will need the last three years' profit and loss statements and balance sheets

If you are permanently handicapped, a Vietnam-era veteran, or a disabled veteran, you may be eligible for an SBA direct loan.

Quite apart from all of the above, it requires salesmanship to secure a loan. You have to sell yourself and your plan during your interview with a loan officer and in your written plans.

BUDGET AND CASH FLOW PROJECTIONS MONTH BY MONTH

You may want to break out your projections into monthly figures during the process of demonstrating to lenders or investors your ability to plan and repay. You will certainly want to do the monthly projections for your own business planning purposes. It's not enough to have income equal expenses at year-end; you must also plan for paying your property tax in April, for example, even though it's at the end of your absolutely dead season. Copy and complete the format in Appendix 4 for your own projections.

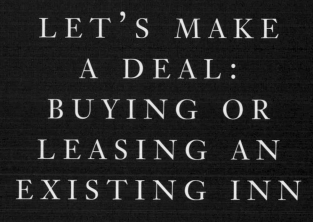

LET'S MAKE
A DEAL:
BUYING OR
LEASING AN
EXISTING INN

▨ BUYING AN EXISTING INN

*T*wenty years ago, if you wanted to be an innkeeper anywhere but in New England, you almost had to start an inn. Not so today. There are plenty of inns around the country, and some of them are for sale.

Like other small, largely owner-operator businesses, inns change hands with some regularity. There is little quantitative measurement of this activity, but a seven-year ownership is the rule of thumb. A limited study by Oates & Bredfeldt, an inn consulting firm in Brattleboro, Vermont, tracked eighty-five inns, mostly mature properties with dinner service, over a four-year period. The average length of ownership was seven years, four months, twenty days, and twenty hours!

Start-ups may turn over sooner, often because of cash flow problems. In most cases, though, inns sell for positive reasons: the owners have achieved their original goals, lifestyles and family relationships have changed, or a new challenge has become more attractive. More inns sell because of success than because of failure, and even problem properties can be turned around by a new owner with the necessary reserves of money and energy.

WHY BUY AN EXISTING INN?

There are several advantages to buying an existing inn. In the first place, you will be dealing with a known quantity with a measurable track record of income and expenses, occupancy rates, patterns of seasonality, and sources of business. Of course, what you'll be buying is the future, not the past. The previous performance of the inn will naturally be affected by your new style of operation. You will, however, have a starting point from which you can—and must—do your own projections.

Second, you can easily verify the existence of necessary licenses and permits. Again, do your own investigation. Permit procedures vary considerably from place to place. As the codes change regularly, the mere existence of a permit is not sufficient. Health department licenses are in some areas issued to a location; in other jurisdictions, to individuals. A sale may or may not trigger fire marshal inspections. If you buy a place that serves alcoholic beverages, you will probably need to apply for a license transfer or a new license, and that often involves investigation into your moral character and finances.

A special word of caution: You'll often hear of "grandfathered" conditions or exceptions. This term is used correctly to refer to nonconforming, preexisting uses in regard to zoning. It's often used incorrectly in relation to health, safety, parking, and fire codes. Waiver of conformance to codes may occur through forbearance, persuasion, or ignorance, but none of those has legal standing, and new ownership may be a signal for the authorities to act. Still, the existence of current licenses and permits does indicate the likelihood of their continuation. Before purchase, make that a certainty.

A third important advantage is that you will be in business the day the sale closes. An income flow, however meager, is strong psychological support, and real guests activate the learning curve in a hurry.

Fourth, you'll start out with market recognition. The 1994 biennial survey by the Professional Association of Innkeepers International indicates that repeat guests and their referrals of friends account for about 40 percent of the business of mature inns. An additional 24 percent comes from inn guidebooks. Neither of these categories, amounting to 64 percent of a mature inn's business, is available to a start-up inn. Most people underestimate the time it takes to build a critical mass of guests sufficient to ensure a strong repeat business. Most guests try a variety of inns. Those who do return rarely come frequently. The average inn guest, according to a *Yellow Brick Road* newsletter survey, visits an inn once every eighteen months.

A critical recognition factor for inns is inclusion in guidebooks. Many of the best guides are, like the inns they review, reaching maturity. They are full, and inclusion of a new inn in a future edition will wait upon the exclusion of another. *Mobil Travel Guide*, for example, limits their new entries to those in areas where none are presently listed. American Automobile Association (AAA) and Canadian Automobile Association (CAA) inspections happen just once a year, and your timing may not mesh with their schedule. Even when new editions are published, travelers are slow to replace their travel-worn but note-enhanced previous editions.

The fifth owners of the Glenborough Inn in Santa Barbara, California, found that, even after the turnover of three owners in four years, the guidebook listings of the founding owners still produced 25 percent of their business.

A fifth reason to buy an existing inn is that, contrary to popular wisdom, you can often put together a better financing package. Since you can describe the business more completely, and most major renovations are already in place, financing needs are more clearly definable. A relatively mature inn will have a demonstrable cash flow to convince lending institutions of your ability to repay a loan. Finally, the selling owner will often wish to, or at least recognize the need to, participate in the financing in the form of a second mortgage or second deed of trust.

The final advantage is the availability of transition help: ongoing, hands-on advice and assistance from the original owner, for a time you can specify in the contract, often two weeks to a month. This can help ease transition jitters, though success, of course, is in your hands alone.

As you can see, there are many good reasons to consider buying an existing inn. It's even possible, in some locations, that current zoning and other restrictions may prohibit development of new inns, limiting you to the purchase of an existing inn—and that's not bad!

Are there reasons *not* to buy an existing inn? It does limit you to the inns that exist and to those that are for sale. And you may face difficult price negotiations with owners who have an inflated idea of the value of their business.

Nevertheless, done right, buying an existing inn can provide a quicker and, in the long run, better economic return with less risk.

FINDING AN INN FOR SALE

The best inn you can buy probably isn't for sale—but you can still buy it. What do we mean? Just this: It's highly improbable that you will drive up to the inn of your dreams and find a For Sale sign in the front garden. But it's still possible that the owners might be interested in hearing your proposition, even if they hadn't thought about selling.

That's one reason why the best places to find an inn for sale are innkeeper publications. Write an ad describing the inn you hope to find, and it's just possible that an innkeeper will decide to sell it to you. Among the inn industry publications that have classifieds are *innkeeping, Innquest,* and *Inn Marketing* newsletters and *Country Inns/Bed & Breakfast* magazine (See Resources).

You can also check the business opportunities section of the *Wall Street Journal* and of the local and major metropolitan newspapers in your target area. Business and real-estate consultants who specialize in the inn field are beginning to show up around the country.

If you've targeted one or two specific areas where your inn should be located, contact local innkeepers by mail or telephone for their advice on what might be for sale.

Whichever of these methods you choose, you'll be taken most seriously if you have a clear picture of what you want. Use the checklist below to "build" your model inn.

Number of rooms
Nature of innkeeper quarters
Monthly income necessary for personal needs

Type of breakfast (sit-down, formal, in bed—affects space needs)
Ambience and decor
Geographical requirements (weather, beach, city, rural, etc.)
Amount of renovation you want and can afford
Architectural style
Special features (pool, acreage, etc.)
Services to provide (dinners, baked goods—affects kitchen requirements)
Extent of your involvement in the inn operation

VALUATION

How do you know what an inn is worth? Well, it's a complicated question.

Size is a factor. Michael Yovino-Young of Berkeley, California, who has specialized in inn appraisals for more than ten years, says, "Small inns, under six or seven rooms, are perceived as highly personal businesses, with revenue vulnerable to the whims and abilities of a particular owner-innkeeper. Thus the ability of the inn to sustain income from year to year is judged to be at risk." A small inn is sometimes perceived to be worth its real-estate value as a residence, and not much more.

Age is a factor. Bill Oates, inn-acquisition consultant from Brattleboro, Vermont, says, "Rarely is there any business value to an inn until it is at least three years old. There are exceptions for certain very high tourist areas where the number of inns is too small for the existing market."

But the truly critical factor for any potential buyer is whether the property makes economic sense for him or her. The most practical approach to determining this is to do a return-on-investment calculation.

To figure this, take the up-front cash you will have to invest, plus a figure for the value of your time in running the inn, including the time spent during any renovation. Divide this into your projected net profit, including your salary and the value of your personal benefit income. The resulting figure is the rate of return on your investment.

For example, say you buy an existing inn for a $125,000 down payment and spend an additional $30,000 on renovation and furnishing. You project a net profit of $12,000 the first year, plus $18,000 in personal benefit income, including your living quarters. To determine the return on your total initial capital investment, divide $30,000 (net profit plus personal benefit income) by $155,000 (down payment plus renovation costs); the .19 result translates to a 19 percent return on investment.

In some very desirable areas of the country, property values are so high that this kind of simple return-on-investment calculation is discouraging, but there are other factors you need to consider.

First, buying an inn and becoming an innkeeper are, to some degree, emotional decisions. If being an innkeeper is what you really want to do, it may be worth it to you, in effect, to buy yourself an innkeeping job.

The second factor is property value. When we buy homes, we don't expect any yearly return on our investment, but we do look forward to reaping a gain when we finally sell. This same opportunity should exist with an inn.

And, finally, in those cases where an innkeeper has substantial income in addition to that from the inn, the inn can provide considerable tax deductions, allowing the innkeeper to keep more of that other income in his or her pocket.

You need to feel good about all the money and time you'll put into your inn, so if you're going to make less on your investment than you would in United States Treasury bills, think again. If the figures only look good when you donate all your labor, think about how much you're paying to buy yourself a volunteer position.

On the other hand, keep in mind that it's not the total value of the inn that is used for this calculation. It's the actual out-of-pocket cash—and that makes the rate of return look better.

These are the practical considerations involved in making a decision on an inn's value to you. By contrast, here is inn appraiser Michael Yovino-Young's glossary of terms appraisers and banks use to explore inn value.

OPERATING EXPENSES: Operating expenses, for a seasoned, well-run bed-and-breakfast/country inn, will fall into a range of 40 to 60 percent of gross revenues, excluding reserves, debt service (principal and interest of mortgage), any expenses not necessary for operation, transient occupancy and sales taxes, and owner draw. The smaller the inn, usually the higher the operating expenses in relationship to income.

CAPITALIZATION RATE INDEX: This calculation gives you the Overall Rate of Return on your investment—much like figuring how much return you will make on other investments. You will want this to be between 8 and 12 percent. Use this formula to figure:

Total Income – Operating Expenses = Net Operating Income

$$\frac{\text{Net Operating Income}}{\text{Purchase price of property}} = \text{Capitalization Rate}$$

GROSS RENT MULTIPLIER (GRM): This is income based and, though time-honored in real estate transactions, must be tempered with inn purchases with the other valuation indices listed here. This is running 4.7 to 6.4 in the West and 4.5 to 12.7 in the East. The lower the GRM the better. Use this formula:

$$\frac{\text{Sales Price}}{\text{Gross Annual Income}} \qquad = \qquad \text{GRM}$$

PRICE PER GUEST ROOM: This all-inclusive index assumes the building has a kitchen, common area, and innkeeper quarters; and includes fixtures, furniture, equipment, and intangible assets of the business, such as goodwill. This is figured as follows:

$$\frac{\text{Sales Price}}{\text{Number of guest rooms}}$$

Examples of prices per guest room of bed-and-breakfast/country inns actually sold:

Area	Average prices	Source
West	$64,000-140,000	1989-1994 (Yovino-Young)
East		
B&B Inn	$35,000-90,000	1992-1994 (Oates & Bredfeldt)
Dinner Service	$36,000-104,500	1992-1994 (Oates & Bredfeldt)

COST APPROACH: In the absence of any other possible approach, say when there are no sales of inns in the area and no income data to analyze, an appraiser may be forced to rely on replacement cost or reproduction cost methods.

The cost approach is essentially a real-estate value. What are typical ratios of real-estate values to other assets of a going concern? Based on a Yovino-Young sample of more than sixty inns appraised since 1983, the ratios vary as follows: real estate, 85 to 93 percent; personal property, 7 to 15 percent; and other intangible assets, 0 to 5 percent.

Placing a value on a business, particularly on an inn business, is not an exact science. There is no one way to do it, but there is one certainty: Sellers will always want more than buyers want to pay. That's not surprising. Sellers have conceived and nourished a property and business, perhaps since its inception. They're almost like parents. How do you place a fair value on something this personal? This part of your inn-search process may be the most difficult and exasperating. Owners tend to value their inns on the basis of what they've put into them, rather than on what a new owner can get out.

Hire your own value consultant or appraiser if you're uncomfortable with the price being asked. Listing agents for inns are not always well informed about the inn business and lack the resources to gather market data on comparable properties.

A word of caution: Don't commit yourself to an expensive appraisal—and they can cost $5,000 to $10,000—before you consult with your lender. Lenders usually have their own lists of approved appraisers and will not act upon reports from others.

Your appraiser or consultant should look at the inn for quality of location, the facilities themselves, and the consistency and reliability of the income history. Your adviser should also be able to inform you about the inn's desirability from the viewpoint of local institutional lenders. Unbiased answers to these and other practical questions are usually worth the cost of hiring independent experts.

ACHIEVING FINANCIAL GROWTH

How can you project the income effect of positive changes in the inn? Very carefully! Consider the ideas below, and make educated cost projections of the expense to implement them—don't ignore the cost of lost income if you need to close for remodeling—and the additional income from new rooms, more expensive rooms, higher occupancy, and additional sales and services. Be specific, and don't spend money you don't expect to get back in higher income.

Increase number of rooms
Increase room rates
Increase occupancy
Decrease expenses
Upgrade quality
Add capital improvements
    Hot tub
    Swimming pool
    Private baths
    Fireplaces
    Curb appeal
Increase profit centers
    Retail sales
    Additional food service
    Wine and beer license
Special promotions
    Marketing changes
    Expand markets
    Small group/conference site

Business travelers
Seniors
Foreign travelers
Travel agent–generated business
Bicycle groups

NEGOTIATING FOR PURCHASE

As a prospective buyer, you can't expect a seller to reveal detailed financial data until you have demonstrated that you are a qualified buyer. You are entitled to summary financial information, however, which may include gross receipts, net operating income, and occupancy percentages for the most recent year. On the basis of this data, you will be expected to make an initial offer. This often includes price, terms, management contract, covenant not to compete, disclosure requirements, and contingencies.

At this point, you will also want to specify the detailed material you will need to review during the escrow period. Naturally, it's essential to protect your interests with contingencies that make the offer invalid if the comprehensive data you receive later fails to support the summary. Now the negotiation begins.

This stage is always touchy, and you'll want to use your consultant or broker in the process. The cardinal rule of negotiation is to determine what you want and what the other person wants and to try to achieve both: a win-win deal. Of course, you must decide first what exactly you need as a bottom line. Keep that foremost in your mind as you make decisions during the negotiations.

Remember that this is a process. No major negotiation results in immediate agreement. Everyone feels hurt or insulted at one time or another during the deal making, but going back and forth is a necessary part of the successful agreement.

And often, when you think all the negotiations are finished and the papers are ready to be signed, more demands are forthcoming and the process begins again.

During the negotiating period, try to maintain some distance from the owner and let your consultant or broker do the talking. This can keep the normal animosities and personal feelings separate from the working relationship you will want later. During this time, many things change or come up unexpectedly to cause both parties distress. This is normal, but keep your consultant out front and your bottom line in mind.

THE PHYSICAL PREMISES

You will want a contractor or person knowledgeable about old buildings to walk through the inn to be sure there are no surprises and that you are planning adequate financial resources for renovation in your business plan.

It is also important to double-check that the inn is licensed, approved, and zoned for all the business being done: number of rooms, bathrooms, pool or Jacuzzi, kitchen, fireplaces, parking, septic.

Most states have laws requiring the sellers and their agents to disclose all information relating to any significant historical problem the property may have suffered, such as flooding, foundation settlement, fire, wind-storm damage, and so on. You are entitled to know these facts and should protect yourself by asking direct questions. If in doubt on any point of concern, ask for a written statement from the sellers.

Once you have reached agreement and have signed a contract spelling out all the contingencies, you will want to be sure to obtain the following:

Real estate transfer disclosure statement from seller and agent(s)

Use permit

Zoning ordinance and assurance your building is in a properly zoned area

Building permit and final inspection

Health Department inspection and county ordinance for kitchen

Copy of recent tests and county reports

Bed tax ordinance and assure inn records payment for last three years

Business license

Structural pest control inspection

Contractor's inspection of building

Resale license and record of present owner's payments

Liquor license

Copy of local or state Americans with Disabilities Act requirements

Copy of local or state Fire Code requirements

Any correspondence with city regarding bed-and-breakfast use

Look at competitors' rooms rates and occupancy

IRS tax returns of present owner for last three years and evaluate: Will your expenses be the same?; Is there unreported income?; Are discretionary costs included—not necessary for operation of the inn? (For example, dog grooming, auto purchase); Does it include capital expense or non-recurring costs?; Have maintenance and repairs, or linen expenses been deferred?

List of all furniture, fixtures, and equipment to be transferred. Include pictures, linens, dishes, pots, pans, silverware, appliances, lawn mowers, tools, etc. It is a good idea to get a list of what is not included at the same time.

List of where sellers advertise and promote the inn and how much it costs:

Guidebooks; How advertised, in which media; Yellow pages; which chamber of commerce; local and regional organizations; referrals from other inns

List of local suppliers and labor, including plumbers, carpenters, house-keepers etc.

Accounting of pre-paid reservations

"Bewares" from an Old Pro

Owner financing—A seller may offer very attractive terms in order to sell an inn at a price over market value.

High cash down—If you have to put high cash down, the inn may not be economically feasible.

Projections—Carefully examine all assumptions for projections. If the local area and nearby inns do not have comparable occupancy or income, how will your inn meet these projections.

Resale value—If you pay too much or buy on projections, the next buyer may be more sophisticated and unwilling to pay for your mistakes.

Use—Be sure that your intended use and number of rooms is authorized by USE permit or the zoning ordinance.

Disclosure—Use the disclosure check list so you can make an informed decision.

Local market—Real estate is generally set by local conditions. Do not be misled because a property is cheap compared to your area. Notice the differences between high and low prices in the examples.

—from Lyman Robbins, CCIM, Santa Rosa, California

MAKING THE TRANSITION BETWEEN OWNERS

If all has gone reasonably smoothly prior to closing the sale, your working relationship with the former owners will be off to a good start. Most selling innkeepers have invested a great deal of themselves in what you have just made yours, so they will want to share with you what they know about the business and the quirks of the property.

Of course, you will want to make changes and to approach the inn from a fresh viewpoint. Remember to be kind. Usually the former owners know all the things that are wrong and had their own reasons for not changing them. Your ideas may not be as revolutionary as you think. If you approach the former owners asking for feedback on your plans, they will probably be able to warn you about pitfalls or suggest places to turn for more information.

To be sure you get all the information you want from the former owners, make a list, using this book as a guideline. Also, encourage the former owners to make a list of what they think you need to know. Be sure to go through both lists thoroughly, writing down the information for future reference.

STAFF

Staff transitions are especially touchy in inns, because the personal nature of an inn carries over into the relationships between staff and owners. Staff will usually feel loyal to the former owners, and it will take time for you to win that loyalty. On the other hand, staff people will often have ideas for you that they couldn't get the former owners to try.

A change in ownership is naturally threatening to employees, but regular communication and clear renegotiation of job descriptions and your needs will usually lay the groundwork for a strong relationship.

If you want to replace staff, however, make a clean break. (See Staffing in "Up and Running," page 255.)

PROMOTION

If the former innkeeper is well liked and has long been an integral part of the inn operation, you may want to ask him or her to write a letter inviting former guests to "come meet the newest member of the Long Lost Inn family." You might make a special discount offer to former guests when you send the letter, as an extra encouragement for them to come.

New owners are news, so try to get local press coverage about the transition. Your aim will be to highlight yourselves and any new exciting direction you plan to take, such as adding dinner service or restoring the original gardens.

You may wish to foot the bill for a transition party, where the former owners will be guests of honor, and invite local merchants, media, and restaurateurs. If they're willing, ask your predecessors to make a formal presentation of a certificate acknowledging you as the only people to whom they would entrust their old place.

What if you want to disassociate yourselves and the inn from the old ownership? Even so, it will be valuable for you to understand what kinds of promotion have worked for the inn in the past, so you can develop new promotional angles along those lines.

A final caution: Do not change the inn name without a lot of thought! If you need to disassociate your inn that completely from its past, be aware that you put yourself in the position almost of a start-up operation from the viewpoint of recognition.

No Dough, No Go?

If you don't already own the building, owning an inn can be a very expensive proposition. But if that yearning to serve up coffee cake and welcome guests just won't leave your heart, you do have options.

More and more inns are hiring managers or assistant innkeepers. (PAII has a staff locator file for members.) Usually owners are happy to train you, but they will be more likely to take you seriously if you have studied this book, of course, and perhaps taken an innkeeping workshop, attended appropriate innkeeper conferences, or taken restaurant and hospitality courses. Inn management is a serious position; be careful to clearly define your hours and duties with the owner. Because innkeeping is such appealing work, it's easy to sign on for more than you can really handle. You can set yourself up for burnout that way. Be realistic about your abilities and also about your salary needs, keeping in mind that this is generally not a get-rich business. Salaries are not high, but many inns have good, unusual benefits, like great locations, simple lodgings in a terrific inn, and overnights at other inns at no charge to you—for research.

Or what about innsitting or relief innkeeping when the innkeeper wants time off? This is a separate business for which you need all the skills of an innkeeper, plus insurance and self-promotion skills. To get innkeepers to leave their "babies" with you, you need references from other innkeepers.

How to get the necessary experience? Volunteer for a few weekends or a month at a nearby inn to see if the work appeals to you. After you learn the ropes and the innkeeper feels comfortable with you, offer to innsit for a weekend or a week, for pay. If all goes well, you've got a reference!

As you consider these options, keep in mind too that few inns have large innkeeper quarters, so if you have a family, two dogs, and a llama, you're limiting your market considerably. (For more information and ideas, see Staffing in "Up and Running," page 255.)

Existing Inns

Santa Barbara has been a bustling inn community since the first inn opened there in 1980. Here's what has happened during the last fifteen years to its fourteen inns.

✳ *The first inn opened with four guest rooms and shared baths. Two of the original four owners remain, having bought out the other two. The innkeepers purchased the building next door, adding five guest rooms and better innkeeper quarters. Later they converted a ninth room and added phones and private baths and a Jacuzzi in one room.*

✳ *Eight inns have sold to new owners. One inn changed its name to project a new image. Two were sold for a purpose other than an inn. One sold to another innkeeper. One ended up in the original owner's hands due to misrepresentation of the financial information at the time of sale.*

✳ *One inn was built for speculation and as a decorating experiment. It was on the market at a very high price throughout the 1980s until it was reclaimed by the bank, not because the inn was not able to be profitable, but because the investor's other properties were in trouble during the recession.*

✳ *In four cases, the inns were developed from property already owned by the innkeepers. One of these went out of business after two years, returning the building to its original use. Two others have steadily expanded and are successfully operating still. The fourth is so substandard that other inns do not refer overflow to this innkeeper, who has never visited an inn, read an innkeeping resource book, or attended a conference.*

✳ *Four inns sold within three years of opening due to the owners' unrealistic views of the business.*

✳ *One nine-year-old inn with a leased property sold rather quickly — three times — because the price was so much lower than for inns where the price included the property. The three sales were all prompted by disillusionment or failure to run the business professionally.*

✳ *One innkeeper filed bankruptcy, unable during a recession period to sell other property he owned to finalize the inn purchase.*

✳ *Two inns have been for sale off and on for five years. Rarely has an inn sold in less than two years.*

✳ *In at least two cases, the selling innkeepers carried part or all of the loan.*

✳ *Six of the inn owners have moved off premises, though they are still intensely involved with operations, often answering evening telephones, for example.*

Pat Hardy, co–executive director of the Professional Association of Innkeepers International, sees the Santa Barbara experience as a "microcosm of what's happening with inns nationwide. Losing partners, adding baths, becoming disillusioned, or *running a poor business are not unusual. It's also interesting that disillusionment occurs early on with people who really weren't cut out to be innkeepers — and say so themselves when they leave the business. Finally, here as elsewhere, inns take a long time to sell and rarely sell at the price the innkeeper originally asked."*

CHOOSING AND WORKING WITH A REALTOR OR CONSULTANT

Before you sign a contract with a realtor or consultant, interview your prospects. Ask questions and get references. Ask innkeepers or friends to recommend possible agents, but avoid working with close personal friends or family, unless you are very good at keeping your business life and your personal life separate. Check references carefully and beware of fast talkers, pushy people, and those who guess at answers rather than admitting that they don't know the answers.

Remember that not all realtors work with "business opportunities." The gap between evaluating real property and valuing a bed-and-breakfast inn is enormous.

Once you decide on a consultant or realtor, make him or her work hard; your future depends on it. But don't rely solely on your agent's judgment. You will have to do a lot of the work yourself.

LEASING AN INN

Leasing an inn is a viable method of becoming an innkeeper when you do not have enough cash to purchase. Two leasing modes are presently used in this industry. One, you purchase the business portion of the inn outright and lease the inn building and, often, the furniture and fixtures as well. Or, two, you negotiate a lease with an option to purchase at a scheduled time.

Leasing, though less expensive than buying, will still involve a substantial cash investment and with it a serious commitment to the business. The risk from the sellers' viewpoint is great: If you destroy their business, they will have to come back and correct your mistakes after they have moved on to another life.

Leasing works well in several situations.

✳ When property values make it difficult to purchase real property at a price that makes running an inn profitable. It's not unlikely that an inn purchased five years ago may have appreciated so much that a new owner cannot afford to operate the inn and make mortgage payments.

* When you know you need a ten-room inn, but only have cash for a down payment for a five-room place.

* When the seller's depreciated basis is small in relation to value, meaning any monies received in a sale will be subject to significant capital gains taxes.

* When the current debt is small in relation to the current value, normally less than 25 percent.

* When owner financing has roadblocks that prevent complete transfer of title, such as an outstanding debt that needs to be paid off first.

LEASE/OPTION

According to Bill Oates, many creative people have discovered that a lease with an option to purchase solved many of the problems of financing a going concern. Here is an example from his *Innquest* newsletter (Vol. X, Issue 1, 1993) of how he structures a lease-option arrangement.

Assuming a going concern inn with a current value of $895,000, there would be an up-front payment of $125,000 (or 14 percent of the price). Normally, an option of this type would be 10 to 15 percent of the value. This sum buys a five-year right to purchase the inn at the option price of $895,000, less the option payment. The option agreement to purchase may be exercised at any time in the five-year period. The option would cease if the concurrent lease were terminated by a default on the lease.

The option payment goes to the owner and is not refundable, nor is it taxable until the option is exercised or expires by time or default.

A concurrent five-year lease would be executed at the same time. This would be a triple-net lease (all real-estate taxes, insurance, and maintenance expenses would be the lessee's responsibility). The base lease payment is normally comparable to a mortgage payment for the balance between option payment and purchase price. In this case, the balance is $770,000. Interest on that at 8 percent (prime plus 2 percent) equals $61,600 per year. A mortgage of that amount on a twenty-year amortization basis with an interest rate of prime (6 percent) plus 2 (8 percent) would require an annual payment of $77,287 ($6,440.59 per month). Of that, $16,275 is the principal in year one; the principal portion of the payment increases slightly each year.

Each year a portion of the payment would be construed as an additional option payment similar to a mortgage. Payments start low to ease cash flow and rise in later years to encourage exercise of the option. If the option were exercised at the end of the third year, the additional purchase price would be $740,000 as follows:

Option price	$895, 000
Less option payment	125,000
Assigned option per schedule:	30,000
Due	$740,000

At the end of year four, the amount due to exercise the option would be $725,000, and at the end of year five, $710,000.

For the lessee–prospective buyer, the advantages of a lease-option arrangement are:

✳ It achieves the objective of being an innkeeper when it might not be possible through normal means.

✳ It is much cheaper to get in: no bank fees, no appraisal fees, no property transfer tax, smaller legal and accounting fees.

✳ It is much faster.

✳ The risk is not total, though it is substantial.

LEASING THE PROPERTY, OWNING THE BUSINESS

When an owner does not want to sell the family homestead or you do not have enough money to buy a property, leasing the building and land and buying the inn business may be a good choice to consider. Be sure you consult a real-estate attorney and your accountant when you set up a lease for your dream inn.

Leasing the real estate is the way most businesses operate, including hotels, so this is not a new idea. While 83 percent of all inns are owned lock, stock, and barrel by the innkeeper, 17 percent of all inns are leased, and that number is increasing. Unfortunately, poorly structured leases can put the lessee in a difficult financial situation, making success problematic and default probable. The best way to prevent such failures is to create a win-win lease that insures the owner won't get greedy and the lessee will be eager to maintain a fair agreement.

In negotiating such a lease, consider the following issues:

GETTING OUT   Always check on how you can get out of the lease at the time you are getting into it. The length of the lease should protect your investment long enough for you to see a return and should allow you time to run the business to a level that would be attractively profitable to a prospective new owner. In some cases you can build in a series of points when the lease can automatically be renewed or ended. Build this into the lease in your favor.

LENGTH OF LEASE   Stagger the options; three, ten, or twenty years are possible periods of duration. The three-year option protects you if you decide to get out of the business completely. The longer time periods give you an opportunity to sell at a profit, having established the business to a level attractive to a new owner.

PERCENTAGE OF SALES If you agree to pay the lessor a percentage of sales, be sure that the base amount of the lease is very low. This type of provision makes sense in a retail operation, where foot traffic is high, but can be crippling for an inn where the number of rooms, and thus the amount of business, has little flexibility. If you must accept such a provision, design it so as to assure the lessor an amount covering basic costs and a reasonable extra. Then the innkeeper should receive a comfortable profit, with the remainder divided between the lessor and innkeeper.

REPAIRS AND RENOVATION Who pays for what? This part of the lease can get very detailed. One option is for the innkeeper to pay for inside work and for the lessor to pay for outside work: care of the roof, trees, and driveways, painting, and so on.

Another possibility is for the building owner to pay for renovations that would increase the value of the property, but for the lessee to cover the costs of extra baths, carpeting, or health-code work in the kitchen, which would benefit the inn business alone.

OPTION TO BUY If you have any hopes of buying, get this in writing. Try to lock in a sales price, unless housing prices seem to be falling. In most cases your business operation will increase the value of the property, and you don't want to pay the seller for your efforts.

Build into the lease the opportunity for a future buyer to purchase the property at the time the inn business is sold. Structure this clearly, so as not to confuse a live prospect.

TRANSFER OF LEASE You should be able to sell the business to a qualified person and transfer the lease with no unreasonable limitations imposed by the lessor.

SALE OF THE PROPERTY If the property is sold, the new owner must be obligated to honor your lease. If possible, also negotiate that you get a percentage of the profit over the value when you first leased it, especially if you are paying for renovations. You may also want a clause giving you first right to buy the property if it is offered for sale (right of first refusal).

Leasing an Inn

The partners in the subchapter S corporation of the Inn on Mt. Ada had no other option than to negotiate a lease to use the former Wrigley Mansion and its fantastic location—it is perched on a hill overlooking the tiny town of Avalon on Catalina Island, twenty-six miles across the sea from Los Angeles. All the rooms have ocean views. The former owner used to watch his Chicago Cubs during spring training from the downstairs office.

The innkeepers and friends signed a thirty-page thirty-year lease (renewable for another thirty years) for the building and the property with Santa Catalina Island Conservancy and the University of Southern California. The lease payment is 15 percent of the annual gross room income and 7.5 percent of the annual food and beverage gross sales with a flat fee paid monthly. The flat fee is adjusted according to the consumer price index annually. At year end, the difference between the annual percentage and the monthly fee is paid to the owners. For the first five years the monthly fee was lower to allow the inn to get on its feet. A $10,000 deposit was paid to the lessors refundable at the completion of the lease. The inn paid $1.6 million renovating the property, landscaping, and furnishing the four common rooms and six guest rooms and suites. Room rates range from $230 to $590 American Plan and include evening appetizers, wine, champagne, and a personal golf cart for trips up and down the hill to town.

Innkeepers Marlene McAdam and Suzie Griffin recommend making the lease very clear, leaving nothing to a gentleman's agreement. The people with whom they initially signed their lease are no longer with the university or the conservancy. The lease defines such things as when the lessor must be consulted about lessee spending plans and the AAA or Mobil quality levels the inn must maintain. Good ongoing communication has helped the lessor-lessee relationship of ten years to work well. Though Suzie and Marlene receive a salary and housing from the corporation, the inn did not make a profit for seven years. They point out that since they won't have any real-estate value at the end of the lease, they will need patience to make back their money during the remaining twenty-three years on the lease.

Special thanks to Bill Oates and Michael Yovino-Young (see Resources) for their invaluable assistance on this chapter.

114

GETTING
INN SHAPE

When you make your plans about who will do what before the inn opens, be sure to keep in mind that time is money, and this cuts two ways. On the one hand, you can save the cost of hiring people to do the tasks you're willing to take on yourself. On the other hand, every day that you spend getting ready to open means one more day that you have no paying guests.

Say you plan to do the remodeling first, then the decorating, and then the promotion. You're planning on lots of time. Hiring a contractor to do the remodel while you get started on the brochure, or vice versa, can be very cost-effective, if it gets the inn open a month early.

You can calculate roughly how effective hiring help will be. For example, hiring a public relations firm to prepare a logo, brochure, stationery, signs, and a press kit might get you open four weeks early. Since most of your costs are fixed whether or not you're open—mortgage, insurance, auto—the income you receive from room rents can be applied pretty directly to your costs. You might want to reduce that income figure by the projected costs of food, supplies, and staff, if any. But the basic point is this: Since your major costs are constant whether or not you're open, delaying your opening costs you money.

AMBIENCE

Ambience is character, atmosphere, and mood. It's the consistent carrying out of a theme, such as the Victorian Mansion or Ye Olde Ski Lodge. Ambience planned and achieved with clarity during the renovation stage can be a major marketing tool over the lifetime of the inn. But before you even consider the marketability of an image, you need to be sure it fits you. You'll look as silly as an orchid at a hoe-down if you wear ski boots in a Victorian mansion.

The classic advice to aspiring authors is "write what you know," and there's a corollary for aspiring innkeepers: More than anything else, your inn should be your own personal favorite, the place you would most like to stay. It must reflect your personality as well as your fantasy. Design it so that it feels true to you.

How do you see yourself? Ask your partner and friends to describe you. Does their view match your own? Do you need lots of private time in the mornings, or do you love to sit down to breakfast with a crowd? Do you prefer that friends call before they drop by, or do you keep a big pot of soup bubbling to encourage impromptu gatherings? Everybody needs private time, but do you need more than the average? Are you formal or casual? Are chats around the fireplace, feet up, your favorite way to spend the evening? Or do you prefer long gowns and tuxedoes in a setting that sparkles with elegance? Do you think a little clutter makes for comfort, or do you tend to empty the ashtray before the cigarette is extinguished? Any of these styles can be a success. The question is, which one is for you?

What about your community? Who comes there, and for what purpose? Is it a mountainous, rustic area, or a city that hums all night long? The personality as well as the geography of your inn's community must be taken into account.

What's your inn building like? It's difficult to do art nouveau in a Federal-style building. The appearance of the structure is one of the biggest elements of the ambience your guests will experience. Inappropriate decor is an assault on the senses, but the range of acceptable choices is wide. The look of the inn exterior can enhance the mood, creating a quality that draws passersby to stop and stay. The way you set up your property, for example, can be expansive and open, or you can landscape to provide privacy and intimate corners. The entryway can determine what guests feel in the first thirty seconds outside and inside your door. While they wait for you, do you want them to feel formal or relaxed?

What's your family like? Do you have small children or teenagers? Who will be your helpers? Do you need very separate space and physical privacy? Will you feel comfortable with guests wandering into your quarters during family arguments or while you're trying to reprimand your children? And how will your guests feel about it?

Finally, what's the field like? What are industry expectations? What's your competition doing? You'll get the best idea of the range of what's offered at inns by traveling and staying in them. Some are elegant and expensive; others have a warm family feeling; still others exude an energetic sense of the outdoor activities available or offer a romantic, intimate atmosphere and fantastic views.

These questions should help you establish a set of givens against which to evaluate image options. Keep in mind that your ambience will be a marketing tool. The more clearly you know what you are, the easier it will be to project that image.

As you visit other inns, analyze how their approaches work or don't work. Adapt ideas that you like to fit your own objectives. Visit inns with an open mind and adventurous spirit. Let yourself absorb the unique flavor of each establishment, and don't prejudge on the basis of your own great concept. Don't try to make an inn what it isn't. If you prefer a mountain cabin, don't reject a place because it's a formal city inn. Neither one is "better," but each needs to be special.

The inns you like best may differ tremendously from each other, but probably each of your favorites will communicate a definite something. Try to describe it as a starting point for taking stock of what you want. Don't even think about renovation until your unique ambience is clear to you.

Ambience

Chris and Denny Becker at A Teton Tree House in Wilson, Wyoming, are former white-water rafting guides who decided, while on a trip through South America, to settle down and raise children. Denny gradually built their hillside inn, with each room offering a view of the trees or valley below. There are ninety-four steps up to the inn's two-story living room, but the climate is worth it to reach the roaring fire in the stone fireplace and the collection of books and clever puzzles. Denny (Chris has gone back to teaching) serves on a hand-carved log table a hearty and heart-healthy breakfast of local-grain hot cereal, several fresh fruits, an organic homemade granola, and at least three freshly baked breads. His knowledge of the area makes for great conversation and is invaluable to guests who need information about local activities. Denny helps people select their day's adventures in Yellowstone Park, providing advice on what to wear and where to hike, and providing maps and loaner backpacks. When guests return, he encourages them to replenish the fluids lost on the trail with Gatorade from the refrigerator. In the inn's tiny gift shop area, guests find hats, T-shirts, maps, and guidebooks that augment their appreciation for the nearby Jackson Hole area.

"GREEN" ROOMS

As public consciousness is raised and individuals grow increasingly committed to environmental action on a personal level, lodging properties are taking steps for both moral and marketing reasons. Your efforts toward environmental preservation will be appreciated by 80 percent of your guests, according to a survey by *Yellow Brick Road* newsletter. Creating green rooms is more than a guest room issue; it involves actually setting up a sustainable system. In developing any green program, the bywords are *reuse, recycle, reduce.* Letting the public know the concrete ways you live out your commitment to earth stewardship will bring you business—at least until green becomes the norm.

Here are some ideas.

* Use natural fabrics.

✳ Install low-flush toilets, low-flow showerheads, and faucet water-flow restrictors. Eliminate drips; keep plumbing repaired.

✳ Use china, cloth, and glass rather than plastic, Styrofoam, or paper.

✳ Recycling bottles, cans, and newspapers is routine for many people; make recycling containers available to your guests. Even flight attendants collect newspapers!

✳ Your guests will enjoy your special biodegradable soaps and probably won't mind a bit if you don't replace them daily for stay-over guests. Using sink dispensers as well as smaller bars of soap gives guests an environmentally sound choice. *Eurobath* dispensers for soap and shampoo in tubs and showers eliminates the proliferation of little plastic bottles; ask your local hotel supplier about it. Or have a central butler's basket of larger containers of luxury-type shampoo, conditioner, lotion, and so on. Give your used soap to charity.

✳ Give your guests an option on laundry. A Munich hotel posted this message: "Can you vaguely guess how many tons of towels are unnecessarily washed every day in the world? This means enormous quantities of washing powder polluting and burdening our water. Please decide for yourself and help. Towels on the floor mean, 'please change'; towels hung back on the rack mean, 'I will use once more for the sake of the environment.' Thank you." Do be sure you have enough towel rack space in bathrooms to dry wet towels.

✳ Wood furniture not plastic is the norm in inns. Because furnishings are often antique, the innkeeper is not endangering rain forest woods. If you purchase new furniture, choose environmentally appropriate woods.

✳ Envirosafe cleaning products have been tested and are being used safely throughout the lodging industry, and are even required by OSHA to protect employees' health.

✳ In-room Jacuzzis and wood-burning fireplaces create a quandary for environmentally conscious guests and innkeepers. Consider an outdoor, enclosed tub that guests can use on a private reservation basis, and look at the new gas-log fireplaces that light in an instant, do not pollute, and look good. But also remember that your guests may lead Spartan lives all year and treat themselves only rarely to the luxury of an inn; that's an acceptable ratio!

✳ Use metal trash baskets so that you can avoid plastic bags in trash containers.

✳ Use metal or wicker containers and laundry baskets rather than plastic ones.

✳ Buy only containers that are recyclable.

* Start a compost heap. If you are not in the country, anaerobic containers are available that do not smell or attract flies. Or find a local pig farmer who will take your garbage.
* Patronize a local organic farm or farmers' market.
* Insulate.
* Keep your heater and air conditioner tuned and filters changed. Providing individual room temperature control can actually reduce the cost of heating.
* Use long-life light bulbs, including the new warm-spectrum, screw-in fluorescents—you want green rooms, not green guests! Consider installing a switch that turns on lights only when someone is in the common rooms. Consider also motion-activated outdoor lighting.
* Print all of your inn materials on recycled paper with as much post-consumer waste as you can find and afford. Use soy ink. Be sure to put the "recycled" logo on these materials.
* Plan low-water landscaping, and use a drip system and/or a laundry-water irrigation system for lawns.

At the Riverwalk Inn in San Antonio, Texas, a sign offered by Green Hotels Association gives guests an option: Fresh towels daily, or use them another day for the environment's sake. Guests like having a choice; 90 percent of them at Riverwalk will hang towels up for another day, making a substantial saving in laundry time and money, as well as in polluting detergents and bleach. Using a front-loading washing machine is another way to save on water and detergent; it also saves wear and tear on linens.

The biggest challenge to going green is educating the innkeepers and staff. Include everyone in the process. When people understand the *why*, the *how* is often not so difficult. Remember the underlying message of *Fifty Simple Things You Can Do to Save the Earth*: You don't have to be neurotically regimented about environmentalism—every little thing you do helps. Eliminate one throwaway plastic bag a day, and you'll save boxes of them over the year.

Once you're committed to creating a green room or a whole green inn, more ways of refining this vision will be suggested by guests and staff. And guest appreciation will show on the bottom line.

❖ RENOVATING

This is what you've been waiting for: the difficult and expensive task of making a promising structure into the inn of your dreams.

And it can be fun! Some innkeepers find after several years of operating an inn that the most fun of all was creating it. If you've done the groundwork in visiting other inns to develop a strong sense of what you like and don't, if you have financing in hand so you can hire adequate help, and if you have allowed adequate time, then you're off to one of the most creative challenges of your life.

Renovating an inn is different from renovating a personal home. At home, we usually do one room at a time, at our leisure—sometimes during vacations, often when we've decided to sell. With an inn, you'll do all the rooms at once, with a timetable and an opening date in mind, and you'll be attempting to please many different people, not just yourself and your family.

Depending on the size of the project, hiring assistance can make the difference between a challenge and a nightmare. If the job involves little more than choosing new furnishings, you may want to do it on your own. If you feel safer with the advice of a decorator, but haven't the budget or the inclination to put the whole project in a decorator's hands, you'll find many competent designers who will be happy to act as consultants for an hourly fee.

If you are adding rooms, changing the exterior, or doing anything that will require the approval of the local government building department, you will probably need an architect and a general contractor. General contractors run jobs, bringing in carpenters, plumbers, electricians, roofers, drywallers, and so on at the appropriate times. If you decide to act as owner-builder, you will do the job of the general contractor.

Before you decide what you'll do yourself and what you'll hire others to do, complete your financial projections and get the money. Determine and outline the following features precisely.

✳ The number of guest rooms you want, from the viewpoint of staffing and serving.

✳ The number of rooms you need, financially speaking.

✳ Kitchen and dining facilities.

✳ The types of amenities, such as whirlpool tubs, fireplaces, hot tubs, wet bars, bathrooms, balconies, decks and outside living areas, or a swimming pool.

✳ Innkeeper quarters.

✳ Laundry facilities.

✳ Parking.

✳ Common areas, living room, TV room, or library.

✳ Bathroom and other accommodation for employees and nonresident guests.

Sketch out your renovation ideas. You can buy drafting paper and templates for bathroom fixtures and furniture. Play with placement in relation to entrances and windows. Consider ventilation of the rooms and bathrooms. Spend time in each room at various times of the day to check lighting and heat needs.

Use the numerous valuable resources available for information on restoring old homes to avoid serious and costly mistakes. (See Resources, page 305.)

Once you're clear on what you need, you need to find the people to help you do it. You find competent, reliable, and honest decorators, architects, and contractors in much the same way that you find other support people.

✳ Architects, designers, or contractors can often recommend people for the other jobs.

✳ Look at older homes, inns, and restaurants that have been successfully renovated, and ask owners and managers for their recommendations. If you see homes being renovated, stop and talk with the people working at the site.

✳ A historical society or landmark committee may also be able to give you names of people who work on older homes. Sometimes, though rarely, a building department will give you names.

✳ Lumber companies, wholesale hardware stores, and other building supply providers may have recommendations.

Select two or three good prospects for each job area. Call them and briefly describe your project and timetable. If some prospects are not interested, they may be able to recommend others. Set up initial consultations at the site with interested people. Usually there is no charge for this, but don't waste the time of a bidder you have no intention of hiring. Present your list of jobs and your sketches, but also be attentive to the ideas of these pros. They can often solve in a moment a problem you've grappled with for weeks. Don't be afraid to discuss money. Whether you're buying an hour's consulting time or spending thousands on an architect, get rates and bids.

If your project requires an architect, he or she will probably send a draftsperson to measure your house and site as the first step in preparing working drawings. Be sure your architect is familiar with the local building and zoning departments' requirements for setbacks, zoning requirements, site plans, landscape plans, and so on. Established inns that have already gone through the process can be very helpful in this regard. Provide the architect with what you consider to be the items to include in renovation costs. Use the sample list that follows on page 129 to draw up your own list. Ask for a preliminary design and cost estimate.

When the preliminary design drawings arrive, study them closely. Go over them with someone who is familiar with all the trades and understands the symbols for plumbing and electrical work. Think through these aspects of the project in the preliminary design phase, not after working drawings have been prepared. Every change costs money. When the changes in the preliminary design are complete, the architect you have chosen will prepare final drawings for the approval of the building department and any necessary review boards.

If you have done your homework, visited many inns, and talked with other innkeepers, you probably will be more knowledgeable about what is required for a bed-and-breakfast inn than most architects. They tend to specialize in projects that are either strictly residential or commercial, and inns don't exactly fit either category. Several years ago, a prospective innkeeper we know allowed her architect to convince her that shared baths are part of the B&B ambience! This may be true in England or Germany, but in the United States, guests want private baths.

Your architect is a good resource when selecting your contractor. Before hiring a general contractor, you should take the following steps.

∗ Obtain additional recommendations from innkeepers, building suppliers, the local building department, and owners of houses you admire.

∗ Verify the contractor's license; obtain copies of the general liability insurance and workers' compensation policies.

∗ Discuss fixed bid versus time-and-materials contracts. Discuss the payment schedule. Discuss liens and lien releases.

∗ Evaluate the size of the construction company; discuss concurrent projects.

∗ Obtain a list of previous projects; visit them and talk to owners.

∗ Discuss completion of project as promised, costs, and time; the availability of the contractor to correct problems; the reliability and quality of subcontractors.

∗ Make final selection and sign contract. You may want to seek legal advice prior to signing papers.

Read the sample contract in Appendix 5 and use it as a model for your own contract. Add a specification sheet detailing your choice of fixtures and supplies by brand names.

When the work is completed and you are settling the bills, ask each party to sign a "lien release for work done and release upon final payment" form. This form acknowledges that you have paid in full for the work performed and that the worker (plumber, electrician, painter) cannot file a mechanic's lien against your property. A mechanic's lien is where someone with whom you have done business (purchase of labor, services, equipment, and/or materials for the purpose of improvement upon real property) files a form with the state, declaring that they have not been fully paid. This lien is recorded against the property and shows as a claim against the property's title. You will realize how much this affects you when attempting to refinance or sell the property. These liens surface in a title search and all must be satisfied.

If there is a contractor supervising your renovation, and you are paying him directly for work done, have the contractor sign off upon final payment that all monies owed to each subcontractor (list them all) have been paid in full.

The term for a mechanic's lien may differ from state to state, but the concept is the same. The release form can often be picked up in your local stationery store.

Renovating

One of the most common complaints in hotels, bed-and-breakfast inns, and country inns is the lack of soundproofing. "Nothing is less romantic than hearing someone else's romance," quipped Sandra Soule, author of America's Wonderful Little Hotels and Inns at the 1994 PAII conference. When renovating, heavily insulate between rooms and floors. If you're already in operation but are concerned about sound, apply soundproofing wallboard, well-padded carpets, and more fabric on tables, windows, and chairs. Special culprits are the doors between connecting rooms, which carry sound very easily.

Bathrooms

Coauthor Mary Davies opened Ten Inverness Way in Inverness, California, with five guest rooms and two shared baths in 1980. By 1986, says Mary, "the handwriting was clearly on the wall that, even out here in the country, travelers prefer private baths." That year she and husband Jon made the decision to convert one of the guest rooms into two private baths, thereby creating an inn with four guest rooms, all with private baths. They raised room rates so that nightly income remained steady. "I'm sure we came out ahead financially, because an inn with private baths has a much higher occupancy rate," she says.

Handypersons often think they can run their own renovation jobs. In many cases this is true, particularly if the projects are comparatively simple, like dividing a large bathroom into two or knocking out a non-weight-bearing wall. But when you get into any structural changes or extensive plumbing or electrical work, a general contractor can be a lifesaver.

Most renovations will require building permits. (See the discussion of city and county requirements on page 52.) Local officials are used to dealing with local architects and general contractors and are more inclined to give approvals to known professionals. There is also some owner security in having a third party—the building inspector—examine the work in process. You want your building to meet all the health and safety codes.

General contractors usually add a percentage of the total itemized subcontractor bids for their overhead and profit. For this fee, you are buying their knowledge, construction management skills, and the work of subcontractors they have used successfully for other jobs. Negotiating with subcontractors requires extensive experience in that field; a general contractor can usually get a better price. Timing is also critical, and a subcontractor would rather disappoint a one-time owner-builder client than a general contractor who can bring him or her many more jobs.

If you decide to take on your renovation as an owner-builder, the following hints may help you. If you decide to hire a general contractor, these hints will give you an idea what to expect from him or her.

∗ Plan to work every evening and early in the morning scheduling subcontractors and deliveries of supplies.

∗ After approval of final drawings, order enough copies to get three bids from major subcontractors: framers, plumbers, electricians, drywallers, finish carpenters. When possible, get fixed bids, not time-and-materials contracts. (Time-and-materials contracts mean you pay an agreed hourly wage for the actual number of hours it takes to complete the job, plus the cost of materials.) Insist upon product specifications in writing; a written contract should include time frame, progress payment schedules, costs for changes, guarantees, warranties, and so on.

∗ Do not schedule everything at one time. Plumbers do not like stumbling over electricians, and painters don't want sawdust in the air. Develop a master schedule for subcontracted work. Understand the order of the work to be done. This is the typical order for an addition: clearing the area and demolition, digging the foundation, laying the foundation, framing, rough plumbing, rough electrical, outside siding, sheet metal, roofing, insulation, doors and windows, drywall, painting, wallpapering, finish plumbing and tile, finish electrical, and finish carpentry.

＊ Use a large calendar and estimated schedules from your subcontractors to figure the length of the project. Anticipate delays.

＊ Hire manual laborers for regular cleanup. Arrange for a bin for trash. Rent a chemical toilet for workers, if necessary. Supervise the demolitions.

＊ Have a truck available; space for stacking lumber and supplies conveniently and safe from theft and water damage; and a ready supply of pinup working lights and heavy-duty extension cords, brooms, hoses, nails in a range of sizes, demolition tools, hammers, screwdrivers, and so on.

＊ Develop a master schedule for ordering materials. Some special-order items like doors, windows, and plumbing fixtures have long lead times. Prepare space to store them when they arrive.

＊ On the one hand, it's awful to live in the house during renovation; on the other hand, it's a good idea to have someone on the site. If you are in the house, store as much furniture as you can away from workers, dust, and dirt. Have a telephone on the site.

＊ Remove windows, if necessary, and have them reputtied by a reputable glazier. Paint them prior to reinstallation. Before doors, windows, and walls are in place, consider moving into the structure large items like four-by-ten drywall sheets, one-piece shower units, armoires, and the like, which are sometimes impossible to get in later.

＊ Get temporary workers' compensation insurance during construction, to cover your manual laborers and anyone else you hire on an hourly basis.

It is important to determine who is an employee and who is a contractor. Independent contractors have their own businesses, provide their own tools, and establish their own work parameters. For example, it's not up to you to set a contractor's hours; they are arrived at by mutual agreement. Independent contractors pay their own social security, taxes, and unemployment and disability insurance. If your contractors have not covered their employees for workers' compensation, you're responsible if they're hurt.

At year-end, you need to fill out an IRS Form 1099 for each contractor to whom you have paid $600 or more. Copies must be sent to the IRS, the state income tax agency, and the contractor. The rules defining independent contractors are specific; when in doubt, check with your accountant on whether your planned arrangement applies. Always sign a contract, such as the one shown here or the one in Appendix 5. Ask all subcontractors to provide certificates of liability insurance and workers' compensation policies; make copies for your files.

Injuries to employees of one of your subcontractors are your responsibility if your subcontractor does not carry the necessary insurance.

Subcontractors who have no employees should show you certificates of business liability coverage. These are a defense for you should they claim they were your employees, as well as a backup for them if a suit arises as a result of their work.

Note: Both your workers' compensation and business liability insurance companies require you to obtain certificates of insurance from subcontractors. Both are within their rights to charge you premiums for these contractors and their employees if you fail to have the certificates on file.

What to Consider in Initial
Renovation and Set-up Costs

Estimating costs and obtaining adequate funding to create your inn are two of the most difficult parts of the process of setting up an inn.

It often costs as much per square foot to renovate a building as it does to build from scratch. Furthermore, many contractors hesitate to give you firm bids on renovation since they don't know what they are going to run into. So take whatever figure you are quoted for the work, and double it. This may seem high, but take it from innkeepers who have been down this path: The job will cost *at least twice as much* and take twice as long to complete as the contractor estimates.

As you plan your renovation and landscaping, keep in mind that you are creating something today that you must be able to maintain tomorrow—and forever. It's worth a little extra expense for long-lasting paint and a high-quality preparation job. It's worth working with a designer on a low-maintenance landscaping plan. And it's worth selecting appliances and plants that minimize energy and water use. Before you begin making changes, survey the features listed below and set some priorities.

Outdoors
Parking area: cleared, paved, striped
Lights along paths, porches, parking areas
Enlarged sewer, water, gas lines
Sign and light for sign
Timers to turn lights on and off
Landscaping: design, labor, materials
Fencing
Sprinkler system and timer
Outdoor electrical outlets for gardening equipment, party appliances
House: scraped, blasted, painted
Roof: repairs, reroof (tiles, shakes, shingles), skylights
Rain gutters: plastic, metal, or aluminum
Stairs and walkways: improve for safety, access for wheelchairs,
    crutches, canes
Door locks: rekeying exterior locks, dead bolts, peephole
Alarm system
Outdoor barbecue, spa

Indoors
Electrical/Appliances
Shaver, blow-dryers (short cord, ground fault interrupters)

Reading lamps
Electric blankets
Lamp switch close to door
Washer and dryer
Stove, oven, ventilation
Dishwasher
Vacuum cleaner
Separate circuits for coffeemakers, other small appliances
Heating, cooling systems
Televisions, cable
Stereo systems
Intercom
Smoke detectors
Doorbells

TELEPHONES
Jacks in rooms
Portable phone
Two lines or more, or central console
Electronic credit card processing and computer, modem, or fax lines

COMMON ROOMS AND BEDROOMS
Windows and doors: double-glazed, easily and safely operable, keyed, private, screened
Decorating: wallpaper, paint, molding
Floors: carpet cleaning, floor refinishing
Soundproofing and insulation: between bedrooms and baths, between bedrooms, between floors, above common rooms, insulation for energy conservation (everywhere you can!)
Sinks in room: plumb while walls open, even if installation is in the future
Fireplaces: add units, stack units, repair, clean and outfit, plumb for gas, permanent screen, heat output improvements, such as Heatilator, woodstove
Closets: linens close to rooms, cleaning supplies close to rooms
Smoke detectors (battery operated or AC)

BATHROOMS
Layout/Floor plan (Design): stacking or back-to-back saves plumbing costs
Shower stalls: Tile or modular, combination or tub/shower
Shower fixtures, hand-held showerhead

Tub: refinishing or painting
Lighting near mirrors
Grab bars for entering and exiting tub, access for the handicapped
Soap holders or dispensers
Bathroom features: Jacuzzis, Jacuzzi with shower over, shower only, tub
    only, combined, toilet and sink
Towel racks: heated or not
Ventilation: fan, window (frosted glass?)
Heater or heat lamp
Hot-water heater, adequate size, wrap pipes, circulating pump
Toilet: water-saver, commode with pull chain, type of seats
Pipes: galvanized (quieter) or PVC
Fixtures and stoppers: sink, tub, and shower
Water-saver fixtures
Counter space: vanity, antique piece, additional dressing table
Handicapped requirements

LAUNDRY
Electrical outlets
Gas
Plumbing
Machine space for extra dryer
Laundry chute
Dumbwaiter
Table for folding

Shopping List for a Bed-and-Breakfast Inn

RECEPTION AREA, COMMON OR PUBLIC ROOMS

Furniture
* *Desk or reception counter*
* *Sofas and armchairs*
* *Occasional tables and chairs*
* *Bookcases*
* *Sideboards, cabinets, or shelves*
* *Serving carts*
* *Game table(s)*
* *Guest refrigerator*

✳ Equipment for guest self-service beverages
(carafes, instant hot-water faucet, cups, glasses, etc.)

Accessories
✳ Reading lamps, general lighting
✳ Draperies and curtains
✳ Carpeting or area rugs
✳ Pictures and decorative items
✳ Plants, plant stands, and vases
✳ Fireplace screen, tools, wood box
✳ Doilies, throw pillows
✳ Fans, air conditioners
✳ Wastebaskets
✳ Magazines, books, games, cards

Optional
✳ Key cabinet or holder
✳ Hat and coat racks
✳ Stereo system, compact discs, cassettes
✳ TV(s)
✳ Writing desks for guest use
✳ Ashtrays
✳ Books and maps on community
✳ Emergency lighting system
✳ Formal coffee or tea service
✳ Napkin holders
✳ Candlesticks, candles

Required
✳ Fire extinguishers
✳ Smoke detectors

Dining room and kitchen equipment
✳ Dining table(s) and chairs
✳ Tablecloths, placemats, napkins
✳ Knives, forks, spoons, serving pieces
✳ Plates, bowls, fruit cups, saucers
✳ Glasses, pitchers, wine goblets
✳ Champagne and ice buckets
✳ Sugars, creamers, salt and pepper shakers
✳ Butter dishes, jelly dishes, bread baskets
✳ Coffeemakers (with timers)

* Teapot and thermos containers for regular coffee, decaf, and hot water
* Usual kitchen equipment and small appliances
* Commercial dishwasher or—truly the poorest choice—three-bin, stainless-steel sink
* Ice maker
* Refrigerators (most inns have at least two; many have a guest refrigerator)

BEDROOMS
* Doors with locks and key, master-keyed. If you wish to be listed in the AAA TourBook, dead bolts are required. For details contact your regional inspection office.

Furniture
* Beds (queens; kings if you have room; twins, only if your client base expects it). The best option here is a queen with a twin daybed that doubles as comfortable seating.
* Box springs and mattresses (comfortable, firm, pillow-top mattresses)
* Armchairs or straight chairs (ideally two comfortable chairs minimum per room)
* Tables (especially if you plan to serve breakfast or any meals in the room)
* Writing desks (sturdy enough to handle a computer, placed near an outlet and telephone if you serve corporate travelers)
* Nightstands (one on each side of the bed and easily reached when lying down)
* Dressers
* Armoires

Linens
* Mattress pads
* Sheets, fitted bottom and flat, two to four sets, depending on whether you do laundry in-house or have a service, and whether you have different colors for each room. If sheet sets may be used interchangeably in rooms, you will need fewer.
* Extra flats for triple sheeting (third sheet to use as a protection for blanket)
* Blankets: a light one and a heavier one on the bed, an extra one in the closet, extras for laundry day. Electric blankets can be used for warming up beds, but many people do not like to sleep with them, so plan also to have adequate blankets.
* Pillows (one soft, one firm for each person), extras in the closet. If you use feather pillows, be prepared for allergic guests by having a nonfeather set on hand.
* Pillow covers, pillow cases, two to three sets

* Bedspread, quilt, comforter, duvet covers. Plan for emergency laundering or cleaning by having extra bedspreads that will fit in any room or one for each room.
* Pillow shams
* Dust ruffles
* Runners, scarves, doilies
* Tablecloths
* Canopy

Accessories
* Reading lamps (one for each side of the bed, writing table, and each reading chair). Ideal general lighting is not an overhead fixture, but a minimum of three lamps that will use 100-watt bulbs.
* Carpet or rugs
* Luggage racks (one per person in the room)
* Makeup mirror (with magnifying section, especially as population ages)
* Full-length mirror
* Draperies: curtains and blinds or shades
* Ceiling fans, air conditioner, and an extra fan in the closet
* Glasses and ice bucket
* Water carafes
* Coat hangers (wood, plastic, but not wire, minimum of five per person)
* Plants and accessories
* Wastebaskets (at least one for each room—bath, bed, living area)
* Tissues
* Vases
* Books, magazines
* Ashtrays
* Pictures
* Smoke detectors (fire extinguisher if room has a fireplace)

BATHROOMS

Furniture
* Wall cabinets or shelves (plan three square feet of surface space for overnight kits, excluding back of the toilet)
* Vanity
* Chair
* Storage for extra supplies

Supplies
* Soaps at sink, tub, shower

* Bathroom tissue and toilet paper
* Soap holder
* Liquid soap dispenser at sink. Soap, shampoo, and conditioner dispensers in showers and by sinks are becoming acceptable green alternatives to the wasteful little bottles.

Linens
* Towels, both bath and face, and washcloths. Plan two to four sets per person, fewer for green rooms.
* Bathmats
* Rugs, removable. No carpeting
* Shower curtain
* Window curtain
* Bathrobes—crucial if you have shared baths, an outdoor Jacuzzi, or are planning an upscale inn.

Accessories
* Mirror near light
* Heat lamp or some heating essential
* Rubber tub mat for safety purposes inside tub
* Laundry basket where wet towels for the laundry can be placed
* Wastebaskets
* Drinking glasses
* Plants
* Towel racks enough to hang each guest's towels to dry if they choose not to have them washed daily

Optional Niceties
    Often innkeepers will create "butler's baskets" or an "I-forgot-it cupboard," available in central areas in the inn or even in each bathroom. Stock them with some of these items.
* Shampoo and conditioner
* Hand lotion
* Hair dryer, hair spray
* Toothbrush and toothpaste
* Deodorant
* Bath oil, bubble bath
* Sewing kit
* Condoms
* Razors, shaving cream, shaving lotion

LAUNDRY ROOM AND CLEANING AREA
* Linen storage area

* *Cleaning equipment storage area*
* *Clothes washer and dryer (two, if possible)*
* *Ironing board and iron, for you, and small board for guests*
* *Vacuum cleaners (for each floor?)*
* *Brooms, mops, pails (for each floor?)*
* *Brushes, sponges, rags, cleaning supplies (for each floor?)*
* *Laundry baskets*
* *Trash baskets*
* *Laundry bins or chutes*
* *Cleaning supply containers*

OTHER POSSIBLE GATHERING PLACES
(Each requires special equipment and furnishings)
* *Porches and patios*
* *Lawn area*
* *Barbecue area*
* *Music room*
* *Game room*
* *Recreation room*
* *Swimming pool (plastic glasses, towels, rescue equipment, chaise longues, tables, chairs, umbrellas)*
* *Jacuzzi*
* *Sauna*

UTILITY AND STORAGE AREA
* *Gardening tools: lawnmower, leaf vacuum, pruners, clippers, spraying equipment, edgers*
* *Firewood storage*
* *Bicycle storage*
* *Your own personal possessions*

OFFICE
* *Desk*
* *Comfortable chair*
* *Good lighting*
* *Filing cabinet (four-drawer)*
* *Cabinet or shelves for books, manuals, etc.*
* *Answering machine with multiple-line answering capability*
* *Fax machine (can double as a copy machine if you buy plain-paper fax)*
* *Copy machine (home version unless volume is substantial)*
* *Calculator with tape*
* *Credit-card printer and electronic "swipe" (discuss with credit-card processor)*

- ✳ *Computer with modem*
- ✳ *Printer*
- ✳ *Portable telephone (900MHz, if possible)*
- ✳ *Cellular phone*

⬚ ACCOMMODATING THE DISABLED

"Temporarily Disabled" by Pat Hardy

I'm a person who likes to study up on places I visit, so I can really understand them. This past year, I "visited" being disabled while I was coincidentally researching the Americans with Disabilities Act (ADA). After a hip replacement, I couldn't drive and needed a walker for about three months. The world changed. I had to find someone to take me everywhere I went. Staying home began to look more and more attractive. My independence was largely gone.

And the planning required! Are there stairs? How many? How wide? It is astounding how few elevators exist. Can I navigate safely and unobtrusively between tables at the restaurant or should we go somewhere else? How far do I have to walk from the parking lot to the entrance? Will I be able to maneuver into the bathroom? Will it have one of those slam-it-quick-before-anyone-can-escape door closers?

I will never forget the first time I ventured out. Terrified that everyone would be staring at me, I felt I had to dress and look especially well. In truth, no one paid particular attention unless I had to maneuver around them. To this, I usually got two responses: either wondering stares—without anyone's moving one inch!—as though they were pondering whether I would make it, or else thoughtful helpfulness.

Though I was not in a wheelchair, I still had to find curb cuts, ramps, and elevators as if I were. Since I could not bend down, my range of reachability was also limited as is a person's in a wheelchair. I tried to keep my handy grabber attached to the walker, but it did not go through doors well, so I would inevitably leave it behind, only to search for it when I was the most tired.

My hands became extremely tender, weak, and awkward from using the walker to support myself. Child-proof pill bottles were also Pat-proof.

Even when I'm able-bodied, I struggle with letting people help me. With the walker, I did nothing but receive, able to give little back. I learned that people generally don't mind helping, but I constantly feared their impatience.

I now understand how daunting an inn can be to someone with even limited disabilities! Suddenly I am twenty-eight inches wide and eighteen inches deep. I

think of the inns where just maneuvering into the breakfast room would be uncom-
fortable, to say nothing about the tiny bathrooms or the guest rooms with little
floor space.

    It would be impossible to get into an upstairs room without hard work and
help with my luggage. And then I would never want to leave my room to renavi-
gate the stairs until absolutely necessary!

    Before the 1900s, people like me were hidden in the attic or just sat in one
bedroom until they got well or died. We live in a more enlightened era, but our
buildings are struggling with their limiting past.

People who invite the public into their buildings must consider accommodating the guest who might be physically, visually, or aurally challenged. The Americans with Disabilities Act (ADA) requires you to do so.

When you purchase an inn, it should meet ADA requirements. If it doesn't, then you should ask for some adjustment in the price to allow you to make the necessary changes. If you are starting an inn, build into your budget the cost of necessary accommodations and equipment for this growing public.

The largest hurdle in coping with the ADA is attitude. Think of it as an opportunity to attract not only the present guests who might be disabled, but also a growing senior-citizen market as our population ages.

Start by learning all you can about the various disabilities you might need to accommodate. Talk to people with those disabilities to find out what is most important to them. While designing your inn plan, visit local independent-living groups or centers that serve the people who are blind, deaf, or physically disabled. Invite them to do an on-site inspection. That experience alone will be enlightening. Or better yet, invite them to spend the night and dine with you. This contact is not only an education, but it also gives you an entrée into a network that can bring you business. Document this research and these contacts, lest you face noncompliance legal action in the future.

THE AMERICANS WITH DISABILITIES ACT: A PRIMER FOR INNKEEPERS

PROVISIONS OF THE LAW

The law does not make unreasonable demands.

   ✳ It exempts an establishment with not more than five rooms for rent, when it is occupied by the owners as their residence.

   ✳ It declares that "all physical barriers in existing public accommodations must be removed, if readily achievable," which is interpreted by attorneys general to mean that removal must be easily accomplished without great expense or difficulty. If barrier removal is difficult, alternative methods of providing services must be offered, if those methods are, again, "readily achievable." You are not exempt just because you have an old building. Be creative in your solutions; a permanent ramp may injure the architectural attractiveness that makes your inn marketable, but a portable ramp won't.

* Elevators are not required in newly constructed or altered buildings under three stories.

* Only one of every twenty-five rooms needs to be made wheelchair-accessible and furnished for the hearing-impaired.

* If you have fourteen or fewer part-time or full-time employees, you are not required by federal law to meet the ADA employment standards. Check your state law for more rigid requirements. In California, for example, the standard is five or fewer employees.

Enforcement is tricky. Individuals may file complaints with the attorney general, who can levy fines up to $50,000 for a first violation and $100,000 for subsequent violations. Individuals may also file private lawsuits. Victims of discrimination are expected to ferret out lawbreakers. In some areas, groups of disabled persons are active in pursuing this primary method of enforcement. Of course, if you alter or build a new structure, local building codes will be enforced by the appropriate regulatory agency.

Tax benefits are available for barrier removal and equipment for persons with hearing and vision impairments; some of these benefits do not apply to new construction. Check with your accountant for full details.

Guests requiring an accessible room cannot be charged extra for accommodating the basic needs provided for all other guests.

NECESSARY ACCOMMODATIONS

Contact your local building department for required accommodations for accessibility in your town. Just so you have an idea, equipment to accommodate the guest who is hearing impaired includes a telecommunications display device (TDD), for making reservations and providing the guest with telephone access, and a combination smoke detector/door-knocking transmitter/amplified telephone handset/alarm clock with strobe and bed shaker, easily movable from room to room. If you provide TVs, a closed-captioned decoder or assistive-listening device is required.

To provide accessibility for physically impaired guests, you'll need accessible parking spaces with short walking or rolling distances; a ramp for front stairs, depending on stairway height; signs; and lever or U-shaped door handles.

In the bathroom, things you'll need as a start are a raised toilet seat, grab bars, a portable bath seat, full-length bathroom mirror, lever-type faucets, and padded plumbing under sinks to protect knees.

In bedrooms, you'll want to have tabletops twenty-seven to twenty-nine inches from the floor with nineteen-inch knee spaces, furniture arranged to allow space for sixty-inch wheelchair turnaround; a thirty-six-inch clearance bedside; and lower clothes hooks or closet bars.

To accommodate guests with visual impairments, plan adequate lighting along all exterior walkways, and large-print or Braille information materials in the bedroom and menus in the dining room. (Go to a local copy shop to enlarge print or contact your local independent living center for Braille material.) Book tapes and a cassette player with headphones are a nice touch. Instead of tape purchases, check with your library and borrow a few when guests arrive.

For everyone's safety, install contrasting color strips on the bottom and top steps of stairways, or on unusual stairways, and be aware of fragile items or dangerous areas that need a special warning, such as low doors, uneven walkways or stairs, or vases or other decorations perched in walkways. Remove them or provide a verbal and physical warning of some kind.

Innkeeper Terrianne Straw, who is blind and operates Flume's End, a successful Gold Country inn in Nevada City, California, offers this advice: Ask your blind guests if they would like you to tell them about the room or the inn to make them feel more at home. Ask if they would like a description of the environment around the inn. It's your sensitivity that will be noticed. Do not assume that every person who has a visual impairment wants this, so ask.

Choosing an Accessibility Consultant

Just being disabled does not make one an expert on the ADA. The following considerations may prove helpful in expert assistance.

1. Individuals who are involved in local disability organizations representing a large population, rather than simply speaking for themselves, often have a broader perspective.

2. The federal government has developed various training programs for disabled individuals, run by the National Institute on Disability Research

and Rehabilitation and administered through regional Disability and Business Accommodation Centers.

3. A person's past experience with architectural-barrier removal or building codes can be useful, since it sensitizes the individual to the realities of compromise necessary in the construction process.

4. Disabled people who own or operate businesses or have experience working with businesses may be more knowledgeable about the needs of, and economic difficulties faced by, businesses.

5. Individuals with construction or building backgrounds may have a special advantage in this area, since they often understand the implications of architectural modifications, their costs, and their difficulties.

There is no perfect person for a project, so a group of disabled consultants representing various disabilities may be best. Look for people with whom you can develop a rapport and who can offer insights into the needs and functional abilities of disabled people. A long-term relationship will be invaluable when the inn expands. Use these contacts to evaluate programs before implementation; you'll want to provide the greatest degree of accommodation to the widest range of people.

FIREPLACES

WOOD-BURNING

Fireplaces and inns belong together. Guests consider a cheery fire welcoming and romantic. Fireplaces are not without cost, however, even beyond the obvious costs to create them. The expense of wood, gas, or special fuel, as well as the time you spend to lay fires and clean or repair fireplaces, must be taken into consideration. In addition, there are environmental effects to consider.

Fireplaces fill guest rooms, and you can charge more for fireplace rooms. So what constitutes a fireplace? Wood-burning fireplaces are universally considered the real thing. In an environment where chimneys are all working and safe, wood is cheap, environmental issues are not yet arising, and the innkeeper is willing to pay close attention to maintenance and safety, wood-burning fireplaces are great.

David Rossell from Colvin Hall in Pratts, Virginia, cuts and splits wood from his property. He has learned which woods work best for certain rooms.

In one room, for example, he uses cedar, because it burns well and resolves the problem of a slow-drawing flue. David says his guests "feel ripped off with chemical logs and are disappointed with gas flame," while he acknowledges that wood is "lots of extra work."

Gene Swett from the Old Monterey Inn in Monterey, California, has solved several problems with his new fireplaces.

✳ First, there's no damper to open or close; glass doors control heat loss when the fireplace is not in use.

✳ Second, the wood-burning fire lights with gas, which is on a timer, so after about five minutes of kindling time, the gas shuts off, leaving a self-sufficient, well-lit fire.

✳ Gene's third achievement is a two-by-four-foot cubbyhole for firewood under the tiled, built-in firebox and hearth. There is no wood mess on the carpet and no clumsy wood carrier that breaks or falls apart.

Because the hearth is elevated, the flames are easily seen from the bed—guests want that.

A wood-burning, minimum-clearance fireplace can be added for as little as $3,000, depending on the venting required. Slatelike, fire-safe hearths come in easy-to-install slabs.

GAS

Gas logs are becoming increasingly popular at inns because of their cleanliness, safety, economy of fuel, easier and cheaper installation, and significant reduction of room heat loss—plus you don't have to haul wood! But how do guests like them? PAII staffer Wendy Denn, who often travels alone, is a fan. "I hesitate to start a wood-burning fire. It's messy and I feel like I have to stay up all night to take full advantage of it. My preference is gas."

Newer models look like real fireplaces and provide instant atmosphere. For fireplaces already plumbed with natural gas, installation is simple. Gas can be vented from the side through a one-foot-diameter hole. These fireplaces are safest when a pilot is part of the set. A new group of gas-log fireplaces are efficient heaters equipped with an ultrasafe permanent glass front with a remote-controlled lighter that guests can use from the bed (though innkeepers report that these remotes can be tricky to maintain).

Guests call with a variety of expectations about fireplaces; how can you be sure they're not disappointed? Most innkeepers are clear about it if their fireplaces are not traditional wood; some don't explain unless asked and find that their guests are delighted with gas fireplaces.

SAFETY

How can you be sure that your entire investment does not burn down because of some overzealous romantic?

* Have a chimney sweep regularly inspect and clean the chimneys.
* Keep a small fire extinguisher by each fireplace. The fire department will not usually require this, but will require a large one outside the room and nearby.
* Know your wood. If you have wet or unseasoned wood, guests will do foolish things to light it. Seasoned split wood is your best bet.
* Lay the first fire. The easier it is to light, the more likely a guest will not try to "help" an unenthusiastic flame.
* Provide clear instructions about the lighting of fires and idiosyncrasies of your fireplace. Verbal instructions during a welcome tour are simply not enough; written directions are a necessary follow-up. If your fireplace draws better with the door open at first, say so. Also include ideas on how to handle problems, such as what to do if it starts to smoke. Drawings help.
* Provide an adequate hearth in front of the fire box to catch sparks from a runaway log. A fireproof rug or mat helps prevent damage and covers up damage already done.
* Put all ashes in a metal container with a metal lid, even if they feel cool. Make sure the container is solid. Never use water to dampen hot wood ashes, says Fire Chief Michael Kotowski. A chemical reaction may cause them to reignite.
* Provide tools and fireplace screens that are effective and easy to operate. Some fireplace tools are not very well designed. For example, giant tongs require dexterity and are generally useless except to take a burning log out of the fire and drop it on the floor.
* Place grates properly to prevent runaway logs; don't forget to tell your staff where and how to replace them after cleaning the fireplace.

What about insurance?
Jim Wolf of James W. Wolf Insurance in Ellicott, Maryland, says that the presence of fireplaces in the rooms makes no difference in premiums. Most fires occur when chimneys have not been cleaned and the fire enters the attic or walls. Jim recommends asking your chimney sweep to inspect not only old chimneys but also new ones, to assure that construction work has been done correctly.

CHOOSING A COMPUTER FOR YOUR INN

What should you buy, *how much* should you pay, *where* should you buy it, and *why* should you have it: these are the questions that plague every first-time computer purchaser—even innkeepers who've been using computers for years. The marketplace is extremely volatile. Prices drop and models change—computer consultants say you just have to reconcile yourself to the fact that the computer you buy today, even when you shop wisely, will be obsolete tomorrow. Nevertheless, many people buy haphazardly, and, not surprisingly, that poor start often comes back to haunt the buyer. Approach this purchase as a business decision.

What are the computing needs of the business? Know what you want your computer to do. Making reservations, bookkeeping, word processing (writing letters, reports), database management (labels, lists), and desktop publishing (brochures, stationery) are all tasks that innkeepers can complete using computers. Defining your computer's function in your business is the most important stage of preparation before computer shopping, and it's important to take the time to be extremely specific.

For example, if you want a database program to help you track guest information, take the time to write up your information form now, longhand. If you want a lot of information, like birthday and anniversary, favorite sport, season they like to come to the inn, and so on, you may need a sophisticated database. On the other hand, if you're never actually going to send birthday cards, it may be enough to include a note about birthdays in a comments section that you'll see only when your guests return—and if the visit falls on a birthday, you can respond accordingly.

Know who is going to use the computer. Will everyone on the staff be taking reservations on the computer, or will one person enter information that is gathered manually? Will you use it chiefly for bookkeeping, so you'll be the only one with your hand on the account? If everyone is going to use it, better keep it simple, to reduce training time and the possibility of errors.

Once you've assessed your needs, determine your budget and set a maximum amount of money you can spend. Read about computer basics and market prices. Talk to other people who own and use computers as you plan to. Decide whether you want a Windows (IBM or IBM-compatible) or Apple (Macintosh) operating system. You will never stay ahead of what is new. The world of computers moves quickly. There is always something newer, faster, bigger, smaller, or cheaper. So go ahead and make your purchase based on your needs.

COSTS

The cost of a computer averages from $1,000 for a decent low-end system to $5,000 for a fully loaded high-end system. Any computer deal should include some software. The midrange to high-end systems usually come with a faster processor chip, better monitor, larger hard disk, more memory (RAM), and perhaps a CD-ROM drive. Since this is an investment, plan for the long-term as well as the immediate future; don't get a system that just barely meets your needs.

What about a portable computer? Laptops generally come with small monitors and a compact keyboard. But are you actually going to take it anywhere? Be realistic about how you'll use it. Some innkeepers prefer the portables because they fit on the kitchen counter, where the innkeeper takes reservation phone calls while she cooks breakfast. Some manufacturers offer machines with docking systems, so that the laptop you take on the road or into the backyard "docks" into your office-based system as if it were a desktop computer.

WINDOWS, DOS, OR MAC?

Choosing a personal computer used to be simpler. If you wanted a friendly machine with great graphics capabilities and could afford a premium price, you bought an Apple Macintosh. If you needed lots of cheap computing power for complicated tasks, or didn't care so much about user-friendliness, you bought an IBM-style PC. There were dozens of brands of PC (and there still are). Since almost all used the DOS operating software, they were able to swap software and data.

These days, Windows endows DOS-based machines with Mac-like qualities. And in the other corner, Apple has reduced the prices of Macs, so prices are competitive with those of the high-quality Windows PCs.

So, which kind of computer is the best to buy? About 80 percent of homes are choosing Windows, but the Macintosh continues to chip away at the buyer marketplace. Mac prices are comparable to those of top-quality PC brands, particularly when you take into account two key factors. First, Macs run more efficiently than PCs and therefore require less processing power and storage capacity to accomplish the same tasks. Second, Macs incorporate features that generally cost extra on PCs.

Without question, the huge popularity of DOS-based machines gives Windows users important advantages. Countless software and hardware configurations are available, and because PCs vastly outnumber Macs, Windows has a built-in ticket to acceptance. And as more hardware and software companies compete to make Windows-compatible products, momentum is against the Mac.

But realistically, any system you buy will be out of date to some degree within a few years, so your computer selection should depend upon which system you're most comfortable with, what software you need, and what you can afford—today.

Computer Moves

Innkeeper Mary Davies bought her first computer, an Eagle(!), in 1984. She used it just for word processing, particularly for letters to publications pitching the promotional angles for her inn, Ten Inverness Way, in Inverness, California. She moved on to an Apple 2c in 1985. She began to use it to keep the inn books, using Managing Your Money software. "I loved that 2c," she says, "and I'd probably still be using it today, except they stopped updating software for it."

She gave in and bought a Macintosh in 1990. She started using Quicken for keeping the inn's books, and now, using her third Macintosh, she prints her checks with Quicken, as well. She uses Aaatrix Paycheck to figure payroll for her three employees, a "lookup" format she designed herself in Microsoft Works to determine sales tax, and Filemaker Pro to take guest reservations and maintain a guest and inquiry database for mailings.

"The ease of use of the Mac is great for my inn, where we all take reservations on the computer. I'm looking at a new database program for the Mac right now, but until I find one that gives me the flexibility to change things myself, like Filemaker Pro does, I'll have to stick with what I have. What I don't have on Filemaker Pro is a link to my reservations calendar that would make it impossible to double book. And I want it!"

TELEPHONE LOGISTICS

The telephone is so much the lifeline of an inn that it pays to plan an efficient, functional, handy system.

Phones should be located where you'll spend a lot of time. Since that's often hard to pinpoint in this business, more and more innkeepers are using remote phones. They'll go with you up to the guest rooms while you make the beds and out to the garden while you cut the flowers. If you take a scaled-down version of the reservation book along as well, you have all the information you need to provide immediate service. Consider a remote phone with at least a 900-MHz range. Although a bit more pricey than others, the extended range will be worth it.

If you choose not to install in-room phones, you will probably want at least three lines: one for incoming business calls, one for outgoing guest calls, and one for your own personal use. Consider lines for a fax and credit card processing machine.

Phones should be located in the office, the parlor, the innkeeper's quarters, and the kitchen.

The personal line should have a different ring from the business line so that the innkeeper can answer calls appropriately; this will let you use a single phone without all the bells and whistles of hold buttons and flashing lights.

The parlor phone should have no bell at all, so as not to disturb guests. This is the phone available for guests making outgoing calls. Your local phone company has a number of options for blocking long-distance calls, requiring guests to use a calling card or to reverse the charges, thereby eliminating any potential abuse. Be careful, though, about toll calls within your area code; these are more complicated to block.

Blocking Long-Distance Calls

If you have a phone system, it can probably be programmed to block local toll calls; check with your phone-system vendor, as each system varies.

Restricting access on single lines is more complicated. Your local carrier should be able to block up to the range where your long-distance carrier takes over. This call-restriction service costs about $2.50 a month, and about $35 for setup. You can buy gadgets that will mount in your phone jack to block long-distance calls. Call your local and long-distance carriers for more information.

A parlor phone is cost-effective for small inns, but only one guest may make calls at a time. Phoning from the parlor is usually not very private, either, but if you provide a portable phone for guests, they can take it to their rooms. If you opt for a portable, be sure it has the necessary range capacity for good-quality communication.

If your inn is large, seriously consider in-room telephones. If you hope to attract business travelers, don't consider anything else; business travelers insist on immediate, private, and continuous phone availability.

A few clever innkeepers provide individual answering machines for their business travelers. This has the advantage of eliminating delays in receiving messages while the innkeeper is out, as well as reducing the number of incoming calls the innkeeper has to handle. Guests return to their rooms, retrieve their messages, and make their calls.

You'll certainly want an answering machine. A two-line model picks up calls on both your business and personal lines. It also records separate outgoing messages for each line. Be sure to have an accurate, current message—it's not good for an April caller to hear about last February's vacancies. Return all calls promptly.

A fax is necessary for business travelers and an innkeeper's friend when you need to get complicated directions to guests booking a same-day reservation or respond instantly to an ad or guidebook deadline. Connect it to one of your phone lines, preferably the one least used or, ideally, a separate, dedicated line so that faxes can arrive or be sent without disturbing anyone. It is inconvenient for the innkeeper to be always running to turn on the fax and annoying for the caller never to get through. If you choose not to install a dedicated fax line, spend the $50 to $100 and purchase a fax-phone switch, which automatically switches to fax mode when it receives the squawk of a fax machine. Some machines come with this feature; local phone companies usually sell switches.

Give careful thought to who will be using the inn's phones, and when, where, and for what. Letting the phone system grow like Topsy is much more expensive than figuring out at the outset how many phone jacks you need and having them all installed at once.

IN-ROOM TELEPHONES

For budget reasons, you may want only a couple of separate extra phone lines to cover all of your guest rooms. Of course this limits guest usage: eight rooms and two lines may mean six guests have to wait to make their calls. There are systems that include a computer and printer; calls may be directed by the innkeeper to specific guest rooms and bills tabulated automatically (if you charge guests for local calls).

There are a variety of telephone systems available for bed-and-breakfast inns and country inns, priced from around $2,000 to $45,000, some for lease and some for purchase. The more options you choose, the higher the cost. Evaluate what you can afford along with what telephone service you want to provide for your guest. For most inns, the high-end systems are overkill, combining computerized reservations, night audit functions, call accounting systems, and so on.

Research the marketplace; the technology and prices change monthly. Don't exclude your local telephone carrier in this research phase. They may have a small-business system that works for your inn and can be purchased in installments. Be sure to check the warranty and upgrade and expansion policies. You may only want four lines now, but be sure the hardware you buy is expandable, just in case. Labor and equipment costs are high in the phone industry.

Cellular Phones

Nancy Saxton of the Saltair B&B Inn in Salt Lake City, Utah, describes a love-hate relationship with her cellular phone. "It totally pays for itself, and I wouldn't be without it," says Nancy—and that's the problem. "Every time I'm away from the inn, I make a reservation using my cellular phone, and that's great. But it also means I'm never really away." When Nancy and her husband, Jan, go to the movies, it's an aisle seat for Nancy; she's always popping up to answer calls. While grocery shopping for the inn, Nancy has one hand on the cellular phone and one on the strawberries. "Once when Jan and I were out of town," says Nancy, "our innsitters took some time off to go skiing. Naturally, they took the phone, and they made a reservation while riding up on the lift! Saltair B&B is forever imprinted in the mind of that guest, who reminds us of the ski-lift story every time he comes back." Nancy's monthly bill ranges from $100 to $180, including four hundred minutes of air time.

WHEN YOU'RE NOT THERE

A warm, skilled person to convey your message, your values, and your style in your absence is the first choice for handling phone calls. The second choice, and only for brief absences—ten minutes or less while you check in the Joneses—is to take the phone off the hook. Then you can be sure to give the Joneses the attention they deserve. Busy signals, within reason, probably whet a caller's appetite.

For longer absences, such as an afternoon or an evening, a high-quality answering machine is essential. Make your outgoing message clear, concise, and warm, but not cute. Cute is too subjective; not everybody wants to hear an imitation of George Burns singing "Reach Out and Touch Someone."

A machine that takes messages on cassette allows you to record one tape with your basic spiel and another with special messages for weekend callers. You might say, "Sorry, but we're completely full for the weekend. We'd love to have you come another time. Please leave your name, address, and telephone number, and let us know if you have a specific date in mind. We'll call you right away if we have an opening for the date; if not, we'll send you our brochure and hope you'll try us again."

Voice-activated machines record caller messages of any length, a good safeguard against losing the last digit of the phone number of a caller who wants to book the whole inn for a week in dark, cold January. If your message tape is limited to twenty or thirty seconds, warn callers about it in your greeting message.

Be honest and realistic. One inn tape says the innkeepers are out grocery shopping. It's a warm touch, until you hear it the fifth time in three days!

Some inns use answering services, others never will. One advantage to an answering service is that they can often locate absent innkeepers and therefore possibly arrange a booking that would otherwise be lost. For example, if a caller has stopped in town on a rainy Thursday afternoon and wants a room *now*, a service could call you even at your bookkeeper's and let you know to get back to the inn or arrange for someone else to do so. Some inns also provide their answering services with information on when rooms are available, so they can tell callers, "Yes, there is a room, and I'll have the innkeeper call you between five and seven this evening to confirm your reservation."

Answering services are risky, because staffing varies. A tired operator may not only lose you a booking for a night, but also may discourage a potential guest from ever calling again. An answering machine message is canned, but at least you control the canning.

Return all calls promptly. Even at that, you will lose callers to other inns. But even if they've made other plans for the imminent trip, your courtesy, professionalism, and warmth may persuade them to try your inn next time.

KITCHEN ORGANIZATION

You may have been a good cook for years, but as an innkeeper, you and your kitchen are going professional. Before you can plan an efficient inn kitchen, you need to make some decisions.

✳ What meals, beverages, and snacks will you serve? Inns variously provide breakfast, lunch, dinner, wine, hors d'oeuvres, bedtime milk and cookies, picnic lunches, high tea.

✳ How extensive will each meal or snack be? Will breakfast be full or continental? Cold cereal or gourmet? Baked, fried, or microwaved?

✳ How will you serve? Buffet, sit-down all at once, sit-down over a set period of time, family-style, individual plates, room service?

✳ What service will you use? Stainless or sterling, china or stoneware, plastic or crystal, paper or linen?

✳ Will guests have a menu choice? Or will you serve one meal to all (allowing, naturally, for dietary restrictions)?

✳ Will you serve large groups such as conferences, weddings, and receptions?

✳ Where will you serve? In the garden, dining room, kitchen, by the fireside, or breakfast in bed?

✳ Who will cook, serve, clean up?

* How will your food service choices promote your overall inn image?
* How much will you actually prepare in your kitchen? Will you buy baked goods? A number of fine inns cook nothing on the premises, serving only fresh fruit, cheeses, and pastries, for example.

Organize the kitchen for its actual use, paying special attention to the preferences and procedures of the person who'll do most of the cooking. If you're designing a kitchen from scratch or making modifications, a few hours' consulting time from a restaurant designer could be well worth the price.

On your own or working with a pro, the second step to a kitchen plan involves listing the centers of use you'll need. For example, a baking center includes baking pans, measuring cups and spoons, flours, sugar, and so on, conveniently close at hand. Other centers to consider are

* Table or tray center: silverware, dishes, glasses, linens.
* Food preparation center: knives, cutting boards, food washing, garbage disposal.
* Coffee and tea: cups, spoons, sugar, lemon, and cream, available out-side your main work area if guests are welcome to help themselves.
* Desk area: for planning menus, answering phones (convenient but out of the way of traffic), making shopping lists.
* Family eating area.
* Guest eating area.

Some kitchens may need all of these; others will need very few. Kitchen centers often overlap, but do consider effectiveness. Draw a plan and play with it until it works well for you.

The needs of an inn kitchen will be somewhat different from those of a home kitchen, so think about the following ideas when you plan the renovation.

* Health department requirements.
* Dishwasher: portable or commercial
* Instant hot-water spout on sink.
* Water purifier on sink spout.
* Extra plugs for electrical appliances.
* Coffeemaker directly attached to water supply.
* Garbage disposal.
* Three-bin stainless-steel sink.
* Vented hood with fan over stove.
* Adequate, easy-to-clean counter space.
* Storage: open shelves for frequently used items. Space to store items so that they are all ready to use again: coffee cups, sugar and creamer, and spoons set out for the next morning's service or individual breakfast tray set

up; wineglasses on trays for evening hours. Room to store cleaning equipment and items purchased on sale and in volume.

 * Adequate refrigerator and freezer space for inn needs and family needs.
 * Restroom for innkeepers and kitchen staff. (Health department requirement in some areas.)
 * Good lighting.
 * Comfortable colors.
 * Adequate hot-water heater.

You've probably noticed a heavy emphasis on function in this section, and there's a good reason for it. Experience teaches that brass fixtures show water spots and fragile wineglasses can't be safely popped into the dishwasher. Don't furnish your kitchen with cute antiques that aren't functional, or supplies that require extra work to maintain. In the inn kitchen, form should follow function.

BREAKFAST IDEAS

The last thing most aspiring innkeepers need advice about is breakfast. Everybody seems to have good ideas regarding what to serve. But innkeepers find that some foods and serving strategies work better than others and contribute more to the overall image of the inn.

AN ELEGANT BUFFET AT A QUEEN ANNE VICTORIAN   The setting: An ornate mahogany sideboard. A delft vase of daffodils. Serving dishes of fine antique china and crystal and a silver coffee service. Guests help themselves, then take plates to tables for two or four in the dining room and sun porch. The tables are set with linen, ornate silver service, antique china and crystal, and nosegays. A discreetly available hostess refills coffee cups and prepares soft-boiled eggs on request.

The food: Three choices of home-baked breads with cream cheese, butter, and jam. Fresh fruit compote of berries, citrus fruit, pineapple. Various domestic and imported cheeses. Crystal pitcher of fresh juice.

A COUNTRY BUFFET   The setting: An antique Hoosier kitchen cabinet displays a help-yourself breakfast, served from antique crockery. The hostess serves hot beverages in country-style mugs from her kitchen counter. Guests carry their matching pottery plates to a heavy oak table set with handwoven placemats, overlooking a stream. A dried-flower arrangement is the centerpiece.

The food: Bananas in a basket or fresh strawberries to slice over a choice of cereals in crocks—granola, Raisin Bran, Shredded Wheat. Bagels and English muffins to toast yourself, and steaming hot bran muffins. Bowls of berry yogurt. Large crockery pitchers of milk and juice.

FAMILY-STYLE BREAKFAST   The setting: A sunny breakfast room. A large table set with a red-checked tablecloth. Bouquets of daisies, simple white china, and stainless-steel flatware.

The food: As sleepy guests appear, they help themselves to a bowl of stewed fruit or homemade applesauce. Hot beverages are served by the innkeeper. When everyone has arrived for the nine-o'clock meal, a huge platter of the inn's special scrambled eggs, fortified with everything but the kitchen sink, is served; a warm loaf of homemade whole-wheat bread and a cinnamon nut ring are brought out at the same time. The guests pass the food while the innkeeper keeps mugs filled. Homemade marmalade and fluffy sweet butter are on the table.

ELEGANT SIT-DOWN BREAKFAST   The setting: A dining room table set with sterling silver, linen napkins, an antique lace tablecloth, crystal juice glasses, and antique china. A fire glows in the dining room fireplace. The innkeeper wears a period costume.

The food: First, a salad plate of fresh fruit, perhaps kiwi with brown sugar and sour cream or melon and pineapple. Hot beverages and juice are offered. The second course is spinach frittata, served with a basket of hot breads and muffins in a linen-lined silver bowl to pass. There are crystal and silver bowls of jams and butter.

BREAKFAST IN A BASKET   Delivered to the guest room at a prearranged time is a willow basket filled with specially designed pottery, some pieces heated to keep the decadent French toast (topped with fresh blueberries and sour cream) warm and gooey, and others chilled to keep the banana-pineapple fruit bowl fresh. A quart vacuum bottle of hot coffee and a carafe of juice are tucked in under the quilted placemat cover, along with tableware wrapped in napkins and a tiny pottery sugarbowl and creamer. Cups are tied to the basket handle with grosgrain ribbon. Guests can enjoy breakfast in their rooms or carry it to the garden or the beach.

CONTINENTAL BREAKFAST IN BED   A tray set with unique embroidered napkins holds a coffee carafe and mugs, freshly squeezed juice in stemmed glasses, and a basket of large, flaky croissants with raspberry jam and butter.

PRACTICAL CONSIDERATIONS

Breakfast is a wonderful opportunity for creativity, but there are unexpected parameters. The first is local government health standards. For inns with only a few guest rooms, it's usually not worth investing in a complete commercial kitchen so that you can scramble eggs. Be sure you find out about government restrictions in this area. The second constraint is timing. Business travelers often want to eat early, by seven or eight o'clock. Vacationers are usually happy if breakfast is available a bit later. Guests who must leave very early are sometimes offered coffee and rolls that have been set out the night before by the innkeeper.

If you decide to serve everyone at once, say at 8:30 A.M., remember that this can be a great strain on plumbing. Also, plan ahead for gentle ways to cope with late arrivers. Perhaps you can offer them at least coffee, juice, and breads from your leftover pantry.

If you choose to serve breakfast over a range of time, say from nine to ten, whatever you provide needs to look and taste as good at ten as it did an hour earlier. Those lovely puffy German pancakes sink fast, and they take about twenty minutes to bake, longer than you may want to keep unfed guests waiting in the dining room. Make another choice.

If you are willing to serve breakfast in bed, select foods that will still be warm or cold by the time they're delivered. Think of this kind of breakfast as a buffet. Can the foods be cut with a fork alone or picked up with the fingers, or are you expecting guests to deal with thick slices of ham on a tray full of china that is balanced on their knees—over your antique quilts, too!

Be bountiful! Croissants and jam can look like a feast when the rolls come by the basketful and the jam is generous. It's much better to raise your rates by a dollar a person and serve more food, than to charge less and scrimp.

If government regulations allow it, baking your own coffee cakes is usually much more economical than buying pastry, and at the same time, it adds a homelike touch. Colette Bailey at the Grey Whale Inn in Fort Bragg, California, is always winning blue ribbons at the fair with her coffee cakes, promoting the inn as a side benefit and providing breakfast guests with a very special treat.

Innkeepers are more likely to get tired of serving the same old thing for breakfast than guests are to tire of eating it. Experimentation is not always greeted with delight. If you want to serve a Guatemalan breakfast with refried beans, you had better make granola available for the more conventional eaters. Also plan to have simple things on hand—whole-wheat toast, cereals, yogurt—for vegetarians, diabetics, or others with diet restrictions, if your usual menu won't meet their needs.

Within the menu on a given day, plan variety in color, temperature, and taste. Don't serve hot spiced cider, warm dried-fruit compote, and pancakes with syrup at the same meal.

Guests who are willing to try anything in the food line with great goodwill are nevertheless finicky about coffee; you just can't please everyone. The best guide is to serve coffee the way you like it, assuming that that means it's fresh, hot, and flavorful. Offer brewed decaf as well as regular coffee, herbal tea as well as black tea, and honey and sugar substitutes.

Make your table setting creative and attractive. Garnish the plates with sliced fresh fruit or fresh herbs and flowers from the garden. Make the taste and the look of breakfast another enhancement of the overall image of your inn.

Plan breakfast time so that you can enjoy it. A frantic innkeeper makes guests uncomfortable. Don't offer what you won't be happy about delivering. If you hate to cook, don't offer a full breakfast; serve bakery croissants with a flair. Don't offer breakfast in bed in your brochure if you're going to begrudge it to the guest who wants to take you up on it.

Food should be memorable: how it tastes, where it's eaten, how it's served, and who eats with you. All these are memories guests take along and pass along to others.

THE WAY TO A GUEST'S HEART

Guest hearts are a little tougher to please today, with more people taking seriously a variety of dietary restrictions. A couple of years ago, innkeepers often found that guests who stuck religiously to fat-free bran muffins all year long were ready for eggs Benedict by the time they got to the inn, and spurned the innkeeper's special low-fat preparations. While this still happens, innkeepers find more and more a demand for accommodating special needs. Guests are grateful and delighted when you make them something special. It's a good idea to have a vegetarian cookbook on hand for ideas, but start simple by stocking your cupboard with special items for guests who say "I can't eat that." Make life easy for yourself by having tricks up your sleeve and ready ingredients for diets that are fat-free, cholesterol-free (but fat is acceptable), wheat-free, dairy-free, egg-free, and sugar-free.

It's often easy to please particular palates with simple substitutions: warm corn tortillas instead of toast for people with wheat allergies; scrambled tofu for folks avoiding eggs; unbuttered toast with jam instead of coffee cake for people avoiding fat; grilled sliced polenta instead of pancakes or french toast for people who eat neither eggs nor dairy.

Just understanding what these restrictions mean is a big hurdle for those who've never had to live with them. While understanding general definitions is important, finding out what they mean to the guest is more important. Mac Noyes of the Manor House Inn in Bar Harbor, Maine, finds this question works best for him when dealing with special diets: "What do you normally have for breakfast?" He then goes out and buys it. This reduces second-guessing and creates a base for creativity.

But be careful about creativity here. Mary has regular guests at Ten Inverness Way who cannot eat wheat, dairy products, or eggs—or even tofu. They love her chicken-apple sausage with polenta and her Amazaki rice pudding, but have actually told her they are relieved that she doesn't get too creative: It's too risky for them not to know every ingredient they're eating!

Ideas:
Sprinkle nuts, coconut, sunflower seeds over vegetables, fruits, oatmeal.
Stir-fry tofu with vegetable salsa and serve with a warm tortilla.
Serve oatmeal with a choice of toppings: chopped dried apricots or dates, warm pecans, coconut, toasted sesame seeds.
Beef up breads by baking with nuts and seeds in them.
Blend even amounts of peanut butter, honey, and margarine, spread on whole-wheat toast, sprinkle with sesame seeds, bake ten minutes at 325°, then quickly broil until lightly toasted.
Broil rice cakes (which have a long shelf life) with applesauce, peanut butter, honey, or cinnamon sugar and butter. They do not fill you up, though, so make several per person.
Offer peanut butter, sesame butter, or other nut butters.
Use two egg whites or Egg Beaters instead of an egg.

Or try:
Black beans as a side dish.
Sliced potato/cheese casserole.
Breakfast pizza or burrito.
Yogurt, granola, nut, and fruit parfait.
Grilled fruit and cheese sandwich.
Fruit with yogurt smoothies.
Pancakes made with extra oatmeal and wheat germ or walnuts.
Cornmeal/whole-wheat waffles.
Egg-free French toast: dip whole-wheat bread in a mix of blended cashews, milk, and dates. Or substitute water for milk for dairy-free diets.

Mary's No-Fat-Added Granola

MIX TOGETHER:
2½ pounds rolled oats
¾ pound wheat germ
1 pound unsweetened grated coconut
2 to 3 cups sliced almonds

MIX TOGETHER:
3 cups firmly packed brown sugar
2½ cups water
3 tablespoons vanilla extract

Combine the two mixtures. Transfer to a shallow 11-by-17-inch baking pan. Place pan in a 350° F oven until mixture is golden, stirring every 5 to 10 minutes. The total oven time should be 40 to 50 minutes.

Glenborough Shirred Eggs

This is an easy dish to prepare when you have just a few guests or an odd number of them.

1 teaspoon fresh bread crumbs*
2 to 3 slices Swiss cheese
1 slice tomato
1 egg
2 slices fresh mushroom
1 tablespoon heavy cream or half-and-half
Parmesan cheese, as desired

Grease a 1-cup ramekin or custard cup with butter (or spray with a nonstick coating). Sprinkle the bread crumbs over the bottom. Arrange the cheese in the ramekin so that it reaches up the sides of the dish, forming a cup shape. Top the cheese with the tomato slice and break in the egg. Carefully place the mushroom slices on top of the egg and drizzle with cream. Finally, sprinkle with Parmesan cheese.

(continued)

Place ramekin in a preheated 350° F oven and bake 15 to 20 minutes, or until egg is firm. Makes 1 serving.

*Pat likes to use the crusts left over from making French toast to make the bread crumbs.

PAT'S DECADENT FRENCH TOAST

Put this together the night before, so you can sleep a little later in the morning.

2 tablespoons corn syrup
1 cup firmly packed brown sugar
5 tablespoons margarine or butter
16 slices inexpensive wheat sandwich bread, crusts removed
5 eggs
1½ cups milk
1 teaspoon vanilla extract
About ½ cup sour cream
1½ cups strawberries, hulled, or one 10-ounce package
    frozen unsweetened strawberries, partially thawed

Combine corn syrup, brown sugar, and margarine in a small heavy saucepan and heat, stirring, until bubbly. Pour syrup mixture into a 9-by-13-inch pan. Nestle the bread slices into the syrup, making two layers. Mix together eggs, milk, and vanilla, and pour over the bread.

Cover pan and refrigerate overnight. The next morning, remove the pan from the refrigerator and remove the cover. Place pan in a preheated 350° F oven and bake 45 minutes.

To serve, loosen edges of bread from pan sides with the blade of a knife or a thin-bladed spatula. Invert the pan onto a serving plate so that the caramelized portion of the French toast is on top. Divide into serving portions and top each serving with a tablespoon of sour cream and some strawberries. Serve immediately. Serves 8.

SUSAN'S SOUR CREAM COFFEE CAKE

¼ pound (½ cup) butter
½ cup vegetable shortening
1 ½ cups granulated sugar
2 eggs, beaten
1 cup sour cream
1 teaspoon vanilla extract
2 cups less 3 tablespoons all-purpose flour
1 teaspoon baking powder
½ teaspoon baking soda

TOPPING:
½ cup finely chopped nuts
2 tablespoons granulated sugar
½ teaspoon ground cinnamon
Powdered sugar

In a mixing bowl, cream together butter, shortening, and sugar. Add eggs, sour cream, and vanilla and beat well. Combine flour, baking powder, and baking soda and gradually add to butter mixture, mixing thoroughly. Combine topping ingredients and set aside.

Grease one 9-inch cake pan and pour in one half of the cake batter. Sprinkle one half of the topping mixture over the batter. Add remaining batter to pan, and sprinkle with remaining topping.

Bake cake in a preheated 350° F oven 1 hour, or until a cake tester inserted in the center comes out clean. Remove from the oven. Sift powdered sugar over surface of cake. Cut in wedges to serve. Makes one 9-inch cake.

Bagels and cream cheese.
Whipped nonfat evaporated milk in lieu of whipping cream.
Low-fat ricotta cheese instead of cream cheese.
Grape Nuts instead of nuts.
Turkey sausage, bacon, or ham rather than pork.
Substituting cinnamon, fruit, or fruit juice for sugar in many dishes
    such as baked apples, crepes, breads.
Pancakes with sliced fresh fruit instead of syrup.

Getting Inn Shape   159

Baked whole pears in pure apple, orange, or cranberry juice and spices.
Waffles with a fruit sauce.
Breakfast nacho with corn tortilla, beans, scrambled eggs, salsa, and
    cheese.
Potato, green pepper, and onion casserole or stir-fry topped with
    cheese.
Corn pudding.
Breakfast risotto.
Crustless quiche.

Two final points: Ask about restrictions while taking a reservation, confirming it, or at least upon arrival; don't just hope the guests will either tell
you themselves or suffer in silence. And keep in mind that these folks may
eat funny, but they eat big—plan on plenty.

ROOM PLANNING

Hauling home the perfect armoire only to discover that it doesn't quite
fit any of your guest rooms is a disaster. But you can easily avoid it with

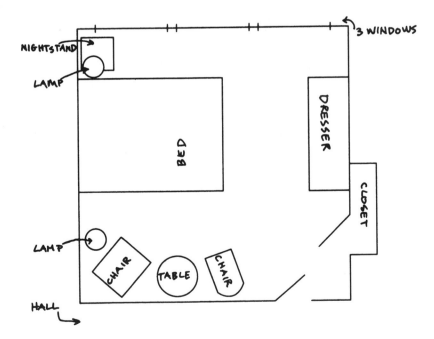

some careful planning. Since you'll have to keep all this information some-where (and keeping it all in your head will result in a great deal of crowding), follow the plan below for making the whole purchase and decoration opera-tion run smoothly and economically.

Develop a folder for each room that includes:

* A scaled floor plan for placing furniture (see sample).
* Swatches of fabric for drapes, upholstery, quilts.
* Carpet swatches.
* Paint chips.
* Wallpaper samples.
* Photos of furniture owned or purchased; use a Polaroid camera.

This is especially important when you order furniture to be delivered months in the future.

* A list of measurements of furniture acquired for the room.
* Photos from magazines that convey something of what you want for the look of the room.
* A room planning sheet (see sample in Appendix 6).

Carry this folder, a measuring tape to measure the furniture you may buy, and a small ruler to measure how pieces will fit in your scale plan.

The room planning sheet can be used in planning your decorating for each room in the inn. A blank form is included in Appendix 6 for you to copy as necessary.

LAUNDRY

There are three basic options for getting inn laundry done: do it your-self, send it out, or contract with a linen service, which will supply clean linens from their own stock.

In most areas, a linen service is a last resort. The sheets provided are often worn and mended; the towels tend to be small and the washcloths thin. But if your inn is in a rural area without a laundry, and if water is scarce or laundry space in the inn impossible, you have to go with a service. Shop them for quality, price, and frequency of delivery. Plan plenty of space to store the clean linens and the bags of dirty ones in an area accessible to a delivery truck.

Doing your own laundry takes a lot of time, and it's heavy work, with all the folding and lifting involved. Before you decide to take it on yourself, calculate the cost in energy, water, and time, then compare this with the estimates you get from laundries. Remember that working with a laundry has its own time constraints and demands, like tracking inventory every week, which must be considered before reaching a final decision.

Before contracting with a laundry, check their references carefully. When you've made your choice, try to find one person at the laundry to be your contact. Reward good service with a small gift at holidays.

If you purchase linens for the inn, the number of sets you'll need depends on how often you want to wash or how often your laundry will deliver. You'll need at least two sets of linens per room, probably more. Light colors spot with mascara and rust from water. Dark towels sometimes show lint. Sheets in prints, unlike solids, show spots less.

Contact hotel linen supply houses in your area and compare their prices with department store sales. Look for quality, price, and consistency of supply. Will you be able to get more washcloths in this same red next January? Linen supply houses sometimes carry products you won't be able to locate elsewhere, such as heavy feltlike mattress pads that last for years. You may be required to order a minimum of half a dozen or more of each item.

If you decide to do laundry at the inn, design your work area carefully. Plan for storage of dirty things as well as clean ones. You'll need a heavy-duty washer, at least two dryers (if you have more than four rooms), shelves for supplies such as soap and fabric softener, space for folding, adequate light, and baskets. Locate the area convenient to kitchen and office.

And make the space attractive. You'll spend a lot of time there.

SHOPPING: MAKING THE LIST, CHECKING IT TWICE

Shopping for your inn is one of the fun tasks, but there's so much to buy that it's easy to forget essential things—until a guest asks for them.

The best way to make your list is to go through an imaginary day at the inn, beginning with check-in time. Start with the entry: What is the location? Is there a desk for holding your cash box, room keys, and reservation forms? Where is the guest registry book? Are those items on your list?

Is there enough seating in the common room for all your guests at once, and do you need it? Where will they set a drink? Do you need coasters? What will you serve drinks in? How will you keep the drinks warm or cold? Will you serve only one beverage, or will any beverage you serve work appropriately in the glassware on your list?

That's the merest beginning of making your list! Now, in your mind, follow your guests to their rooms, then to the bathroom, to outdoor seating areas, and to breakfast. If you'll serve several menus, picture serving each one and list what you'll need.

Here's a long list of things to think about when choosing specific items as well as items you might forget!

✳ Smaller plates make food look more bountiful.

✳ Consider how the color of your china will look with the food and with your guest room (if you'll serve breakfast in bed) or dining room decor.

✳ Containers for ice cubes and for chilling bottles.

✳ Glasses and openers for beverages guests bring themselves.

✳ Spares of big things: bedspreads, tablecloths, mattress pads, shower curtains. You will need these to make emergency replacements without having to wait for the laundry to finish.

✳ Outdoor furniture in inviting spots.

✳ Fancy dispensers for liquid hand soaps: they look good longer than the containers the market sells.

✳ Bud vases for when flowers are sparse, bigger vases and bowls for midsummer.

✳ Adaptable tissue box covers so that you can buy tissues in the cheaper, less-attractive packages.

✳ Attractive baskets in all sizes for clutter: menus from local restaurants, other inns' brochures, matches, kindling, coffee filters, plants in from the garden for a week of show, cleaning supplies.

✳ Large canisters for baking ingredients.

✳ A powerful vacuum cleaner lightweight enough for quick cleanups.

✳ A battery-powered vacuum for smaller, even quicker cleanups, such as vacuuming up a line of ants.

✳ Cleaning supplies that are multipurpose, for efficient storage and carrying.

✳ China, flatware, and glassware in patterns so that you'll be able to replace them when broken.

✳ Or wonderful old mismatches of china, flatware, and glassware to use in gay profusion!

✳ Thermos-type servers to keep hot beverages hot.

✳ Trays for serving beverages in the evening, taking breakfast to rooms, and for guests who make a special request for a tray even if it's not your normal serving plan.

✳ Flashlights, candles, and other emergency equipment.

✳ First-aid kit.

✳ Kitchen things: skillets large enough, potholders you won't be ashamed to use to carry a warm plate to a guest, a lemon zester for making neat garnishes, one of those tools that will core and slice an apple in one push, and food and serving things for people who won't be able to eat your regular menu.

A mere beginning!

SOMETHING OLD, SOMETHING NEW:
A COMPENDIUM OF DECORATING IDEAS

What a guest sees in an inn reflects planning that began long before that guest's arrival, often even before the inn was selected. If your dream inn is a Victorian with large airy rooms, you may have problems finding it, since Victorian homes in reality tend to have small, dark bedrooms and larger but also dark parlors.

Once you've chosen a structure compatible with your dreams, you must take care during renovation to ensure that electrical outlets are in the right places, that beds and other furniture will fit between doors and windows, that the floors—whether you're refinishing hardwood or underlaying uneven floors for carpet—will fit with the whole decorating scheme, and that fixtures for bathrooms and hardware for cabinetry complement the rest of the decor.

Remember that you can't be all things to all people. Mary says she was excited at first about decorating at Ten Inverness Way, but then she became "catatonic," as she puts it, because she was trying to decorate for some unknown public. "I finally realized that that can't be done well," Mary says, "and decided to decorate as I would for myself. It turns out the public likes it, too!"

Be clear and firm about what you want, but temper it with the reality of what people will buy. If your taste runs to black walls and ominous furniture, you should probably either rethink your taste or go all out for a "haunted" image. Listen to the suggestions of others, and there will be many, but measure them against your own instincts.

To assist you in making the myriad decisions ahead, here's a collection of ideas gleaned from the experience and research of innkeepers.

BEDS

∗ Where possible, use queen- or king-size beds. King beds that can be converted to twins provide valuable flexibility in spite of occasional complaints from king-bed users about the bump where the beds have been joined.

∗ A daybed in a spacious room can be made up to accommodate an extra person.

∗ Antique, handcarved, and reproduction headboards are impressive focal points.

∗ Footboards can almost double the cost, but not the effectiveness, of the look. When you buy bed frames, get them without footboards, or use the footboards as heads for other beds. Very tall people can be comfortable in double beds, but not with their feet through the slats of a footboard. Leave it off for tall folks.

✳ Old doors with beautiful wood can be transformed into headboards.

✳ An interesting focal point in lieu of a headboard can be achieved by using a large antique map, a large picture or group of pictures, or by draping the wall.

✳ Forming corners of drapes around the head of the bed creates a cozy feeling and economical canopy effect.

✳ Antique double headboards can be attached to double or queen beds; two antique twin-bed headboards can make one king-size headboard.

✳ Firm, comfortable, quiet beds are an investment in guest happiness.

✳ Sturdy cotton ticking on mattresses helps your sheets stay tight and smooth, unlike brocade covers.

✳ Pillows can be part of the room's accents: shams on bed pillows, small crocheted covers on throw pillows.

✳ One king-size sheet can be made into two pillow shams and a dust ruffle.

✳ Dust ruffles are a country look and hide bedsprings, but they do make it more difficult to make the bed. Invest in ruffles that fit well.

✳ Or cover the bedsprings with a coordinated fitted sheet instead of using a ruffle.

✳ Guests will sleep, sit, make love, and put suitcases on your bed-spreads; choose them with this in mind.

✳ Have a spare bedspread or two for spills and other emergencies.

BATHS

✳ Most Americans prefer shower baths to tub bathing—except at inns, where they frequently request the room with a tub. Use tubs where you can, but plan also to have showers in every room.

✳ Capitalize on the romance of the tub. Position a large claw-foot tub for the river or fireplace view. Jacuzzi tubs are becoming increasingly popular and add to room prices, but here, placement is even more important than jets. The Rabbit Hill Inn in Lower Waterford, Vermont, placed a tub in the sleeping room, in front of the fireplace, overlooking the valley.

✳ Shared baths are a thing of the past. As soon as possible, make them private. Do include a door to the toilet and shower part of the room.

✳ A sink in the guest room (separate from the bath and toilet) is actually a nice convenience, which the owners of the Canyon Villa in Sedona, Arizona, incorporated in the built-from-scratch inn. This works well when space is tight in a closet-converted bathroom.

∗ Dark grout for tile makes it easier for you to hide the mildew.

∗ Corian shower walls are easy to clean and always look fresh, and it comes in a marble pattern.

∗ Fiberglass tub and/or shower units are easy to install and maintain and always look spotless with reasonable cleaning methods.

∗ Rugs in bathrooms should be removable for washing.

∗ Be sure you plan enough towel bars in the bathroom for hanging the wet towels that your environmentally conscious guest has opted not to have washed every day.

∗ All towel bars, grab bars, and toilet paper holders need to be solidly attached either into a stud or with toggle bolts. If you don't do this in the beginning, you will do it in the end.

∗ Brass fixtures in the bathroom are old-fashioned and initially attractive, but they're costly and hard work to maintain.

∗ Install sinks in antique dressers to match your decor.

∗ Waterproof-fabric shower curtains launder well and quickly; apply a spot cleaner to the hem (which shows the dirt first) and put them in the washing machine with towels.

∗ Avoid shower curtain hooks that take both hands. The more difficult it is to unclip the shower curtain, the less often you and your staff will wash it.

∗ For fabric shower curtains to be used with a plastic liner, use a sheet, making buttonholes for the rings.

∗ Smooth glass doors for showers clean more easily than pebbly ones.

∗ Sliding shower doors keep the water in its place, but the tracks are hard to keep clean.

∗ Plan plenty of space in bathrooms for makeup and shaving gear.

If you are using a septic tank or are in an area where water is at a premium, consider installing an outdoor hot tub. Since the water is reused, you will need to meet health department requirements for a public pool. It is very romantic to look up through the trees at the stars. You can enclose the tub, inviting guests to make reservations for it upon check-in, or put a tub on a private guest room patio for that room's occupants only. When the tub is available to all guests, you are likely to increase occupancy, but perhaps not guest room prices. A hot tub has become an expected necessity in ski areas. The Old Miners Lodge in Park City, Utah, has a tub that guests scoop the snow from to climb in and soothe their ski-sore muscles.

LIGHTING

✳ Guests want reading lights on both sides of the bed and lights for shaving and applying makeup.

✳ Plan carefully: Start with light sources for specific purposes like bed reading, chair reading, and applying makeup, and then determine if there's enough light.

✳ A designer suggests that a minimum of three lights is most flattering to rooms and guests because shadows are less harsh.

✳ Overhead lights are rarely installed today, but don't remove existing overheads. Just put in a rheostat to adjust light intensity for the mood, or install a fancy fan and fixtures.

✳ Lamps installed in the bedside wall do not take up table space. Neither do floor lamps, but they're often knocked over.

✳ Modern lamps in brass or china can complement an old-fashioned decor and are sturdier than true antiques and meet UL requirements.

✳ Old lamp shades add a special flavor to rooms, but are difficult to find; it's expensive to custom order reproductions.

✳ Adequate lighting is a problem in most inns and hotels. Be sure you purchase lights that can safely accommodate 100-watt bulbs. A lamp with a higher wattage bulb than approved for it can burn the lamp shade and cause wiring fires in the building.

✳ Dark lamp shades reduce the lumens available to actually light a room. Use them where the light that escapes out the bottom or top is directed where you want it, like over a headboard rather than at bedside.

✳ Candles should not be part of lighting. Fire danger and furniture damage is too great.

✳ Every room should have a romance light that can be turned down low enough to see but not to read. Leave this one on after you turn down the beds.

FIRST IMPRESSIONS

✳ The entryway sets a tone for a stay and can entice a potential guest, so the first impression is important. Use a handsome antique desk, a cabinet, or a cheerful bouquet. The entryway is a priority decorating job.

✳ How your inn looks to passersby involves primarily landscaping and gardens, but don't forget to look from the street at your curtains, for neatness, and your lighting, for warmth. A porch swing or a well-placed armoire visible through an upstairs window can contribute to your image.

✳ Wood and marble surfaces add richness to rooms. Guests appreciate them and generally are careful to protect them. The occasional water rings or iron marks are easily repaired.

✳ Marble surfaces are less susceptible to inadvertent guest damage but are easier to overlook when cleaning; watch for barely visible rings and dust.

✳ Don't be so concerned with being true to the period that you provide no comfortable furniture. A few good pieces with tasteful coordinates can give an impression of consistency.

✳ A round table with a cloth draped to the floor adds softness and an extra surface to the room. Make the table inexpensively from a round piece of plywood and a pedestal foot from the home building supply store, or buy a decorator table from a department store.

✳ Varathane in a satin finish is good protection for fine wood surfaces.

✳ Dressers, shelves, closets, cupboards, and luggage racks should be selected based on the probable length of stay of your guests. Overnighters generally don't need a full dresser; guests staying longer than two days need space to store things outside their suitcases.

✳ If possible, guest rooms should have at least one comfortable chair.

✳ Stripping woodwork: Some of it is ugly and soft. Don't take on a stripping project without carefully evaluating whether the finished product is worth the work.

✳ Window seats are a charming way to add seating and can also be used to store blankets and pillows.

✳ Trunks are another decorating feature that doubles as storage.

✳ Quilted material for window-seat cushions softens hard edges of cut foam, and it's durable.

✳ Velcro makes cushion covers easy to remove for washing.

✳ Cover imperfect dresser tops with crocheted doilies.

✳ Glass covers to protect dresser tops and tables are easy to clean and prevent marks.

✳ Mirrors can solve space problems by creating illusions of distance.

✳ Utilitarian mirror placement: over the sink and long enough for short and tall users; a full-length or large, tilting, over-the-dresser mirror to dress with; a lighted or small, movable, tabletop mirror for makeup and hair.

WALL SURFACES

✳ Painted woodwork: Many old houses are dark and can benefit from tasteful paint jobs.

* Wallpaper can hide many defects in old, repaired walls that might otherwise need resurfacing.

* Wallpaper will take incidental scuffs and scrapes without showing them.

* Wallpaper can set a tone for a room and be the starting place for the whole decorating scheme.

* Wallpaper accents are economical: Paper a ceiling, just one wall, or halfway up the walls.

* Use a strip of wallpaper border in a painted room around the ceiling or to frame a bed, fireplace, baseboard, or doorway. The illustrations in wallpaper sample books are a good resource for ideas.

* Good vinyl-coated wallpaper is easier to maintain than paint.

* Stain and prime woodwork before installing it as trim. Then just fill the nail holes.

* To reduce sound transmission between walls and through unused doorways, consider installing a foam or masonite wall panel or fitted doorway panel covered with fabric.

* Use soft things to absorb sound: Replace shutters with drapes, use tables and tablecloths instead of hard dressers, and hang quilts on the wall.

* Stencil borders on walls and ceilings.

FLOORS

* Paint and stencil a "rug" on a wood floor.

* Wood floors are beautiful, but they're noisy. Plan to use large rugs in the rooms, and runners in hallways and on stairs.

* Before you choose an expensive refinishing job for your wood floors, consider the folk-art look of painting them.

* Different-colored carpets in each guest room add interest.

* Dark carpets show lint; light carpets show spots.

* Investigate the new, easy-care surfaces for refinishing wood floors. In a satin finish, they can produce a look very much like waxed floors.

WINDOWS

* Professional installation of good-quality window shades is worth the money. A shade installed slightly askew will wear out faster.

* An alternative to blinds is an under layer of blackout-fabric curtains on big rings that slide easily behind your regular curtains.

* Use window coverings for energy conservation, noise insulation, privacy, and light control as well as decoration. Line them to extend their lives and accommodate late sleepers.

ACCESSORIES

* Bedspreads can be tablecloths, tablecloths can be curtains, and comforters can be upholstery. Be creative.
* One good old quilt can provide fabric for several pillows, framed wall hangings, and quilted wreaths. Use the little scraps to make Christmas tree ornaments.
* Use wreaths for artwork on walls; make them of vines, herbs, fabric, and so on.
* Frame illustrations from old books. Use photos from family albums. Save handsome old calendars. Use them all for wall decoration.
* Switch plates and outlet covers can be made attractive with wallpaper or brass or wood covers.
* Make or buy linenlike easy-care cloth napkins bordered with lace.
* Solid-color napkins show stains more than print ones. Whites can be bleached.
* If you permit smoking, provide ashtrays and matches.
* Set out books and magazines.
* Plants, dolls, old teddy bears, ducks, and shells and bottles from the beach can make a room look human and inviting. A Victorian dress or hat on a rack is another nice touch.
* However, if a room looks full before the guest arrives, it will be difficult to enjoy. Put objects in spaces guests don't need; hatboxes atop the armoire, for example. Leave valuable surface space for the guests.
* Provide two luggage racks or other accommodation for two open suitcases, since usually two people will use the room.

COLOR

* Color evokes a look, creates an ambience, and changes space perceptions. You can also target customers—upperclass, male or female, and so on—by choosing certain colors.
* Dark colors or patterns make a room smaller but hide incidental spots on bedspreads and rugs. Light colors and white expand space and look fresh but must be cleaned more often.

✶ Guests seem to choose first the rooms with dark and light contrast or rooms that are bright and airy. A monochromatic color scheme is less inviting and less memorable, yet the right single color enhances the serenity of a room.

✶ Accent a simple door with paint, highlighting the panels.

✶ A common color thread running through your rooms will mean you can use the same color towels and tissues for them all.

✶ Avoid ice-blue color schemes in cold climates; avoid red in hot areas. Simple changes in your basic color scheme—different throw pillows and table coverings, for example—can warm rooms for winter and cool them for summer.

MISCELLANEOUS

✶ Make scale drawings of rooms, measuring and marking window locations, doors, fireplaces, and built-ins. Use scale furniture pieces for model arrangements and to help you figure appropriate sizes of pieces to be purchased.

✶ Before you renovate a room, evaluate it very carefully. Don't incur the expense of cutting in a skylight when a lighter color paint would do the trick.

✶ Use closets as part of the decor. Remove the doors, wallpaper them in a coordinated print, and make them dressing rooms.

✶ Keep a notebook on decorating ideas gleaned from visits to restoration museums and other inns, and from reading magazines.

✶ Don't overlook the possibility of involving a decorator or designer, especially if you have more than five rooms to do. You'll save time and possibly money when you consider the decorator's discount purchasing power.

Before you decorate, and then on a regular schedule during your life as an innkeeper, stay a night in every room. Notice noise, cobwebs, ceiling paint problems, lighting, mirrors, water pressure, and hot-water adequacy. These are all areas that affect guest comfort tremendously. And guest comfort is your chief objective.

AMENITIES

The amenities are the extras, and there are as many philosophies about providing these special surprises to your guests as there are innkeepers. The range of possibilities is also very broad. Here are things to consider when planning what you would like to offer.

* What do *you* especially appreciate when you travel?

* What will help your guests be comfortable in your area? Umbrellas and boots may be the perfect surprise for rainy-weather visitors.

* What will make the visit more enjoyable? This could be anything from bikes to hot tubs.

* What is characteristic of your area? Wine glasses, saltwater taffy, or apples?

* What will increase your competitive edge? When people call and ask about prices, what amenities will make your inn look like a good value? What will encourage a guest to come back? Balance the cost of an amenity with its effectiveness.

* Do you have the energy and the money to continue to provide the amenity? For example, bowls of fresh fruit in each room are a cinch when the orchard is full, but expensive in winter. Turning down beds may mean hiring extra staff when you plan to go out to dinner.

* Would guests miss it if you didn't provide it?

* What problems would providing it cause to other guests? Television in a game room is a plus to some guests, a minus to others, and the sound may carry up the stairs to the guest rooms.

* How will you feel if once every two years a guest takes the entire basket of bubble bath envelopes from the bathroom?

Also keep in mind that the amenities you provide can and should reinforce your inn image. Things guests take home should continue to remind them of your inn and their lovely experience there. If you can provide things guests will take to work or share with others, your amenities can extend your marketing program even further.

Here are the pluses, and in some cases the minuses, of various choices.

FLOWERS   The rose garden you established to create curb appeal can also be a good source of cut flowers, as well as petals to dry for potpourri. Fresh flowers make rooms smell good as well as look lovely. When cut flowers are out of season and expensive, consider flowering plants such as poinsettia, impatiens, and flowering bulbs.

CANDY   Some inns put mints on pillows when they turn down the beds. At other inns, a candy jar in the parlor is a sweet stop on the way back from dinner.

TURN-DOWN SERVICE   There's something about returning from dinner to a freshened room with lights low and the bed open that makes you feel pampered. Five-star hotels *must* provide this, so it's a posh service. On the other hand, it can be a difficult service to staff, as you must hire someone to do it if you want to go out for the evening, and they'll have to wait around watching for guests to leave for dinner. It can cause problems for guests: interrupted naps, lovemaking, and so on. On the other hand, it can give the innkeeper an opportunity for a conversation with quieter guests, as well as a chance to remove wet towels from antique furniture pieces.

MENU BOOK   Guests really appreciate a menu book or basket of current best-restaurant menus. It also saves hours of innkeeper time making recommendations! Consider also a blank restaurant critique book in which guests can write their impressions.

EVENING BEVERAGE SERVICE   If your parlor is comfortable, a "wine time" encourages gatherings. Inns should also provide something nonalcoholic, such as soft drinks, mineral water and lime, lemonade, or iced tea. At some inns, guests are specifically invited to this evening gathering; at others, they're just informed that there will be drinks in the parlor at such-and-such time. Some inns serve hors d'oeuvres. This is prime time for innkeepers and guests to spend together.

TV AREA   At the Bath Street Inn, the Olympics were the catalyst for bringing a television into the inn. It's in a third-floor alcove, separate from the guest rooms. Guests watch evening news, favorite programs, or whatever; it's especially appreciated by business travelers there on their own.

VIDEO CASSETTE DECK AND VIDEOTAPES   If there's little to do in your area in the evenings, you might provide a library of classic films.

STEREO AND COMPACT DISCS, TAPES   Choose music that you enjoy to enhance the inn's ambience.

LIBRARY   This can be a separate room or a corner of the parlor, with well-stocked bookcases and a selection of magazines. Your choice of reading material can reveal your personal tastes and also establish an image.

SPA, TENNIS COURT, SWIMMING POOL   Any or all of them, if provided in such a way as not to detract from the peacefulness guests desire, are pluses that will attract people.

TELEPHONE   A small desk, message pad and pencil, directories, and good light make a comfortable spot for phone calls in a private alcove or in guest rooms. See Telephone Logistics (page 146) for more on the pros and cons.

BATHROOM ITEMS Oversize towels or clean towels twice a day are luxurious. You might provide a basket for carrying toiletries to a shared bathroom, or stock your bathrooms with soaps, shampoos, and shaving cream.

PERSONAL NEEDS ITEMS Bathrobes, an iron and ironing board, and a hair dryer or blower all fit this category.

OVERSIZE BEDS Americans who have king-size beds at home will find it difficult to sleep in a standard double bed. You can order converter rails to make your antique double beds accommodate queen-size mattresses. You can also use two twin beds together for a king.

EXTRA PILLOWS Shams for sitting up and reading in bed are especially nice in rooms too small for easy chairs. Fancy neck rolls and heart-shaped pillows are other nice extras.

WELCOME SERVICES Some inns offer a beverage to refresh arriving guests. Others carry luggage and provide airport pickup. A welcome tour of the inn and its services is basic to all inns.

ROOM KEYS Customers like the option of locking their rooms when they're out. You can ask a locksmith to make keys that will open the inn entry door and separate room doors. For example, at Ten Inverness Way every guest-room key opens the front entry door, but no one guest-room key opens any other guest room.

ALL-DAY COFFEE AND TEA SERVICE It's much appreciated and easy and inexpensive to provide in vacuum serving bottles or by piping a hot-and-cold-water faucet in a marble sideboard with a small sink.

DINNER RESERVATION SERVICE This is simple to do and makes guests feel special. Because restaurants get frequent reservations from innkeepers, they often give your guests better service and more attention than they'd otherwise receive. And restaurateurs may return the favor, sending a late dinner guest your way.

BICYCLES This depends on your area, but if it's a nice place to bike, the bikes will be used and appreciated. Check with your insurance agent first and provide helmets. The Bath Street Inn provides a coupon to a bike rental shop handy to the bike path, which is actually cheaper than bike maintenance, fitted helmets, and insurance would be.

PICNIC LUNCHES   Provide them yourself, make arrangements with another supplier, or send guests to a nearby deli for a do-it-yourself picnic.

SOCIAL DIRECTOR   You'll be asked, and should be able to say, where to bike, ride horses, play tennis and golf, jog, hike, find antiques, see the best scenery, and get Burt Reynold's autograph.

POSTCARDS AND STATIONERY   A nice giveaway that does your promoting for you! Some inns provide stamps and do the mailing.

AIRPORT/TRAIN/BUS PICKUP   This can be expensive in terms of time and gasoline and insurance, but if it's practical for you to do, it makes guests feel very special.

REFRIGERATOR   Guests like to have a place to store the oysters they bring back from the beach, to chill the wine they picked up on a tour, and to hold their doggy bags from dinner until time to go home. And both of you will like it when they can get ice at midnight without disturbing an innkeeper.

MISCELLANEOUS   Games; coloring books and crayons; jigsaw puzzles; popcorn maker, stocked and ready; Polaroid camera to take pictures of guests for their albums; coffee mugs to take home; cuttings from your herb garden; and seasonal items, like heart cookies for Valentine's Day, Christmas ornaments, and Easter eggs.

Amenities are a good topic to brainstorm with your partners. Silly things may be perfect for your inn, or you may feel that only the most elegant items reflect the image you've chosen. Whatever your direction, be innovative and have fun with this!

SOURCES AND SUPPLIERS

Before you buy basic inn items, check the Yellow Pages for industry suppliers. Motel equipment in your craftsman bungalow? Of course you won't use motel bedspreads and frames, but under the covers, inn beds are strikingly similar to beds in other top-quality lodgings. You can say the same for soap, towels, and tablecloths, as well as other necessities, and the discounts can be excellent.

If you find the perfect brass fixtures at a retailer's, contact the manufacturer directly and ask about industry prices, particularly when you can buy in quantity—even small quantities. Remember, however, that what you purchase in your small town may be more promptly repaired there as well.

Industry suppliers can also provide solutions to problems that you will not have encountered as a householder. For example, buying hand and body soaps by the gallon to refill attractive dispensers in guest bathrooms is not only cheaper, it is also more environmentally sensitive and convenient than stocking dozens of sixteen-ounce refill bottles.

During renovation, ask your contractors to introduce you to local suppliers of painting, plumbing, and electrical supplies, and then establish with them your own account with a trade discount.

Discount food warehouses are rarely the bargain you would expect. Price food carefully, with an eye to quality. For inns of twelve rooms or less, you're probably better off shopping at a local grocery; discuss volume discounts with them.

Don't buy retail linens until you check wholesale prices. How do you find a linen supplier for your area? Look in the Yellow Pages for "wholesale items" and be sure you find a lodging industry supplier, not just a wholesaler who sells to retail stores. Frequently, you may find that wholesale prices will not beat your local retailer when linens are on sale, but check anyway.

An advantage to using industry linen suppliers is consistency: You can choose a type and color of towel and know you'll be able to add to your stock and buy matching replacements year after year. If you use good quality but simple white or pastel sheets, you can often buy them by the dozen at a good price.

Other ways to identify good suppliers? Attend state or national innkeeper conferences where there are exhibitors serving the inn industry. Ask your colleagues. Check innkeeper publications, particularly the classified ads in *innkeeping* newsletter.

When you contact wholesale suppliers, use your inn stationery. You're a member of the lodging industry, so ask confidently for industry prices, especially for quantity purchases.

SO—
YOU WANT TO
SERVE DINNER

Breathes there a (prospective) innkeeper with soul so dead
That never to herself hath said,
"Why don't we serve dinners?
We already have the kitchen!"

The real question about serving dinner is not why don't we, but why *should* we? As any successful hotelier or innkeeper will tell you, "The bucks are in the beds." You need a very good reason to justify the expense, time, and effort required daily to serve meals, even if only to your overnight guests.

Not-so-great reasons are:
* You throw wonderful dinner parties and have always wanted your own restaurant.
* The previous owners served dinner.
* You have a wonderful space to host dinners.
* You feel pressured to be a "real" inn by serving food.
* You love to eat.

The really good reasons to serve dinner are guest-centered.
* If you have only one good restaurant in town, you might find guests stay longer if you serve dinner. High-quality restaurants are important to attract inn guests.
* If you are located in a seasonal area where few restaurants stay open off-season, consider offering a few special package weekends that include dinner. The meals could be prepared by you in advance during the week; by a local caterer, with you serving; or by special arrangement with a local restaurant or country inn that might be pleased to open and have guaranteed guests for the weekend. Gradually increase the number of weekends as you are successful.
* If you are located some distance from restaurants, making travel at night in bad weather a hazard, consider developing a favorite menu that is easy to prepare and to have ready at the last minute. Offer your guests a hot bowl of chili with homemade bread and a salad, followed by a heaping platter of brownies. A formal, several-course dinner isn't necessary when you are doing this almost as a favor. If the problem is that restaurants in your town normally close early and your guests often show up late and hungry on Friday night, consider offering a platter of fruit and cheese from a local deli with a bowl of hot chowder; you won't want to be up much later than the restaurateurs are.

Look around at local country inns. Ask yourself a few questions. Do other inns in your area comparable to yours serve dinner? Why do they serve it? Are they successful? Do the innkeepers do the cooking or do they have a chef?

Maybe you just love to cook and truly want to try your hand at this new venture. We can't give you all the answers to questions about operating a full-service restaurant or even providing regular dining for guests; that's a book in itself. But we'll give you an overview here of meal service as a possible additional inn feature. Read on.

In Innquest *newsletter (see Resources), business consultant Bill Oates comments on his biennial survey on inn sales in the East: "Amazingly, the price per room averages are almost identical: $68,545 for bed-and-breakfast inns and $69,544 for dinner service inns. This information strongly supports our long-held contention that the purchase of dinner service inns makes better economic sense than buying a bed-and-breakfast inn. The restaurant is essentially free!" On the other hand, this could also mean dinner service has no value at resale time.*

TYPES OF MEAL SERVICE

Formal sit-down dinners with many choices prepared by a chef are not the only dinner-service options, and they are too ambitious and costly for most innkeepers. But before we give you some other ideas, a couple of definitions will clarify how innkeepers approach meal service: Modified American Plan (MAP) means that breakfast and dinner are included in the price of the room; American Plan (AP) indicates that all meals are included in the price of the room; European Plan (EP) means room only; and bed-and-breakfast is just that.

Here are a few of the distinctive ways inns serve dinner.

✳ Guests are invited to dinner in the Victorian dining room. They "dress" for dinner, then gather for a glass of wine in the parlor, a few appetizers, and conversation with the innkeeper. The doors swing open to several intimate tables set around a formal dining room with crystal chandelier. Dinner is served as if you are a guest in someone's home, except you pay for it. It is a fixed-price meal served only to house guests, with a set menu varied only for health or vegetarian reasons, served at one seating. This option provides the greatest possible control over food and labor costs.

✳ Guests of an eight-room inn down a country lane dress casually for dinner after a long day of cross-country skiing. They help themselves to drinks at the honor bar, then are seated at staggered times for a fixed-price meal with their choice of entrées selected when the room was reserved. Wine is offered when guests are seated.

✳ A local caterer dressed in tie and tails brings a romantic dinner to the guest room. Guests select the menu prior to arrival. The table is set and meal delivered as in room service at a hotel, but all courses are left to the guests to serve in the privacy of their room. The inn owner collects the dishes, payment, and keeps 10 percent of the overall charge. Or the caterer brings dinner and serves it on inn china and silver in the inn dining room while the sun sets over the Rocky Mountains. Innkeepers drop in to say hello. The caterer cleans it all up, leaving the kitchen ready for preparing breakfast the next morning.

✳ Guests gather around a roaring fire in the great room that opens to the kitchen where everyone kibitzes with the innkeepers as they prepare a family-style dinner. Guests help themselves to down-home country fare from serving dishes on each table. The fixed menu for the evening is selected and prepared by the innkeepers, served by an abbreviated staff that also cleans up with the help of one dishwasher and the innkeepers while guests dine. MAP only.

✳ In a primarily bed-and-breakfast inn, a six-course dinner is served by a self-trained chef-innkeeper only on Saturday after a social hour. The set menu is posted on the blackboard in the living room or dining room area so that as guests check in they can express dietary restrictions if they have them. Tables can be for couples or combined for those guests who became friends during the social hour. This is the only inn in town serving dinner; it has had more media coverage than others in town because of its fine, though infrequent, dining. MAP only.

✳ When guests arrive, they are asked if they would like to dine at the inn. A reservation is made with the inn's public restaurant. Guests gather at the bar and chat with the bartender. A hostess seats them in a large room that overlooks the lake. A menu with a wide range of items is presented, and dinner proceeds with fine service and food. A bill is presented upon completion and is paid at the time or charged to the guest's room.

Meals other than dinner and breakfast are also prepared by innkeepers to please their guests. For instance, some provide picnic baskets for romantic in-room fireside or outside summer picnics. Also, many inns cater lunches for meetings held at the inn, as well as theme teas for locals.

PERSONAL PREPARATION

Having a restaurant or even serving just ten people will involve you, the owner, even if you plan to hire help for everything. Your inn's reputation will be resting on the success of the kitchen. So consider carefully the following:

✳ Do you want to cook? Without an accomplished chef or great cook, your meals may be ho-hum, from the viewpoint of what is a very discriminating bed-and-breakfast inn and country-inn public. Your food need not be haute cuisine, but it does need to be tasty, fresh, attractive, and well prepared. Everyone who knows how to cook, or even eat, will tell you what is wrong with your style. You need an intact ego to prepare food for people who are paying you to cook. They are not like your family and friends, who can just laugh off the burned rice experiment. At the same time, you must be an innkeeper with the personality to motivate, cajole, train, assist, and interact between the front and the back of the dining room; without this, the food has no soul. Often, innkeeper schmoozing completes the experience for the guests. If you're cooking, who'll be the innkeeper?

✳ Do you have previous food-service experience? How much and in what capacity? Having been a waiter, or even kitchen help, does not give you the experience you need for ordering, pricing, and supervising all aspects of a restaurant. Consider taking culinary and management classes at a local college and working at a local restaurant. Even volunteering to do quantity cooking at a local homeless shelter will give you some practical experience.

✳ If you have a dinner staff, and they are all sick or have quit (which *will* happen), can you pull off dinner yourself at an acceptable quality level without affecting the other parts of your business or the total guest experience? For how long?

✳ If you don't have food experience, do you know someone you can hire to help you? Are you prepared to pay for consulting advice? Are you prepared to take that advice, even if you may not like it?

✳ Running a restaurant is not just cooking and serving. A background in business and accounting is helpful when dealing with the increase in paperwork and reporting to governmental agencies. Handling administrative details and being organized is key. If you have a chef, you may not need to know food, but you must be tremendously organized and a great motivator.

IS YOUR BUILDING READY?

Seating twenty people for dinner requires space not only to dine but also to store, refrigerate, serve, and cook the food, plus do the dishes afterward. Because more extensive cooking is involved in serving dinner, governmental agencies will be more interested in you. Can you handle this?

✳ Do you have an existing commercial kitchen? If not, what would you have to do to make your kitchen dinner-ready? Approval for serving breakfast generally does not assure approval for dinner service.

✳ Are you zoned for dinner service? If not, what is the process? This is crucial, because it generally requires not only additional health department regulations but more parking and additional fire-safety requirements. Often, inns are not located in areas that allow liquor licenses, even if you can serve dinner.

✳ Do you have the equipment, including dishware and flatware, to present dinner? What would you have to buy? How much would that cost? Do you have that in the bank? You will need to subsidize dinner service in the beginning, probably. If you aren't financially ready to open the doors and operate for a while at a loss, think again.

✳ Does a food distributor service your area? If there is only one distributor, will you be a hostage to their standards of quality, costs, and service? If you serve dinner to a small number of people only on weekends, minimum-order requirements may be unreasonable. Many innkeepers drive to discount stores forty minutes away to buy products they are unable to obtain from their local supply house.

✳ Do you have a place to serve dinner that doesn't get in the way of your guests before and after dinner? It is important to evaluate the space accurately, but it is not an exact science, and it's complicated by the odd spaces available in inns. Some rules of thumb apply. Allow twenty-four to thirty-two square feet per seat for the *entire* food-service space, including dining, serving, and dishwashing areas, and ideal kitchen space. Or, to look at it another way, production areas, including receiving, storage, preparation, cooking, and dish and pot washing areas require eight to twelve square feet per seat, while twelve to eighteen square feet per seat is estimated for the dining room. You'll need the larger space for luxury table service, with room on the table for flowers, a variety of crystal, silver, glasses, and side dishes accompanying the main course. Space in the aisles for fine dining needs to be large enough to accommodate iced wine buckets and the wait staff's tray stand.

✳ Would you serve wine? Do you need a liquor license? Can guests bring their own wine? Wine is the minimum service most guests expect, and since labor is less than when serving food, it's profitable.

✳ Are food smells from dinner going to interfere with sleeping? Are noises from the kitchen at night going to keep guests up? Commercial dishwashers can be loud, and they are the last piece of equipment to shut down at night. You need a good fan system in the kitchen, which can also be noisy without proper insulation. And even with insulation, a fan just underneath a bedroom window is annoying.

✳ Can you handle increased garbage and trash accumulation and recycling?

You can reduce your time spent and your costs with a single-price, single-entrée, one-seating meal without taking away from a guest's experience.

KITCHEN DESIGN

Create the menu, then design the kitchen. Or create the menu based on your existing kitchen. The wide range of possible dining service you might provide precludes a detailed list of kitchen equipment and space design. For example, if you plan to serve family-style, you will need ample serving dishes, but not so many side plates; however, if you plan to plate the salads early, you need refrigerator storage space. (See Resources, page 308, for books on designing a kitchen.)

LARGE EQUIPMENT

In most cases you will already have a kitchen in place, with stove, oven, refrigerator, storage, and prep space. Plan a menu and practice preparing it there. If you do need equipment, such as commercial dishwashers or a larger range, buy used equipment. Restaurants are always going out of business (think about it!) and a great deal of good, used, reasonably priced kitchen equipment can be purchased. Replace large kitchen equipment if it's old and doesn't work very well, if it's an energy hog, or if it's obsolete and you can't find parts. Consider first the cost to fix your existing equipment, what its useful life will be after replacement, the cost of a new one over a used one, and how much you'll need it for the present or future menu.

SMALL EQUIPMENT

Your dinner service and the tools you use in preparing the food will depend on what you serve. Here is a basic set for dinners; numbers will be higher, of course, if you do weddings or banquets.

Dishes: two sets per seat if you use different place settings for dinner and for breakfast. Specific pieces depend on your menu.

Silver: two sets per seat. Specific pieces depend on menu.

Linens: three cloths per table and three napkins per seat.

Miscellaneous table items such as salt and pepper shakers, sugarbowl and creamer, vases: average of one and a half per table.

Coffee and tea service, depending on how you plan to pour.

Equipment, such as a cleanup rack for dirty dishes and the container you use to clear dishes from the table, needs to be chosen as you walk through the dining process. Here is where your organizational skills come into play. To serve wine, you need a corkscrew to open bottles and a place to put the bottles. To take food to a room, you will need a tray.

Who Will Do the Extra Work?

Serving dinner is much more labor-intensive than offering a guest room, so estimating the required staff is important. With an inn, if you get the rooms all cleaned in time for check-in, you are pretty well home-free until breakfast if staff don't show up. When you serve dinner, you'll need three times as much staff. More questions:

✳ Do you like to cook? Even if you hire a chef, you will inevitably end up actually cooking at times. Understanding and enjoying the food preparation process gives you a basis for supervising a chef.

✳ Do you have a reasonable labor market in your area for servers, kitchen helpers, and dishwashers? Can you do all the work yourself? A rural inn located twenty to thirty minutes from anywhere else may have difficulty getting staff to come to work. Some inns in tourist areas find that there are not enough wait staff and cleaning staff to meet the needs of all the hotels, restaurants, and inns.

✳ If you are the cook and your partner is the server, is there anyone else to take care of guest needs? Who answers the phone, turns down the beds, or fixes the clogged sink when you are carving the roast?

✳ Do you have at least an extra three to five hours every day to plan, prepare, and present dinner? Or do you have an extra two hours to supervise planning, preparing, and presenting dinner?

✳ Would all guests be required to dine at the inn? If not, how will you know how many will be dining? Keeping a close count for dinner is as important as keeping count when renting out rooms. You will need to know staff and food preparation needs in advance. Including dinner in the room price (MAP) is a way to control the dinner count. You will need to properly present this additional amenity on the phone; otherwise, your price will appear too high as compared with bed-and-breakfast inns. If your guests' average stay is three to four nights, you might want to consider not requiring the MAP every night and encourage guests to go somewhere else one night. (Just be sure you tell them which night it is.)

So, what staff will you need? Here are some basic minimums:

✳ Sufficient housekeeping staff to allow for daily cleaning of the dining room.

✳ One chef or cook, perhaps you.

✳ One server for each twelve diners, more servers for anything greater than a single-plate presentation and wine service, such as serving accompanying appetizer, soup, and salad courses. Server also clears dishes in a small dining room.

✳ One preparation assistant, dishwasher, and all-around helper in the kitchen and dining room. This could be a second server or a kitchen assistant.

✳ One combination host and cashier, perhaps you.

If you are serving dinner to outside diners as well as to house guests, you will need to plan for public bathroom and parking area cleanup.

STAFFING TECHNIQUES

Scheduling servers is one of the most difficult tasks in a restaurant, whether you run a small dining room serving only your inn guests or a larger room open to the public. You may have too many wait people on one night and too few on another; it seems that no matter what you do, either the service or your bottom line suffers.

As you develop your dining room, determine an acceptable level of service and quality. Then develop labor standards, or the number of labor hours required to perform each task to your acceptable level. Time spent analyzing each position and shift will help you accurately determine how many people to schedule on each shift to achieve the desired level of service.

POSITION PERFORMANCE ANALYSIS

For one week, carefully watch the servers during the dinner shift. Daily, note how many people each server handled and the number of hours they worked, thereby determining the number of guests per labor hour. Note the quality of service on your analysis sheet—"service was even," "too rushed," or "not enough to do."

You may be surprised that your standards require more or fewer servers than you initially believed. After the week, you will be able to judge the ideal server-to-guest ratio. This position performance analysis can be done for each job classification: server, busser, runner, even housekeeper.

Don't be afraid to adjust the work schedule. Give your staff advance schedule-request forms to hand in at the beginning of each month (or longer, if you need to prepare further in advance). Try to accommodate staff, and they will usually work better with you. Let staff know that in case of cancellations, more reservations, or staff illness, you will adjust the schedule. Ask for volunteers willing to stay home or to be on call. (Of course, be certain to comply with any legal regulations in your area.) Work daily to keep labor hours under control.

THE STAFFING GUIDE

A staffing guide lists the labor standards you have set during your position performance analysis and shows the number of employees needed based upon your varying business levels. Use the guide with your forecast to create a schedule.

The guide not only helps you in your weekly or biweekly scheduling of servers, but can also aid you in controlling labor costs before it's too late.

After you set up the number of scheduled labor hours, convert hours to dollars and develop a forecasted daily labor cost. By comparing scheduled hours and dollars to actual hours and dollars, you will have a positive or negative daily variance factor. Use this tool to adjust hours as needed to meet projected costs for the week.

Unless you do a single seating per evening, where all servers are on the same service sequence, the business flow is rarely constant throughout a shift. There will be busy, slow, and steady times. To avoid staff's standing around waiting to rush, consider staggering work shifts. One server should arrive early to set up the room, with the second server arriving just before the guests do, giving you maximum coverage when needed. The server who arrived first leaves first, the second server handles the last table(s) and dining room reset. This method gives you greater efficiency and fewer wasted dollars.

Labor hours can be an invisible thief. An extra labor hour a day at $5 times seven days means $35 a week or $140 a month more than you projected. Did you really need that extra hour? You can lose money without being aware of it. Your dinner is served from 6 P.M. to 10 P.M. and you have always scheduled your three servers from 5 P.M. to 11 P.M. even though your busy time is 7 P.M. to 9 P.M. Schedule one server from 5 P.M. to 9 P.M., one from 6 P.M. to 10 P.M. and one from 7 P.M. to 11 P.M. You now have twelve labor hours instead of eighteen hours, with essentially the same coverage.

CROSS TRAINING

On evenings where your staffing guide shows you to be right on the edge of needing another server or requiring a host, cross training can help.

Sample Variable Staffing Guide

(Based upon Position Performance Analysis)

Number of Guests	Beakfast (7 to 10 A.M.)			Dinner (6 to 10 P.M.)		
	Host hours	Server hours	Busser hours	Host hours	Server hours	Busser hours
1–10	0	4	0	0	6	0
11–20	0	8	0	0	12	0
21–30	0	12	0	4	12	4

If a busser has been properly trained, he or she can pitch in and take a table. The assistant innkeeper or dining room supervisor can fill in as host during a busy hour in lieu of another person who would need to be scheduled for a full shift. Cross training allows you to trim a few hours here or there, which can add up to a significant amount of time over a period of a week, and certainly throughout the year. In some inns the wait staff also turn down beds during slower seasons or in lull periods of dining.

USE THE TOOLS

Forecasts, staffing guides, and schedules are tools to use daily, not merely weekly exercises. Too often, innkeepers create the forecast, guide, and schedule, and then forget about them. Learn from your business and use the tools to make adjustments that are more efficient and effective. Spending a little bit of time each day for analysis of available information will save money and improve service. And service is key.

HIRING A CHEF

Even the most experienced innkeeper seems to dread the prospect of hiring and managing a chef. It is a serious task, but nothing to panic about. True, an inn chef is an extremely important member of the staff, and qualified applicants will rarely walk through the front door. But if you need a chef, there are some easy steps you can take to find potential candidates.

WHAT IS THE JOB?

Before you do anything, pour a cup of coffee and close yourself in the office with no distractions. Answer these questions.

* What do you want the chef to do?
* Will he or she cook only dinner? Will the chef ever have to prepare breakfast or special parties?
* Who will do the ordering? Is this the chef's responsibility, your responsibility, or is it done jointly?
* Who does the inventory? Who manages other kitchen staff or wait staff?
* Who supplies uniforms?
* Who creates the menus?
* If you do all of the menu planning, is there any room for the chef's creativity?
* How much are you willing to pay?
* Is there any bonus or incentive for increased revenues or lowered food cost?

Too often, we hire someone after describing only part of the job. In fairness to yourself and your employee, think about the scope of the job in advance, so your new chef can begin with realistic expectations. Create a job description based upon your consideration of the position and your answers to the above questions. Here is a model position description to use as a start; modify it for your needs.

THE SEARCH BEGINS

In some areas, running an ad in the local newspaper is enough to generate applicants. If you do this, remember that the respondents will likely be from your area; in other words, you may be taking your neighbor's staff person. If you run ads in big-city newspapers to draw more people, remember that ads in New York, Boston, or Chicago will draw individuals with higher salary expectations. If you don't want this response, consider some other possibilities. Contact culinary schools in your region. Classes graduate regularly, and you may be able to interview some excellent people. New graduates will not have the refined management skills that come with years of experience, so you'll need to be more involved in training, but they should have great technique and may be more affordable.

Another idea is to call your local chapter of the American Culinary Federation. Chefs in your area will generally belong to this association. Like innkeepers, chefs network and may know of someone to refer. Find the number for these associations in your telephone book.

POSITION DESCRIPTION

Position Title: Executive Chef
Reports to: Owner/Innkeeper

POSITION SUMMARY: The department head responsible for
any and all kitchens in a food service establishment.
Ensures that all kitchens provide nutritious, safe, eye-
appealing, properly flavored food. Maintains a safe and sanitary work environment for all employees. Other duties
include menu planning, preparation of budgets, and maintenance of payroll, food cost, and other records. Specific
duties involving food preparation are the establishment of
quality standards and training of employees in cooking
methods, presentation techniques, portion control, and
retention of nutrients.

TASKS

1. Interviews, hires, evaluates, rewards, and disciplines
kitchen personnel as appropriate.

2. Orients and trains kitchen personnel in property and
department rules, policies, and procedures.

3. Trains kitchen personnel in food production principles
and practices. Establishes quality standards for all menu
items and for food production practices.

4. Plans and prices menus. Establishes portion sizes and
standards of service for all menu items.

5. Schedules kitchen employees in conjunction with
business forecasts and predetermined budget. Maintains
payroll records for submission to payroll department.

6. Controls food cost by establishing purchasing specifications, storeroom requisition systems, product storage
requirements, standardization recipes, and waste-control
procedures.

7. Trains kitchen personnel in safe operating procedures
of all equipment, utensils, and machinery. Establishes
maintenance schedules in conjunction with manufacturer's
instructions for all equipment. Provides safety training in
lifting, carrying, hazardous material control, chemical control, first aid, and CPR.

8. Trains kitchen personnel in sanitation practices and establishes cleaning schedules, stock rotation schedules, refrigeration temperature control points, and other sanitary controls.

9. Trains kitchen personnel to prepare all food while retaining the maximum amount of desirable nutrients. Trains kitchen personnel to meet special dietary requests, including low-fat, low-sodium, vegetarian, and low-calorie meals.

PREREQUISITES:

Education: Degree from a postsecondary culinary arts training program is desirable.

Experience: A minimum of five years as sous chef, plus three years in another food preparation position.

Physical: Must be able to speak clearly and listen attentively to employees, dining room staff, and guests. Must be able to stand and move about quickly for periods up to four hours in length. Must have the ability to lift pots, pans, etc., up to forty pounds in weight. Must be able to read and write.

Local hotels, restaurants, country clubs, catering halls, and other inns are also good networking sources. Applicants will often go to these places looking for work, and if you have developed positive relationships with your fellow businesses, they may refer people to you. If you belong to a state, regional, or national association, let them know of your recruitment plans.

The key to finding the right person for the job is to reach out in a number of different ways and then to interview respondents thoroughly before making your decision. This can be a lengthy process; be sure to allow yourself enough time so that you do not make the wrong choice out of desperation. If you need to hire for your summer season, consider starting in the fall.

Once you have applications that interest you, begin the interview process. Talk with each candidate frankly. Do not exaggerate the position. Be honest about your needs and expectations. Listen, and answer questions thoroughly. After all, you are hiring an integral part of your team, and you want this person to be around for awhile. After you have spoken to the applicants, go to where they work now, if possible, and taste their food. Would you want it to be served at your inn? Invite the candidate to come into your kitchen and prepare a meal for you. This will give both of you an idea about whether the job will work out. This also allows you to have another conversation in a different environment. If you find a person you are excited about, check all references. If you are comfortable with every-thing, offer the job. Do not be afraid to set up another interview if you are not completely sure. Be absolutely certain now and avoid problems later.

Congratulations! You have hired a chef. Now is not the time, however, to breathe a sigh of relief and leave the kitchen; your most important job is just beginning. Your new staff person deserves and expects your manage-ment and time. Positive strokes as well as constructive criticism are vital.

Too often, innkeepers who have gone through all the right steps in interviewing and hiring cannot understand why the perfect person does not live up to their expectations, or quits. Frequently, little or no time was spent with the employee after hiring. It is only natural that if your new chef feels you are not paying attention to, or do not care about, his or her perfor-mance, habits will become sloppy and motivation will disappear.

Innkeepers who have the best relationships with their chefs are not nec-essarily the ones with food background, but the ones who are excellent communicators, not intimidated by a chef's expertise. Talk, listen, and be consistent with praise as well as criticism. Do this well, and you'll be rewarded with a happy team member for a long time. These relationships take time to grow. Give yourself time.

▦ BUDGETING

You will need to budget for the expenses of your food service. You may have twenty seats in your dining room, but sometimes they'll be empty, and sometimes you'll wish there were two hundred.

There are two basic ways to treat profit at budget time. First, the tradi-tional approach, which regards profit as "what is left over from sales income after subtracting expenses." It looks like this:

Profit = Sales Income - Expenses

The second treats profit as if it were a "cost":

Sales Income - Required Profit = Allowable Operating Expenses

Since inns are likely to be on a tight budget and use the food service as a marketing opportunity, it's easy to figure that you do not need a profit. This is dangerous thinking, considering that your own time is generally not built into the budget. To be more realistic, look at the profit as owner time spent on food service, and build it into the budget at the outset.

How to Project Sales

* Analyze sales histories to determine your heaviest season, the most popular type of meal, and the trends that have developed over the past couple of years. Are desserts being ordered more? Are appetizers passé?
* Review current factors over which you have no control, but which may affect sales, to give yourself a broader understanding of sales. Is there new competition or is the street being repaired? What about the effect of local special events?
* Consider economic variables may affect the public's habits and lifestyles. As inflation rises, guests may demand greater value for their money.
* Also consider room occupancy projections.

Figuring Expenses and Operating Costs

Once sales volumes are known and profit requirements determined, estimate the expenses required to generate the projected level of sales. To simplify this, operating costs are broken into three categories.

* Fixed costs, which remain constant in the short run, even though sales volume may vary. Include management salaries, rent, insurance, property taxes, interest, and depreciation.
* Variable costs, which change according to the volume of business. These include food and beverage costs, linen laundering, labor, music, and some supplies used in food production and service areas.
* Mixed costs, which contain both fixed and variable cost elements, such as the telephone service, with its fixed basic charge and its variable charges depending on call volume.

Operating costs to consider:
Food
Labor
Supplies
Utilities
Marketing
Rent
Depreciation
Insurance
Property, business, or other taxes

The term *prime costs* is often used in the restaurant business. Prime
costs are food and labor costs only; they should represent no more than 65
to 70 percent of your gross income. If you figure profit, then, at 25 percent,
the other costs run about 5 to 10 percent, which is why you want to avoid
waste in your kitchen.

Operational businesses often use two methods for figuring expenses, neither of which is really recommended for a new entrepreneur. The "simple mark-up method" adds a percentage increase in costs over the previous year. In the "percentage method," food and beverage costs are calculated as a percentage of sales income. Both systems have the potential disadvantage of perpetuating an inefficient operation if the current budget cost percentage is higher than it should be.

A third method, zero-based budgeting, avoids the errors of the other two by starting each year's budget from zero, giving you the more direct experience of developing each category based on today's costs and knowing your budget much more intimately. To a newcomer in this field, this will be time-consuming, but the exercise will yield priceless knowledge. Do not, however, disregard previous expense histories if they are available; they are a valuable reality test.

Remember, always estimate expenses high and income low; you never know when a blizzard will blow away all your projected profit.

FINE DINNER SERVICE: *MISE EN PLACE*

Mise en place (pronounced "mees-on-ploss") is a French phrase which, if translated literally, means "putting in place." In the food service world, *mise en place* is the organization and completion of every behind-the-scenes task to prepare the smoothest possible service for the guests. It is more than just folding and placing the napkins correctly. This physical readiness is the setting of the stage and the costuming that prepares your actor-employees to be their very best.

You need the right number of employees at the right time, so no one ends up scurrying around doing tasks that should have been done last night or early in the afternoon. Efficient staffing will make money for you, when your people are prepared and poised enough to sell your wine list, gush knowledgeably about the menu, and charm your guests into dessert.

This preparatory work is vital, for once service begins—the moment the guest walks through the door—staff must be able to devote their full attention to the needs of the guest. When guests are in the room, it is no time to fold napkins, fill salt and pepper shakers, or adjust lighting. Guests come for a magical experience and pampering, and the magician needs to be physically and mentally prepared.

Wendy Denn, a PAII country inn consultant, wrote this after a summer visit to New England. "This is my favorite time of the year, when I jump into my car and visit inns. I write this at the end of an excursion, and overall I'm as enthusiastic as ever about what I see, but my experiences also remind me of the importance of *mise en place* and what can happen when you don't get a chance to put the rabbit in the hat.

"I arrive at an inn mid-afternoon, full of anticipation. I walk into a beautifully appointed reception area, every detail surpassing my expectation. At 7 P.M. I arrive, as expected, for dinner. After several minutes, I seat myself. I watch two other couples wait awkwardly and then seat themselves as well. We all wait.

"My table is set with flatware for three courses plus dessert, and two wine glasses. The cup and saucer have been pre-set, not really appropriate for fine dining, and I have no napkin nor a water glass. Clearly, there has not been time for sufficient *mise en place*. Suddenly the music comes on, the lights dim, and a waitperson rushes into the room with an armful of napkins, menus, and glasses. Gasping an apology, she thrusts a napkin onto my lap.

"Ignoring the difficult beginning, I ask several questions about the menu. I receive answers such as, 'I don't know what type of salad dressing; the chef hasn't made it yet.' *Mise en place* is lacking in the kitchen also. The evening ends, however, with an absolutely lovely dinner.

"Another evening I am graciously greeted, seated at a table with a wonderful view of the sun setting behind a swan-filled pond. The sunset is overshadowed by spotty glasses, mottled flatware, and a smudgy picture window. *Mise en place* is missing here also. I believe that all these problems are probably the result of innkeepers cutting staffing just a bit too close."

PRETEND YOU ARE THE GUEST

Walk through your inn and dining room as if you were a guest and ask yourself the following questions.

* Do you know where to go and what to do?
* Do you feel comfortable?
* Do you sense a warm innkeeper presence?
* Do you want to get up and help the server?
* Do you want to fix that dripping candle on table six?
* Are you the only one who notices the couple at table three who has no butter?
* Do you wonder why the man at table four just pushes the fish around on his plate?
* Would you come back?

The essence of *mise en place* is complete emotional and physical readiness.

Innkeepers Karl and Lynn Buder of Thorncroft on Martha's Vineyard operated a fine restaurant in conjunction with their inn for four and a half years. They started off leasing the restaurant to a young, newly married couple recently out of culinary school. The relationship started positively, with both parties feeling that the innkeepers were doing the new chefs a favor by giving them their own restaurant at what seemed like a good price. The inn paid the lessee a per-head amount for serving breakfast and tea, and the lessee paid the inn 40 percent of the dinner revenue. After a year the chefs began to feel that they were doing the inn a favor. Without a written contract, nothing could be changed as the situation evolved. The dirty kitchen became a sore point to Karl, who was the relief breakfast chef. The lessees began dramatically cutting food costs (and as a result, quality) on the tea and breakfast served to inn guests. When, in the middle of high season, the husband of the chef team became surly with Lynn, Karl terminated them.

Karl and Lynn subsequently ran the restaurant themselves for two and a half years, hiring chefs to cook. Karl recalls many sixteen-hour days when he was waiting tables, bussing, and hosting the dining room—after having served breakfast in the morning. "I missed a thousand Little League games," laments Karl, who later took stock of the whole thing. "The restaurant is nice in concept," he says, "but here on Martha's Vineyard, guests come to explore restaurants and the town. We found that less than 9 percent of our guests actually ate dinner here. If you don't have a large restaurant or do MAP, requiring all your guests to dine with you, it's hard to make it fly." In a village where there are lots of choices, the quaint country inn where all the guests settle down to enjoy the evening together just doesn't happen, even for this Mobil 4-star and AAA 4-diamond property. Although they made money the last year they provided dinner (previous years they put money earned back into equipment), they stopped. Karl sees every Little League game. "The best thing we ever did was to deep-six the restaurant," he says.

Chef Nancy Donaldson of the nine-room Old Yacht Club Inn in Santa Barbara, California, has always liked to cook, and seriously looked at opening a restaurant before becoming an innkeeper. Her partners have encouraged her because it promotes the inn. Although Santa Barbara is known for its fine cuisine, Nancy has established her own reputation and market niche in a competitive inn community. Serving only to guests (the city wouldn't allow her to expand to outsiders), Nancy provides a fixed-price, five-course, sit-down dinner one weekend night a few times a month. "I have a server, sometimes two. Along with my business partner,

Sandy Hunt, and my faithful sous chef and dishwasher, we all pitch in to clean up after the dessert is served."

Rooms are MAP for that weekend, with the rate including two nights and dinner—and, of course, two breakfasts. Guests gather for champagne before the dinner bell is rung. They can order from the wine list at dinner, for an extra charge. After sixteen years in business, Nancy still loves preparing dinner and has achieved quite a reputation.

Fair Haven, Vermont, innkeepers Shirley Stein and Bea and Richie Taube, in their search for the perfect country inn, found a "restaurant with rooms upstairs" and a bad reputation. Originally serving primarily locals and adventurous inngoers who would accept poor food and shared baths, this property was transformed into a Mobil four-star and AAA four-diamond inn. They reduced the restaurant from sixty to thirty-five seats, creating more space between tables and returning the drawing room to its original glory. Ninety-five percent of their diners are MAP. Locals tend to be awed by the new Vermont Marble Inn, frequenting the dining room only on special occasions or to impress a business associate.

Each of the owners is intimately involved in the restaurant at some level. Shirley describes herself as "dowager queen of hearts," overseeing all the activity of the restaurant, as well as creating the after-dinner chocolates. Richie maintains their fine wine list and tends bar. Bea is known for her baking, producing famous rolls and prize-winning desserts.

An additional room has been added for dining room overflow, meetings, and private parties, and the "Celebration of Romance." For the gentleman proposing marriage, anniversary celebrants, or visitors celebrating other special occasions, Shirley sets up this private room with a dozen long-stemmed roses and a bottle of chilled champagne before the fireplace, with a private server, for just $100 extra.

The closest quality restaurant is thirty miles away, so Shirley and partners do not have the choice of being just a bed-and-breakfast, which they would prefer. Shirley, who is also the breakfast cook, says her day starts at 7 A.M. and doesn't usually finish until after midnight. She tries to nap midday. She says, "The restaurant is extremely exciting, tasting all the foods and keeping up with everything, but it's a lot of work."

This chapter would not have been possible without the expertise and gentle guidance of Wendy Denn. With her vast experience in food service and smaller properties, and as the on-site innkeeper for Trinity Inn and Conference Center, CT, Wendy brings a great depth of knowledge and understanding of the MAP and full-service country inn.

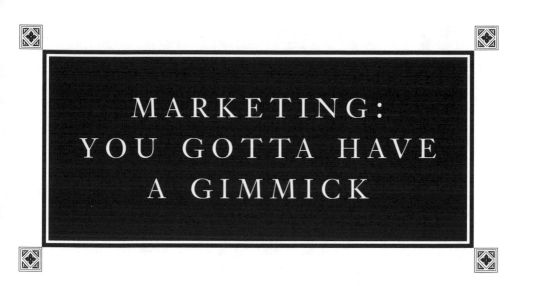

MARKETING:
YOU GOTTA HAVE
A GIMMICK

*I*f you're not careful, the opening day you've so long anticipated can be the longest, loneliest day of your life. Where are all the friends who asked you every two weeks when you'd be ready? Where are the neighbors who stopped by to check your progress? Where are the guests who are going to pay for the months of renovation you've just completed?

Marketing is how you let people know what you have to offer, and it's how you make them want it. Marketing is critical to success. You'll lose business if you don't do a good job of getting the message out there.

Marketing includes many things, from the obvious ones like advertising and publicity to the less obvious concept of creating an inn image that can be presented to potential guests in an exciting, compelling way. To make sure your opening day isn't an anticlimax, put your marketing program together as you proceed with the other business of getting ready to open.

ESTABLISHING AN IMAGE

You'll have set the tone for your image before you began renovating, when you made decisions about inn ambience. The difficulty in the increasingly competitive bed-and-breakfast and country-inn market is to define your image so clearly that you stand out from your competition in the guests' minds. You want them to remember a unique experience. Yours could be the place that serves the champagne breakfast in bed, or boards your horses, or where you can walk to the beach or visit the barn. Notice that all of these are descriptions of the guests' experience. The more you build your image around what happens to guests when they visit, the more likely they are to think of you when they want to vacation or tell a friend about a great place to stay.

Capitalize on what your guests do within your community by adjusting the amenities you offer. In California's Napa and Sonoma wine regions, for example, inn rooms often provide wine glasses. But don't offer something just because everyone else does, or, if it's an important service in your area, offer it in a different manner. The Old Yacht Club Inn in Santa Barbara is a block and a half from the beach. They provide beach chairs and towels and picnic baskets for breakfast. They capitalize on their relationship to the ocean in every way they can, including the name of the inn.

You can dress to reinforce an image. Santa Barbara's Simpson House staff all wear similar outfits to present a more formal, upscale look to their four-diamond property. At the Garth Woodside Mansion in Hannibal, Missouri, the innkeepers give guests a chance to dress the period by offering an old-fashioned nightshirt in each guest room. Of course, guests are given an opportunity to purchase them, complete with inn monogram. Innkeepers Irv and Diane Feinberg are also known to show up in their nightshirts at local radio stations with breakfast for the DJ.

Don't overlook the contribution of your staff to your inn's image. If you have an old English country house image, hire someone with an English accent. If you emphasize hiking and the outdoors, recruit staff from the local gym or Sierra Club chapter.

You'll want to maintain and extend the image of your inn throughout its lifetime, responding to the interests of your guests. If you have decided to emphasize history and a guest suggests that a library of books about the history of your area would be interesting, consider adding one. Be willing to research the history of your inn building if guests are interested in it.

Your guests will often tell you what they like. Look for moments when you can ask for their opinions.

Don't let your inn image just happen. Once it's established, it's very difficult to change. Consider carefully what your inn image should be and how you will project it. Your inn guests will return in large part for your particular style.

SELECTING A NAME

Inn image and inn names are vitally related, of course, so the work you have done on developing an image concept is a good start on choosing the name. But there are a number of additional opportunities and limitations. Let's review them one by one.

The Davy Jackson Inn in Jackson, Wyoming, uses a hospitable alternative to the typical but somewhat harsh No Vacancy sign. Their sign by the front door says in two-inch letters, "Rooms Available." When they are full, a sign goes on top that says, "Sorry No." It's a convenience to travelers not to have to climb the stairs or the path to find out if there's a room. A basket of brochures by the front door also gives a future guest a chance to take home a reminder of the inn, now that they have seen it from the outside.

LOCATION

Use a reference or allusion to your location to evoke a mental image for potential guests. The Inn by the Sea is a name opportunity for a coastal location, but since inns along hundreds of miles of American coastline could claim it, you might include the name of your town and make it the Kennebunkport Inn by the Sea. Maybe your inn's proximity to a landmark can lead you to a name.

HISTORY

Is there a historical event or personage that hints at a name for your inn? Many inn names are taken from the former owners of the residences. The Glenborough Inn considered this approach. According to Pat, "A Mr. Brooks was the original owner. But in Santa Barbara, there's a Brooks Institute, so Brooks Inn would have been confusing. The most famous person who lived at our inn was named Fowler. Fowler is an okay name, except fowl can also be foul, with obvious negative connotations. So we decided the historical names didn't work for us."

But consider the Captain Lord Mansion in Kennebunkport, Maine. All three parts of that name connote authority and even wealth: captain, lord, and mansion. The word *captain* also brings to mind the sea, which the inn overlooks from its top floors, where no doubt a waiting wife once paced.

SOUND

The Captain Lord Mansion is pleasant to say and to hear, both important tests for the inn name you select. How will it sound when you answer the phone? Will callers say, "What?" The Bath Street Inn often gets mail addressed to Bass Street Inn. Susan makes a joke of it, telling callers it's "bath—as in taking one."

Does the name feel good coming out of your mouth? Does it sound crisp, clear, inviting? Does it come trippingly off the tongue? Chambered Nautilus is an inn name that does, and it also brings to mind the sea, chambers, and even aquariums, all appropriate to the inn and its Seattle location.

The Jabberwock, an inn in Monterey, California, evokes immediately an image of playfulness from the moment the name rolls off your tongue. If you know the Lewis Carroll poem "Jabberwocky," you're propelled instantly into the innkeepers' image of gentle fun.

Each room name comes from the poem, and so do names for the bathroom, the telephone room, and the common refrigerator. Even breakfast foods have Lewis Carroll names. The property is landscaped in trills and trolls. The logo is ornate and intriguing; if you look closely, you'll see the Jabberwock. The playful theme is carried through with cookies and milk at bedtime and a stuffed bear tucked between the sheets.

Because the reference to the poem is rather erudite, while the poem itself is sheer fun, the Jabberwock appeals to both the sophisticate and the child—of any age.

CONNOTATIONS

Be sure the name you choose doesn't mean something different to others from what it means to you. The Bath Street Inn chose not to be called the Bath House because bathhouses have specific, inappropriate connotations in some areas of California. Nevertheless, people still occasionally call the inn the Bath House. So when you name your inn, consider whether the name will have for others some implication you don't like, or whether it invites unpleasant wordplay.

To test this, try the name out on friends and strangers. Tape record it. Experience the name in the context of your building and the atmosphere you want to have. For many people, the word "parsonage" evokes warm feelings about their parson and their relationship to the church. For others, negative past experiences predominate. On the other hand, a name like the Parsonage has more historical connotation and softness than Minister's House. Since the name should strengthen the image for prospective guests, you wouldn't want to name an authentic British pub-style inn the Parsonage.

INNOVATION

Moving the words around in a name can sometimes create something fresh. For example, say a couple named King is opening an inn that they want to call King's Bed and Breakfast. By changing it just a little, to Bed and Breakfast with the Kings, they've made it more of an invitation. The

Kings, determined to use their name, can make a rather conventional choice something different by changing the order of the words.

▦ DESIGNING A LOGO

Your logo should be a strong visual statement of the spirit of the inn name, image, and ambience. It can be as simple as a typeface or as extravagant as an artist's design, commissioned and copyrighted for your inn alone. Whatever way you go, the trick for maximum effectiveness is repetition, using your logo in the same way on all your visual material, from brochures to T-shirts. This strengthens the image in your prospective guest's mind.

Whether you want the challenge of designing a logo yourself on your computer or prefer to work with a designer-artist, there's some basic conceptual work you need to do first.

First, can you tie the logo image to the name of your inn? to a drawing of it? to the street it's on? to the skyline of your city? to the tree in front of the inn? to your locale? to a special service you offer? Capitalize on the concept that will give you the strongest image. In general, the simpler, the better. For instance, if you're the Cuckoo's Nest Inn on Pine Street, you might be able to come up with a stylized cuckoo in a pine tree.

Second, do you want or need something more than just a typeface? Why? Do you have the budget to have a logo created for you? Is your budget so limited that it would be wise to do a less-ambitious logo very well, rather than try to do an ambitious one poorly?

Third, make a list of specific uses for your logo, along with the minimum and maximum sizes required for those purposes. Remember that as you reduce an image, the lines become thinner. As you enlarge it, the lines become thicker. To maintain the original quality of the design for each use, it's wise to have the art work done in several sizes, for both large and small reproduction.

Consider the appropriateness of the overall shape of the logo. For example, a long name on an essentially horizontal logo may take the entire area of a one-inch display classified ad, leaving you no room to describe the inn. An emphatically vertical logo may be a problem on a sign for your front yard.

You will want to put your logo to a variety of uses, some immediately, others several years into the business. Apply it to your letterhead, ads, brochures, signs, postcards, T-shirts, matchbooks, soaps, and displays at conferences.

When Maureen and John Magee bought the Rabbit Hill Inn in Lower Waterford, Vermont, the rabbit name was already in place, but they made it work—hard. Their logo is a bunny; stuffed bunnies sit next to the salt and pepper shakers on their dining room tables and perch on guest beds, on shelves, and in all sorts of unexpected places. Guests bring them rabbit gifts. Their telephone number is 800-76-BUNNY. Sound a little too cute? Not after you've stayed at the inn and discovered how serious they are about making you feel as pampered as a beloved childhood bunny.

PRODUCTION

Start by finding a designer you can work with. Artists or public relations firms may recommend creative people, willing to share ideas and ready to give honest feedback. Talk to a few prospects about prices and procedure, and ask to see their work. You may want to do some initial design work on your own computer, experimenting with typefaces. Many firms have flyers or booklets that show their typefaces in available sizes. If not, ask them to photocopy samples of your favorites for you to take home. Look them over carefully. Maybe you can combine them in an interesting way. For example, an ornate initial letter can set off an otherwise straightforward, readable typeface. Be sure to look at the individual letters in your inn name; some of them may be hard to read in some typefaces.

Once you've narrowed the typeface choices to three or four, have your inn name set in a larger size than you'll use on a business card. If you want more than just a typeset name in your logo, review clip-art computer files or books for border shapes or illustrations, like an apple or a tree. A designer can put art and type together as you request, make useful suggestions for snazzing up or simplifying the design, and give practical advice regarding the different sizes you'll need for your uses. Even if you decide to do much of the developmental work yourself on your own computer, work with a designer on the final product: Your logo is the basic building block in your entire portfolio; don't let it look amateur.

Think, too, about reproduction costs. Your basic logo design should print well in black-and-white, without halftones to reproduce shading. There may be times and purposes for color or halftones, but using a logo that requires special printing techniques and inks is costly in the long run.

Show your prospective logo designs to your partners and friends for their opinions. Ask them to choose a favorite. Do some reality testing, too.

Ask what each logo says to them, what ideas and feelings are evoked. Does it say hominess, elegance, softness? Don't prompt the answer you want to hear.

When you've made your choice, get stats in a variety of sizes at the typesetter's or from a lithographer. Stats are camera-ready art, and it is handy to have a file of them to respond quickly to a good ad price or to use on a urgently-needed flyer. If your designer can scan your logo and store it on computer disk, it can easily and quickly be resized as needed.

PRODUCING A BROCHURE

Producing a good brochure is astonishingly time-consuming, and it's easy to let the project slip when you're up to your armpits in sawdust. But your brochure must be ready at least as soon as you open the doors of your inn. The brochure is the basic tool in your promotion kit. It represents you to prospective guests who may never have seen your area or your inn. The words, pictures, and format you choose can make or break you.

You'll almost certainly be surprised and frustrated at how long it takes to get everything done: a month or more for design and typesetting, a couple of weeks for drawings, time for you and your partners to review and react to everything, a week for the printer, and another for the bindery. The operational decisions that precede these mechanical steps can be even more time-consuming: setting inn rates, establishing deposit policies, and deciding whether to accept credit cards. Give the entire process plenty of time.

To start with, you need a good grasp of what you want to convey and how you want to convey it. It helps to be very analytical here about what can become otherwise too personal. You're choosing your appropriate approach within a spectrum of what other inns do, so at least six months ahead of opening day, begin collecting brochures you like from other inns. Keep a collection to review for ideas on layout, color, typefaces, and the ability to project a feeling.

At the same time begin collecting the promotional materials of the big spenders in your area—the chamber of commerce, the department of tourism, and big hotels or motel chains. Analyze the way they sell the area and their businesses. This can give you a good idea of why people come to your community. (However, please don't use the materials developed by neighbors as obvious models for your own! You'll want your colleagues to be friends, you know.)

About four months before opening day, start considering how much energy and expense you want to put into developing your brochure. There are a number of approaches you can take to getting the job done. You can do it yourself, with or without a computer, drawing the illustrations, hand-lettering the copy, and doing the layout and paste-up. If you're very good at it, this can be successful. But the truth is, a complete do-it-yourself job fails more often than it succeeds, especially in today's competitive market.

You can take the opposite approach and hire an agency to do the whole job. You tell them what you want, and they write the copy, commission the artwork, choose and order the type, and furnish you with printed brochures. You can build in stopping points along the way when they will ask for your approval. Naturally, you will want to know the price of the project before you make any agreements.

Then there's a middle ground, which you design to suit your own needs and skills. Perhaps you want to write the copy, supplying it on computer disk to be modified by your designer, who will do the rest. Or you may want to render the drawings. Another option is for you to handle the leg-work, hiring someone to write the copy, someone else to take photographs, arranging for the typesetting, and choosing a printer. In a sense, it's like being your own building contractor.

Be careful about working with friends. Your brochure is so important that you don't want courtesy to require you to accept something less than terrific. It must be easy to say no firmly.

⟨⟨⟨⟩⟩⟩

Brochure guru Roberta Gardner offers innkeepers this advice about working with color:

If you want to work smarter, not harder, use a color brochure and color postcards to market your inn. Color is twice as expensive as other printing, but if the work is quality, marketing in color is four times as effective.

To prevent wasting time and money, here are pitfalls to avoid at all costs.

✳ A color brochure can hurt you if it outshines your inn. If you don't show truthful photos, your guests will feel duped, and they will be unhappy. And there's nothing worse than an unhappy guest.

✳ Don't tell everything, and don't show everything in your brochure. One of the great joys of inn travel is discovery. Show enough to attract guests, but allow them to be pleasantly surprised by the unanticipated details.

✳ A simple message is essential. Today we have less and less time to do more and more. If recipients of your marketing materials have to scratch their heads to figure out what you're saying and what you're selling, you've lost them. Be clear, simple, and direct.

❋ Don't allow your designer to get carried away with a design concept at the expense of your business—design for design's sake rather than for your inn's sake. Looking at good design is like walking into an uncluttered room—a pleasant, easy experience.

❋ Before hiring a photographer, review his or her previous work. Photographers specialize, just like doctors do. You wouldn't go to an eye doctor for knee surgery. So don't assume that all professional photographers can shoot interiors of buildings. Once you're certain your photographer can shoot buildings, ask yourself if you like the look of the work. Some photographers use even lighting from top to bottom for a clean, still, editorial look. Others evoke mood, emotion, and romance. There is no right or wrong style; it's a matter of taste.

❋ If you can't afford the best-quality design and printing, don't use color. A thoughtfully designed one- or two-color brochure (ideally with a color postcard insert) will be far more effective than ho-hum color.

❋ If your guests say, "Your inn is so much nicer than your brochure," know that you must make a change, and quickly. For every guest who gave you the benefit of the doubt, you can count on many potential guests who chose not to take a chance on your inn.

COLOR

Color brochures advertising inns are becoming more common, but they're not a good idea for everyone. First, they're expensive. The printing process itself is more time-consuming, and that costs money. Second, only the very best color photographs will convey a professional image, and good photography is not cheap. Third, color brochures raise an expectation in guests' minds that the inn will be more than a simple B&B; the innkeepers must be ready to meet those expectations.

Why do inns choose color? Some do so to keep up with neighboring inns. Some believe their guests expect it in a high-quality place, and international guests certainly do. Some hope to increase occupancy. Some have settings or buildings that simply must be seen to be believed. Innkeepers report that the number of reservations increase in response to color.

Old Miners Lodge in Park City, Utah, uses full-color watercolors in their brochure rather than photos. This is a very comfortable, well-run inn located in an upscale ski area where luxury properties abound. Rather than try to compete with them head-on, innkeeper Hugh Daniels has created an honest, beautiful yet unpretentious variation on the color theme.

If you decide a color brochure is too expensive or inappropriate for your inn, you might consider enclosing a color postcard with your line-art brochure. You can have your own made or use a commercial one that shows off your area. Or you may also enclose color reprints of articles that have been written about your inn. (Remember to get permission from the publisher.)

CONTENT

Put yourself in the position of a future guest. What would you want to know if you were shopping for a getaway inn? Why would you want to visit your inn? How would you benefit from staying there? You want your potential guests to be able to picture themselves at your inn, waking up to the smell of baking bread, opening their eyes to sun-dappled treetops. Sure, they want facts, but mostly they come seeking an experience. Don't give them a furniture inventory.

You want your inn to appear unique compared to all the other choices the guest may have. When you're writing copy, eliminate every descriptive word that can be found in someone else's brochure. Eliminate nonspecific terms like elegant, charming, historic, and cozy. Always remember that the brochure is about the guests, not about the inn. For example, don't say, "There is a cozy window seat in the elegant, historic Abigail's Room." Instead, say, "Like Abigail herself in 1832, you'll burrow down into the pillows on the window seat to watch the sun set over the river. While you're there, see if you can find the secret hiding place where she kept her golden coins!"

Content has a more mundane side as well. Make a list of the questions you have as a traveler. Ask your friends, partners, and guests at the inns you visit what questions they have. Using the list as a guide, three and a half months before opening, start to draw up the categories of information you want to include in your own brochure. Here are some suggestions.

✳ Should you include prices? The trend is to put them on an insert card that can be altered less expensively than the entire brochure. Some inns list a range of room prices, while others price and describe each room individually. Whether from your brochure or on the phone, guests will want to find out what their room costs and what it includes.

✳ How will your guests find the inn? Most will be from out of town, many from other states or countries; it will help them to know where the inn is in relation to the state or region of the country. Plan to include both a map *and* directions; not everybody is good at deciphering a map. It will reduce the time you have to spend on the phone, repeating the same instructions. When you've drafted your instructions and drawn your map, have them tested by a friend who easily gets lost.

* How much space should you devote to describing your area and activities? Guests are selecting your inn partly because you know your community. Describe your area as helpfully as possible, so they'll know, for example, that you're three blocks from the Shakespeare festival or within walking distance of ocean-view hiking trails—and of course, let them know that you provide free maps!

* Should you describe each guest room? This is an area of some controversy, but innkeepers seem to succeed, whichever course they follow. If you have sixteen rooms, it will be difficult to describe each without losing your audience; you might group descriptions by room features and prices, like "fireplace suites with Jacuzzis, $185; private bath, queen bed, $85 to $110." But if your inn is small and there is a substantial difference in room decoration and prices, detailed descriptions will save you telephone time and help the guest fantasize about the place. It's to your advantage to promote those fantasies. In some inns, the guest rooms aren't the main draw, the common area is. In that case, that is what you want to focus on.

* Should you use the brochure to promote special services? Meetings and weddings, on-site therapeutic massage, bikes to rent, tours, gift certificates, and package deals are services you might offer. If some are integral parts of your inn image, mention them in the brochure. If you're not sure how certain services will be accepted, plan instead to promote them with brochure inserts. This gives you a chance to try ideas and discard them if they fail, without dumping your whole brochure.

* What about mentioning the innkeepers' names? It adds a nice, warm touch, and guests like to know the names; it's something hotels generally don't provide. But some guests will be disappointed if they don't meet the "real" innkeepers during their stay.

* How much of your policies and procedures do you want to describe? Veteran service-oriented innkeepers know from experience that clear information saves time, confusion, and unhappiness on all sides, but they include this information on the rate sheet insert rather than prominently in the brochure. In today's market, you don't want to sound like the inn police, but it's only fair to describe your deposit and cancellation policies, check-in and check-out times, and smoking standards.

These are the basic areas you'll want to consider for your brochure copy. You will probably think of others. This is the "function" part of brochure planning; "form" is our next subject.

Brochure Checklist
Things to consider including in your brochure:
Inn logo and name
Innkeeper names, both owners and employees
Address, including zip code
Telephone number with area code
TDD availability
Fax number with area code
E-mail address
Map and directions
Number of rooms
Room descriptions
Local description: what is there to do?
Photos, drawings
Insert sheet
    Policies and procedures
    Prices
    List of services included in prices
One-line catchy word picture
Main copy: brief images actively involving guests
A little history, woven into guest benefits
Environmental actions
Special services offered: weddings, massage, gift certificates
Dining on premises; menu samples
Inspections you have passed: AAA, Mobil, ABBA, state associations
Associations of which you are a member: PAII, state associations
Accessibility for handicapped, with appropriate designations
Space for writing confirmation note

FORMAT

You'll mail thousands of brochures during your innkeeping career. Think about the effect of various formats on cost. Some card-style designs take advantage of one-sided printing for an unusual look, but standard brochures look more professional printed on both sides. In addition, since the costs of paper, design, and postage are fixed, the marginal cost of an additional side of information is very little. If there's a brochure format you like, before you do anything else, take a sample or a description to a couple of printers for informal bids on what it would cost to do something similar.

Black ink is the cheapest. Adding other ink colors or using any color instead of black is usually somewhat more expensive, but it can be effective. Ask your designer about using screens, which use shading to make one or two colors look like more, and other design techniques to make an inexpensive printing job look special.

Choose your paper carefully, and make sure you understand how the color of the paper will affect the color of the inks; your printer can show you samples. Contrast is important. In general, red ink is hard to read and red paper is hard to read from. Remember, you're already competing for your reader's attention; don't put any unnecessary obstacles in the way.

Choose a paper that allows you consistency among promotional materials. Not all papers are available in the weights you may need for your letterhead, business cards, and postcards. Consider whether your paper will fold nicely; heavy stock sometimes won't, unless you pay a little more to have it scored before folding. Consider using recycled paper.

If you're on a tight budget and are evaluating design, ink, and paper choices that vary widely in price, think about whether a potential guest is more likely to choose your inn if you adopt an expensive look. If your image is elegance, the answer may be yes. If your image is more down-home, the extra cost may not be worth it.

Before you take your design to the printer, take it to the post office to get a sense of postal limitations. A size differential of a quarter inch that makes no difference in the effectiveness of the design can nearly double your mailing costs. Putting the return address in the wrong corner of a 5½-by-8-inch mailer can do the same thing. Test how well your design and paper make it through the mails by mailing samples to friends. Do postmarks cover copy or detract too much from the look of your self-mailer? Or if you want a delicate look, is your paper too flimsy to survive the mail? A three-panel, two-fold piece will hold up better with lightweight paper than a single-fold piece.

Typefaces should be easy to read. The accepted wisdom among graphic artists is that printing in italic type is not, all capital letters is not, and reverse type (white letters on a dark background) is not. On the whole, the more you're aware of the typeface, the less you're aware of the words. Type must be clear in small sizes as well as in large. Look at all the characters you will use, including numbers for your address and telephone number.

COPY

Few people feel obligated to read carefully every printed piece that comes before their eyes. The best format then is one that provides the basics in big letters to attract attention and detail in small letters for those who want it. Use short sentences and short paragraphs, with headings that tell the bare bones of your story to readers who routinely give material a thirty-second scan. Estimate how long your brochures will last based on how you'll distribute them. If you include room rates in your copy, you will need to reprint when prices go up, and you don't want to have to wait five years to raise rates.

DOING IT YOURSELF

If you decide to write your own copy or do your own artwork, take plenty of time. Three months isn't too long. You need time to think, to work, to get others to react, and time to put your copy, drawings, or photographs away so that you can come back and review them with fresh eyes.

HIRING WRITERS AND ARTISTS

Even if you're working with a pro, do your homework first. It will save you money because your job will take less time, and you'll probably be happier with the product because it will reflect your inn as you see it. Start by writing out your identity concept. Give it to your artist or writer with a copy of your logo. Also supply any other written descriptions you may have, like the one in your business plan. Your writer will also need a list of what information must be included in the brochure.

Before any work begins, put on paper your expectations and the artist's or writer's fees, delivery dates, and restrictions. Specify whether you are buying the product outright or only limited rights to its use. For example, if you're working with a photographer, will you own a specific number of prints only or the negatives, too? Be clear about what happens if you don't like the preliminary work proposed to you. Your contract should provide for a "kill fee" to be paid by you to end the agreement at a specified stage if you don't like the work in progress.

TYPESETTING

Getting type set for the brochure may take as long as ten days. Material to be typeset must be typed double-spaced with wide margins. Keep a copy so that you can check your original against the type you get back from the typesetter. The errors the typesetter makes will be corrected for free. The errors you make or alterations you request after the material has been set will be charged to you. They can be expensive.

Your typesetter may also provide layout and paste-up skills, or may do all production on the computer, which means you can provide copy on a disk, ready for layout, and avoid errors in type that is reset.

SELECTING A PRINTER

This is a good time to establish a working relationship with a printer, since you'll be doing plenty of printing through the years. Find someone you're comfortable with. Ask to see samples. Check to see that they're crisp and clean, not smudged, not tilted, and with folds sharp and straight.

Printing prices can vary tremendously, so get bids for your first job from more than one printer. Include this information in your bid requests:

* Name of paper, its weight, texture, and color.
* Typeface and distinctive symbols, features, or a logo
* Type of ink and colors, identified by PMS numbers found on printer's ink color wheels.
* Size of finished piece: A rack card? A folded brochure?
* Number of halftones, screens.
* Number of folds and a sample of the finished folding format.
* Number of finished pieces.

Always ask for price breakdowns based on volume; the price per thousand of ten thousand brochures will be substantially less than the cost of one thousand brochures. Think seriously about using recycled paper and soy ink, even if it costs more; guests will appreciate your concern for the environment when they see the recycled logo on your materials.

When you've received the bids and you've chosen your printer, provide painstakingly clear written instructions with your artwork and a mock-up of the finished piece, illustrating where folds go and which end is up. Keep photocopies of the artwork in case it is lost and to make telephone discussions with the printer easier while he or she has the job. Set a date to check a blueline to see how the material will look when printed, before the whole job is run. Make sure everything's coming out correctly at that stage, when changes, although very expensive, can still allow you to salvage a potential catastrophe. Be sure to agree in advance on the final completion date and pickup or delivery.

Then prepare for the thrill of holding your first brochure in your hands—put the champagne on ice!

ONGOING MARKETING

Marketing is one of your most important jobs, and the one that most often gets pushed aside in favor of things like toilet repair. It's a classic example of the urgent pushing aside the important. Don't let it happen to you, or all your urgent work will be complete, and you'll have no guests to enjoy the perfect flush.

The frustrating thing about marketing is the lack of immediate gratification. When you serve breakfast, you get not only the satisfaction of completing a task but also enthusiastic, immediate feedback. Marketing is not like that. Much you produce and pay for will never succeed. Then, unexpectedly, an article will appear in *Gourmet* magazine because a guest liked your coffee cake. Marketing is experimentation with uncontrollable elements, but it can be as creative as it is frustrating. And it's certainly a great educational adventure.

The best marketing you can do is a superb job of attending to details—and loving it—as an innkeeper, but that's just step one. There's a lot more.

Decide who will be the marketing director of your small business. For the first three years, at least, that person should set aside a regular weekly time to market, five to eight hours minimum. Use the time to send promotional material to writers, track patterns of occupancy and demographics, and plan new promotional strategies.

Develop a promotion file of names and addresses of travel writers who have written articles about other inns. Keep copies of the articles, so you'll know the subjects and angles that most interest particular writers; this will help you target letters, releases, and personal contacts with them. Keep copies of information you send anywhere; you can often reuse it as it is, or modify it slightly to send to someone else. Keep a careful record of what you've done, so you won't waste time contacting the same travel writers or guidebook authors more than once.

File art—drawings, logos in various sizes, and photographs—and originals of type used for ads and brochures. Much of this can be recycled, and it's all expensive to use just once. Keep additional separate files for advertising contracts, letters to guidebook publishers, and promotional ideas.

Mailing supplies should be kept on hand. Getting together the envelope, cardboard backing, and appropriate postage, then leaving the inn to mail everything, is not easy. Having all these items stocked away enables you to respond to media inquiries with lightning speed—which is just what the media expect.

As results of your marketing begin to appear in newspaper and magazine articles and guidebooks, keep a scrapbook for your guests in the common room. It will provide them interesting information about the inn and also reconfirm their idea that your inn is the best place to stay.

Keep close track of your marketing efforts, and ask all guests and callers how they heard about the inn. If you don't see the return from a particular ad or approach, stop spending money on it. Computer software will help you track results easily, but don't let the counting and book work keep you from tallying this information, even if you have to do it by hand. The information is essential.

Save all names and addresses from any respondents to your marketing; this is your mailing list, worth its weight in gold for future promotions.

THE BASIC KIT

Whether you are suggesting a story idea to the travel editor of the *New York Times* or asking a guidebook writer to consider including your inn in the next edition, there are basic materials you will be expected to provide.

What do you need? At least one crisp, clear line drawing. If one is all you have, make it a view people will see and recognize as they drive by. You need eight-by-ten or five-by-seven black-and-white glossy photographs of the exterior, a guest room, the common room, and a breakfast, plus a few color transparencies, either slides or four-by-fours. A couple of great color photographs may make the difference between being included in a story or not. Reproduce photos, slides, and transparencies only from original negatives and artwork; bad quality artwork will go directly into the wastebasket.

Black-and-white shots are important for newspaper articles; a well-styled black-and-white can be the center of a press kit sent to papers in your top five feeder markets. A color photo is often unusable in a black-and-white format. Contrasts are important to black and white; cloudy skies are better than blue. If you need to have these photos taken, try your local paper's photographer.

Many writers say they prefer to see people in the photographs, receiving a breakfast tray or walking up the front pathway; after all, these aren't real estate ads. However, you define and limit your audience if you show only young white couples in the photos. Be sure your photographer is familiar with work for publication, so the contrast in the photographs will be good. Your objective is to have such appealing artwork available that editors who must choose to highlight an inn from among several will pick yours so that they can use your great photo. In some instances a fine color transparency provided by an inn has appeared as the cover of a magazine! The byword is, make it easy for the media to make you famous. Have several copies of everything, so you can mail artwork at a moment's notice.

Label it with your inn name and address so that it can be returned. But it's better for the media to keep it, just in case there's an emergency empty space to fill.

Try taping to the back of the photo a typed description or caption that you would like to have accompany the photo when it is published. Always include your inn name, town, and state in the copy. Also tape to the photo a business card or piece of paper bearing your name and address. Handwritten notes smudge or leave marks that could show through.

You will need to provide the media with background material. Your brochure is an obvious source, but a detailed, easy-to-read description of the inn just for writers is a good idea. Describe the history of the inn, the locale, the innkeeper's biography, and local activities. Consider including a unique item that makes your inn stand out from the rest, just to attract the writer's attention: an acorn from your oak tree, rare seeds from your historic garden, or a bit of patchwork in the pattern of your handmade quilts.

Mary Nichols of Hannah Marie's Country Inn, Spencer, Iowa, uses theme teas to promote her inn. "The teas have lots of benefits," says Mary. "They give locals a chance to dress up and see the inn, they produce extra cash flow, and have resulted in great public relations, from newspaper articles to a feature in a book on teas."

Mary researches her authentic teas and has presented them on such themes as Queen Victoria's chocolate tea, tea at the Ritz, Danish tea luncheon, Hannah's country tea, and a Mad Hatter's tea party for mothers and daughters at which Mary and her staff are dressed as Queens of Hearts.

Photographs

"In producing our book, we include two photographs for each inn, and the quality of the pictures sent by the inns is often poor—if the innkeeper even has photos. We wish every innkeeper would invest in quality photos of their inn. Photographs taken by a professional will give you a better chance of being on the cover of a magazine or a book, though some innkeepers have produced good photos themselves by taking many and ruthlessly selecting the best."

Wendy and Jon Denn, The Professional Inn Guide of Inspected Inns

Contracts for advertising

Artwork, carefully stored:

    Line drawings, originals with at least five copies ready to mail

    Logos in various sizes

Photographs, each clearly marked with inn information:

    Eight-by-ten or five-by-seven black-and-white glossy or matte photos (negatives saved and clearly marked), at least five copies of each

    Color transparencies—slides or four-by-fours. Buy five additional sets or the original negative from the photographer

    Color photographs of the transparency shots, clearly marked, ten sets

Plastic organizer for viewing slides and transparencies

Articles written about the inn, five copies of each. Be sure you have permission to reprint.

Recipes with a little background, original plus ten copies

Chamber of commerce materials about area, twenty copies

Written information (ten copies each) on:

    Inn history

    Owner/innkeeper background

    Special packages, events, cooperative marketing

Stories about the inn to help the media write about you

Brochures and rate sheets

Menus from the dining room or breakfast

Mailing materials:

    Twelve nice folders to hold materials

    Twelve large nine-by-twelve-inch envelopes

    Four overnight express envelopes (Federal Express will let you charge fees on your credit card) with telephone number and times for pickup

    Cardboard backing to protect artwork

    Postage stamps

Your special item in quantity: an oak leaf, a bit of patchwork, etc.

Also include a collection of chamber of commerce material about your town and area; there's no need to duplicate material you probably help pay for with your membership.

Reprints of articles on your inn give media people a feeling of security, that they're not alone in being interested in you. Reprints should show dates, the writer's name, and the newspaper or book title. Select the most recent and the best coverage as the quantity grows. Be sure you have permission to reprint articles. Sometimes it is less expensive to get copies of the magazine or buy reprints from them; nevertheless, be sure to ask permission before you copy.

Many inns assemble these materials in loose-leaf binders or cardboard folders to present to writers. Some inns preprint covers with their logo; others find attractive ways to mount a business card or brochure on the cover. Your presentation should look professional, but don't be afraid to be innovative and creative; media people get kits by the hundreds.

Now you're ready to promote. In some cases, you'll want to use your complete kit to introduce your inn to an important writer; in others, you'll only use appropriate materials. Depending on the photos, artwork, and attention-getters your kit includes, it can be expensive. Use it judiciously, but don't be stingy. A major article is worth the price of a lot of kits!

INN GUIDEBOOKS

Innkeepers say inn guidebooks are the largest single source of business, excluding word of mouth and return guests. Because the time lag between selecting inns for a volume and getting the guide to the bookstore can be a year or two, contacting guidebook writers can begin even before you open.

The best approach is to send a letter to the author at the publishing house. Indicate that you're familiar with the author's book and understand his or her particular emphasis, which might be history, cuisine, or quality. Explain why your inn is an appropriate inclusion, particularly if it helps fill an obvious gap, such as location.

Briefly describe a few additional things that make your inn different from others. Being romantic and charming is not enough. Use specific, vivid language that will help your reader imagine your inn. Mention attractions and events in your area and invite the writer to visit. Enclose a press kit or selected material: a brochure and other information that will make a visit irresistible, particularly anything that relates specifically to the author's guidebook angle. You may also want to include some reference to yourself—a hobby, your life before innkeeping, a close relationship to the House of Windsor—anything to convey that time spent with you will be interesting. Your tone should reflect your style as an innkeeper, just as it does with guests or prospective guests.

Keep the letter brief, a page if possible, and before you finalize it ask someone not connected with the inn to read it and tell you what overall impression it conveys. This is a safeguard against the errors occasioned by being too close to your subject.

Naturally, this letter is going to take some time. Once you've written it, though, you'll find that with slight modifications it's a good letter to use for many other contacts, such as those with other media or new businesses in your area that might need accommodations for clients. Modify it to send to writers of several other guidebooks, too.

Keep guidebook writers informed of price or other significant changes, and when they do list your inn, send a thank-you note.

Should you offer a free night's stay? Many writers make it a policy not to accept free nights, to insure their objectivity. On the other hand, it's expensive to visit hundreds of inns a year, and some writers almost have to accept free nights. It doesn't hurt to suggest it.

According to PAII's comprehensive *Guide to the Inn Guidebooks*, less than 30 percent of guidebooks charge fees to list inns, but this number is increasing. Before you pay, ask other innkeepers who keep good guest records whether the listings are worth it. Innkeepers are inundated with offers for listings in books, CD-ROMs, and at Internet sites. PAII maintains a file of offers they have researched for members and a list of good questions to ask guidebook representatives.

When you receive a solicitation from a guidebook writer, check the deadlines and respond clearly and on time with what they want. Most guidebook authors will not visit your inn, so the information you send is your chance to be included.

TRAVEL WRITERS

Coverage in newspaper and magazine travel articles is one of the best free promotions for inns. Sometimes getting a story is just luck, but there are also things inns can do to attract attention. To plan the most effective approach to a travel writer, consider your story from a writer's viewpoint.

Writers need to produce good articles in a reasonable amount of time. Remember that these folks are being invited to all kinds of places, all the time; a getaway is not the thrill to them that it would be to you. The information you provide should reassure them that they'll get a great story without a tremendous amount of work if they take the time to visit. You must provide complete information on rates, directions, special programs and deals, and so on.

Your area is as important as your inn. Innkeepers often mistakenly believe an inn makes a story, but travel writers regard inns as places to stay, not reasons to travel. A large part of your pitch is selling the things to do in your area.

How do you identify travel writers? Start by developing a list of names and addresses of travel writers who have done articles on other inns. Save copies of the articles so that you'll know the subjects and angles that most interest particular writers; this information will be helpful when you write them a pitch. Subscribe to the publications in which you'd like to be featured, and get a feel for what they look for. You might also contact the American Society of Travel Writers for their member list, or Inn Marketing (see Resources, page 306) for their travel writer mailing labels.

Some innkeepers routinely send out press releases to writers; others insist personal letters are the best approach. In either case, keep in mind that travel writers get stacks of mail, and many of them have perfected the art of reducing the size of the stacks at a rate of about an inch a minute. You need to attract attention and make a compelling case in your first paragraph.

On the whole, sending a mass mailing to travel writers announcing your inn opening is probably a waste of time. It would be wiser to send out specific invitations to writers in nearby large cities. Do something catchy to attract attention, like sending a box of cookies along with the invitation to an opening of Grandmother's Inn or delivering a hot pizza along with the invitation to the opening of Albergo Lucia. Use all the pizzazz you can muster!

When you finally hear from your dream writer, what then? Here are some quick guidelines from travel writer Marilyn McFarlane and public relations counsel Catherine Lockwood.

✳ Return calls promptly. Often writers are working to meet a deadline; if you're not available, they may call the next inn on the list.

✳ Show enthusiasm.

✳ Be a good listener who is interested in the writer. You'll learn how best to meet their publication requirements and fit into their articles.

✳ Send promotional information as soon as possible. Use overnight mail or your fax to get it there fast.

✳ Always gets the writer's name, address, phone number, and publication, even if it's just a quick phone interview. You might come up with a great new angle and want this person on your media list.

When the writer arrives:

✳ Always tell the truth. If you don't know the answer to a question, say so.

✳ Be ready with a colorful anecdote about your inn or yourself: a story about the couples that have become engaged at your inn, how many pancakes you've served, the biggest fish caught in the lake, and so on. Write these ideas down when you get them, so you'll be ready for writers.

* Say what is different about your place. It may be the history, the theme, package deals, anything that makes your inn stand out from the rest.

* Give the writer something to take home: cookies, muffins, a jar of jam, flowers, a sachet, any small reminder of your hospitality. A gift of food allows writers to speak of your cooking, even if they're not there for a meal.

* Offer to introduce the writer to other tourist operations in the area, including other inns, restaurants, and attractions. Function as tour guide.

* Don't complain about anything, including guests, overwork, expenses, or even local government. Be positive.

* Don't ask to read and approve material before it is published or ask for a guarantee that you'll be included. (Unless you're paying; that's advertising, a different matter.)

* Don't speak off the record; who says anything good off the record?

What about complimentary lodging? Ask for more information before offering free lodging or a discount, whether you're responding to a letter, call, or a visitor who has arrived unannounced. You can do this gracefully, while ascertaining whether the person is genuine or merely looking for a free room; fortunately there are only a few of these. In fact, few authentic writers actually spend the night, so when they do, treat them like royalty.

It's okay to ask about the project. Who is the publisher? What is the assignment? When will it be published? Ask about previous articles so that you can get an idea of the writer's interests. A professional understands your need for information and will not be insulted. Often a freelance writer can provide you with a copy of the assignment letter. If you're still doubtful, call the publication.

If, despite your best efforts, your inn is not included in an article, don't feel cheated. The writer may be able to use your information another time. Take it in stride and keep the writer on your mailing list.

And if your inn, or even just your area, is included in a story, send a warm thank-you note or letter!

SPECIAL EVENTS

Special events are gatherings organized around a theme, designed to expose people to your inn, create interest, and generate publicity. The big-city paper in your area is unlikely to do more than one travel article about your inn, but if you sponsor an autumn biking tour that goes from inn to inn, mystery weekends, or an annual puzzle challenge, that's news.

The more angles you can come up with, the better. Some inns plan events calendars for a full year, so every article on one event automatically leads readers to send for the full calendar. Sometimes you can get local merchants to cosponsor, saving you money and providing more hands for the work to be done. For example, the bike tour might include stops at new wineries in the area, or it might be sponsored by a worthy nonprofit group that will do much of the promotion for you. Nonprofit sponsorship of events means you can get free public service announcements on radio and television, too.

Sometimes special events are a way to bring in paying overnight guests at slow times of the year; they can also introduce local residents to your inn, who will then think of you first for accommodating out-of-town guests. For some inns, the events themselves have provided important incomes during early years before occupancy could support the operation.

Special events are great opportunities for creative promoters to generate consistent publicity and to develop the image that their inn is the place to be. But they're also a lot of work, so be sure you plan something that's fun for you. Even if it isn't a roaring success, at least you will have had a good time during your slow season.

Creating a newsworthy happening is just the first step; the follow-up of letters, press releases, and phone calls to the media takes a lot of time, energy, and nerve. If you've got all those, you can make events pay off.

Comedy Weekend. Cornelia Niemann of the River House in Boyce, Virginia, uses her theater background to gather a group of guests in winter and early spring for an "Enter Laughing Weekend." She provides the script, and the guests come anticipating an uproarious time with others of the same inclination. What happens is different every time, but Cornelia's flair for the dramatic and ability to bring together strangers and involve them creates a memorable weekend that has guests clamoring for invitations.

Computers and Marketing

How can innkeepers participate in computer marketing opportunities? One option is to become published on CD-ROMs; most computers are now sold with CD-ROM drives. Companies are marketing CD-ROM inn guides; the quality varies just as it does among printed guidebooks, so check the quality. However, the real key here is CD-ROM marketing: A bunch of CDs sitting in someone's garage won't sell your inn. The disks must be advertised in major consumer publications and widely available in video stores to even reach your customer. The real proof of the pudding is in whether you get reservations.

Another opportunity is to take advantage of electronic on-line marketing, which you can do by paying to be included in the on-line listings or by working the bulletin boards yourself, or both.

The two largest commercial electronic services today are CompuServe and America Online. Both contain inn directories to which inns pay a fee to be categorized and listed. More importantly, both contain travel bulletin boards where users post messages in their quest for the perfect travel experience, such as, "Looking for perfect honeymoon retreat in Smoky Mountains." With a computer, modem, and free software connecting them to one of these on-line services (priced around $9 per month), innkeepers can become active in these bulletin boards and post return messages letting the honeymoon travelers know that you have the perfect inn.

You may also initiate contact with your own message, like, "When you want to hike in a secluded woods and view the world's greatest sunset from a quiet hilltop, come to the Miracle Inn: king-size beds, privacy, and great breakfasts delivered to your door."

The Internet is the fastest growing advertising medium ever. Do your homework, as with any other advertising opportunity. And remember, there's no deadline within the Net. The advertiser can go on-line at any time and change, modify, or delete listings. With time, prices will drop considerably. Remember hand-held calculators?

ADVERTISING

"Never buy ads or vacuum cleaners on the first contact." Ad salespeople always sound urgent, but there will always be another chance. Here are some guidelines to help you make wise advertising decisions.

✳ Remember that advertising is only one part of your overall promotion campaign, and that it needs to be integrated into the plan. A number of excellent, one-time articles on your inn won't help for long if readers can't find out how to contact you a few months later when they finally plan a trip.

✳ The reader, or audience, is basically passive. The more difficult it is to read your ad, the less attention it will get. Some marketing studies claim you have all of three seconds to grab a reader's attention.

✳ Arrange the information in the ad as clearly as possible. Use the 60-40 rule: 60 percent art and 40 percent copy, or 60 percent copy and 40 percent art. If art and copy are given equal weight, the reader will be confused about the ad's focus.

✳ The primary goal of an ad is to give your reader the basic facts: what you do, where you are, how to reach you. The size ad you buy should determine how many more details you will be able to share.

✳ Are you primarily competing with inns in your area, and therefore working to differentiate your place on the basis of price, services, quality, and so on? Or is yours the only inn in the area, and you are trying to attract a new market, missionary style? Determine your position—and it may very well combine a bit of both objectives—to help construct more effective ads.

✳ How well will your ad compete on a page? If you are buying a small ad on a directory page, you have a lot of competition for attention. So how can you draw the reader's eye? Use bold borders, bold type, or black background with white type. Is your logo a real eye-catcher, or does it need to be strengthened when it's reduced? Can you use a combination of bold and lightweight typefaces or a combination of type sizes to balance the look of the ad?

✳ Leave room around the words or the design within the borders of the ad so that the eye can focus. This concept is called white space by graphic designers. Consider walking into a room with flowered wallpaper, plaid curtains, striped upholstery, and mirrors along one wall. The eye doesn't know where to look first, it has no resting place, no focus. The only obvious move is to leave the room. For the same reasons you wouldn't decorate this way, you shouldn't design ads this way.

✳ Repetition—alias money, money, money. A one-time placement of an ad is likely to get little or no response. When you've carefully considered all the periodicals in which you might buy space, and you've made your choice(s), give the ad some time. For a reader, it's a disappointment to try unsuccessfully to find in a current issue an ad that was there last month.

✳ When should you advertise? Do you expect a slow time you want to bolster? Advertise before you hit it. In the middle of a lull is no time to make a one-month advertising appearance. Besides, you won't have any money then. If there's a time of year when your area is flooded with tourists, you may want to advertise then, so people take your ad home to plan for the next season. You might also want to run an ad that encourages them to come back at a slower time.

Figure out exactly what the ad's purpose is, and then buy space accordingly. The only way you can gauge the effectiveness of an ad is to be very clear from the beginning about what you want it to do.

✳ Never, never, never let a persuasive sales representative talk you into buying an ad during the first phone call or meeting. Ask for the rate sheets and the demographics information on the subscribing population. A professional publication will have this information for you. Then tell them you'll get back to them after you review it. Check their editorial calendar; it will list the topics to be covered in particular issues, so you can time advertising decisions or submission of copy for stories to be included in appropriate issues. If the publication looks like a good possibility, request the same kind of information from its competitors. Compare them carefully before you select your best buy.

* In general, beware the little, inexpensive ads, those costing thirty to seventy-five dollars. The only truly inexpensive ad is one that brings in more business and income than it costs.

* Advertising lodging in the local paper is usually a waste of money. Instead, get involved in fund-raisers for community causes and advertise the events. This demonstrates your public spirit, and inclines the local media to print your media releases.

* If you're considering a particular ad buy, contact other inns that use the publication and ask about their results. Sometimes you'll get a more helpful answer from inns not in your immediate competitive area.

Advertising shouldn't be an impulse or instinct buy, and it doesn't have to be. Just make sure you know what you want your ads to do, and then run ones that accomplish your purpose and target your audience at a good price. To target your ads, you have to do your homework. Start by reviewing your guest research. From where will most of your guests come? What professions will they represent: doctors, attorneys, teachers, carpenters, artists? Finally, what will your guests come to the inn to do: ski, hike, or eat?

Using this information, develop a list of advertising target priorities. Be as specific as you can about your target goals. For example, maybe your very best market is bird-watching dentists from the Twin Cities, and your next best, also from Minneapolis-Saint Paul, is carpenters who enjoy the hot springs and mud baths. How do you reach these targets?

If your audience is chiefly professionals from the Twin Cities, there may be a business journal most of them receive. If they are in small business, a chamber of commerce publication might be good. If your guest population is very broad in terms of profession and activities, you might consider advertising in the *Minneapolis Tribune's* travel section, a publication that targets a geographic area more than a demographic one.

The next step is designing an ad that will catch the eyes of the people you want to attract. If you're after craftspeople, how about an ad with calligraphy? Professionals may be drawn to a very sophisticated, clean look. (Caution: This may be the toughest one to achieve without the assistance of a pro.)

If you plan to work with an artist on the ad, look at several portfolios to find an artist who already does the kind of thing you like. It's much easier than trying to explain to an artist, no matter how talented, an unfamiliar style that your heart's set on.

Theme Packages

Stuart and Hermine Smith and Jim Kent of the Churchtown Inn in Churchtown, Pennsylvania, are known for their weekend themes and packages, but the weekend exciting the most interest is the one when they join an Amish family for dinner. This relationship was initiated by the community's Amish families. The visit is described when the guest makes a reservation. Just before dinner, guests gather in the inn's parlor and receive gentle directions from the innkeepers. "We respect our hosts' beliefs by dressing conservatively, not taking pictures, and not carrying on any 'doubtful' conversations." Jim and Stuart accompany their guests to set the mood. Guests and hosts alike introduce themselves and a prayer is said. At that point, the family and the guests are generally comfortable, so the evening progresses without the innkeepers needing to provide direction. A bounteous meal is served with several homemade salads and breads, then poultry and meat dishes, three vegetables, and finishes with three desserts and coffee and tea. Sixty-five percent of the Churchtown Inn's guest are repeats, most specifically for this experience. Guests return to visit all three kinds of homes presently hosting: an old-order Amish, a new-order Amish, and a senior-citizen Mennonite.

GIFT CERTIFICATES AND GIVEAWAYS

There's a publicity angle on gift certificates: Inns are frequently asked to donate them as prizes for fund-raisers. Every time your inn is mentioned at a raffle or a silent auction, potential guests hear it. Every guest who comes at no charge as the result of a fund-raiser will be another satisfied customer to spread the word.

To help a good cause without loss of needed income, limit the certificate's validity period to times when the inn won't be full. Track the way your donation is publicized, so you can decide whether you'll want to do it again next year. Feel free to be specific about the conditions of your offer. You can donate for the silent auction only, or perhaps reserve the right to be the only inn featured.

MARKETING TO GUESTS WITH DISABILITIES

Here is an opportunity to expand your guest population to include the over thirty-seven million consumers with a visual, hearing, or physical disability.

Start with checking your language. Of course you wouldn't use words like *retarded*, *crippled*, or *crazy*, but appropriate terminology today can be confusing, even to people with the best intentions. Peter Robertson, a disabilities consultant, prefers the phrase *people with different physical, hearing, or visual abilities*. To Robertson, the rest of the world are TABs, *temporarily able-bodied*, with the idea that everyone is vulnerable to age and accidents.

Other appropriate terms include *physically challenged, disabled, visually impaired*, or *wheelchair-users*. *Lame, wheelchair-bound*, and *confined to a wheelchair* are considered derogatory. *Blind* or *deaf* are acceptable, but *deaf and dumb* is not.

Language is powerful. It reflects, reinforces, and shapes perceptions. Words that inspire positive attitudes and awareness help develop great communication with happy, returning guests.

TO WHOM CAN I TURN FOR HELP?

Find out more about the needs of the otherwise-abled. It is time to walk (or roll, as the case may be) in someone else's shoes—or chair. Understand your inn from their viewpoint. Invite someone from a local organization that provides services for the disabled community or ask a disabled friend to go through your inn and discuss what you need to do to increase accessibility. Talk to someone who actually experiences the disability. An architect generally knows the law, but you want more. You want happy guests.

COMMUNICATION ACCESSIBILITY FOR HEARING DISABLED TRAVELERS

The most effective way of contacting the deaf community is to invest in a Telecommunications Device for the Deaf (TDD). This device attaches to your phone and has a keyboard with a screen. A traveler dials your inn and indicates when you answer that they are on a TDD; you switch to your system. Communication is achieved by typing back and forth to each other.

At a minimum, contact the Teleconsumer Hotline (see Resources, page 307) for current national 800 numbers for TDD service; you can publish these in your brochure. For example, AT&T's TDD number is 800-682-8786; deaf callers can call that number and be connected with you; a voice operator reads their typing aloud to you and types your response to them during the call.

Over 10 percent of the American public is hearing disabled. By listing after your telephone number "voice/TDD," you announce availability to those nine hundred thousand potential travelers and their relatives and friends.

If your inn is barrier-free and has met federal guidelines, then use the blue international wheelchair symbol for accessibility. However, do not misrepresent yourself. This group of travelers has more often than not faced serious misrepresentation regarding accessibility. Be honest and clear about the obstacles that exist. "The bath has no turnaround and the sink has no knee clearance, but the shower and toilet have grab bars, and there is plenty of room to wheel into the bathroom. In addition, there is a one-inch threshold on the outside entry door, but it is thirty-one inches wide and has a ramp. We also have a portable ramp for entering and exiting the dining room."

Architectural and communication barriers are obvious, but attitude is an invisible barrier. You may think, "I won't get much request for this type of room, so there's no need for me to make changes." This may be true, but it may not. If hearing-disabled individuals cannot even call you or physically disabled persons have other obviously safer choices (which advertise and market to them), why would they even bother to contact your inn? Imagine the delight of a wheelchair user when a great place like yours solicits their business!

DIRECT MAIL

Direct mail gives you the opportunity to capture a prospective guest's undivided attention—for a few seconds, at least. Compare this with magazine advertising, where readers may never see your ad at all among the competition.

Successful mail promotion makes a valuable short-term offer that is urgent, personal, and easy to understand. Even offering a percentage discount is too complex. Think about what would make you drop everything and run: "Stay two nights and get the third one free" or "Stay three nights and we'll give you a hundred bucks!" Be sure to describe exactly how a guest can take advantage of the offer, and tell them to do it. Many innkeepers are shy about saying, "Call now," but it works.

How do you know which idea will work best? Print two different offers, randomly splitting your list. Code them so that you know when you get a booking whether the guest responded to the special rate, say, or the free champagne. Stick with the most successful offer on subsequent mailings.

Traditional elements of successful direct mail marketing are an envelope with a two-page cover letter, a brochure, and a special offer. Innkeepers are changing this standard with clever, well-designed postcards, full-color photos of the inn, self-mailing brochures, and newsletters. Naturally, whatever you produce should be consistent with, and extend, your overall theme at the inn.

The *Direct Marketing Association 1994–95 Statistical Fact Book* shows that postcards are the second most likely piece of mail to be read (after newspapers and magazines), and they are the least common piece of mail received, making them stand out. Innkeepers are sending birthday and anniversary cards generated from their computer records of guests who celebrated these events in previous years.

Where do you get a list? Your own list of former guests and inquirers is at least four times as effective as any other list you can use, according to Peppers and Rogers in *The One to One Future*. Of course, if you are just opening, you won't have a list, but if you are taking over an existing inn, be sure you get their list of former guests—even if it is on little pieces of paper in a shoe box. Also consider purchasing lists from other inns and from inn consumer publications, the local Chamber of Commerce, a state association, or list broker. Be sure you focus on zip codes that match the demographics of your inn guest profile.

If you've got a clearly targeted audience and an irresistible idea, mail it! Once you've developed a piece that works, you can use it again and again.

If you mail it, will they come? John Kirby, innkeeper of Sea Crest by the Sea in Spring Lake, New Jersey, is a former direct marketing executive who decided to apply what he learned in his previous career to his inn—with a vengeance. He mails color postcards and brochures to his former guests and inquirers nine times a year. He offers his mailing list free to other innkeepers to send out their newsletters or brochures to his guests. Five innkeepers exchange lists with him. John reports that he can tell when other innkeepers send mailings to his guests because Sea Crest receives additional calls for reservations! The other innkeepers have the same experience when he mails to their guests. He is selective about those with whom he exchanges lists to be sure that the audience is a match and that the inn is actually sending mailings. He also sends only to an area within several hours of his inn, because he has discovered that it is most productive for him. In six years he has turned the small, seasonal ocean town with a single inn open off-season into a year-round resort with ten inns open in the winter. The twelve-room Sea Crest by the Sea quadrupled its January and May business in the first three years and increased annual occupancy by 30 to 40 percent in subsequent years, which they attribute directly to their repeated mailings. Sea Crest's January business is equal to May's in just six years!

For most sectors of the accommodations business, travel agents are a significant (40 percent) resource for booking rooms. Though an increasing number of inns work with travel agents, the 1994 PAII study shows no increase in the number of bookings innkeepers receive over the 3 percent average of the past five years; properties with more than nine rooms do better than smaller ones.

Working with travel agents is a challenge for small properties with few rooms available to rent at the peak times when the agent requests them. If the inn is not charging enough for the guest room to comfortably pay the travel agent, the innkeeper resents paying the 10 percent commission. However, the greatest hurdle is confusion over third-party reservations, because inns are so different from each other; they don't like to miss the opportunity to set the stage for the visit with a hospitable initial contact.

Make it your goal to get organized enough to avoid the confusion. When a travel agent calls (and, with rare exception, they identify themselves) for a double room, be very clear about the unique features of the room, such as bed size, no TV or phone, three floors of stairs, and no facilities for children and policies not typical at hotels, such as cancellation policies and restricted smoking and check-in times. Of course you want to sell the room, but be sure to find out whether their clients will be comfortable. Never book a shared-bath room unless the client has specifically requested it.

Create a warm letter of confirmation with the specific potential problem areas of your inn highlighted in the letter and again in your brochure. Enclose two letters and two brochures, one each for agent and client.

Inns that work regularly with travel agents find they establish a regular clientele of loyal agents, especially when they satisfy the agent's clients and promptly send commission checks. Commissions, usually just 10 percent of the cost of the room, are an investment, not an expense. Travel agents can fill rooms that would otherwise remain empty; the commission is a bargain.

TELEPHONE MARKETING

What is the sound of opportunity knocking? In the inn business, it's the ringing of the telephone. Great beds and great breakfasts are not enough. You need a telephone presence that conveys all that you have to offer.

Skill matters, too. An inviting presence on the phone is simply an empty promise if your guests arrive to find you forgot to calendar their reservation, quoted the wrong room rate, or were too embarrassed to mention the no-smoking policy. Whoever handles the phones should understand the history, development, and relevance of your policies. There's a tendency for new staff members to apologize for policies that seem unnecessarily hard-nosed. Sometimes, too, staff people who don't have to follow the reservation process all the way through can be too casual about recording complete, accurate information. Getting names right, for example, avoids embarrassment and is a way of demonstrating to people that they're important to you. You can and must be professional and skilled as well as friendly and inviting.

Get the details right and you'll find that your telephone can be a great promotional resource—on the customer's dime. You have paid for your callers through your advertising, your brochures, special promotions, word of mouth, and so on. Now this caller is spending time and money to find out whether your inn really is as wonderful as it's billed to be.

The first rule for tapping this resource is to make sure the phone is well tended, by you or someone you have trained. Whoever answers your phone should see it as an opportunity to transform originally interested callers, obviously shopping around by phone, into guests with confirmed reservations, so eager to stay in your inn that you know their deposits will go into the mail without hesitation.

When you or your trained staff can't be at the inn to answer the phone, you have two options: answering machines and cellular phones. The "cell phone" lets you take your reservation book and make reservations wherever you go. Future guests don't know where you are and will make an immediate reservation with you rather than wait for your competitor to respond to a phone message.

Answering machines have become an expected part of today's society, so using one is not a problem for guests. Be sure your message is clear, friendly, and inviting. Give the caller a reason to make the extra effort to get in touch with you. Your prompt return call is crucial. If you leave an exciting message on the tape, the number of people leaving messages and waiting for your return call will be high. The way you handle callbacks can increase your business. Many a guest has said, "I chose your inn because you were the only one who called me back, even when you had no rooms when I wanted them."

Don't fill your message with rules and instructions. Many people are still struggling with voice mail instructions and are turned off by "if we don't have a room we won't call you back, if you want a brochure leave a name and address, if [after all this] you still want to make a reservation, leave your number, and we will call." Assume that the guest knows nothing about your place, and make your message so inviting they will wait with bated breath for your return call.

Voice mail has not taken hold at inns and may not. If you have a large inn and want to install voice mail for nighttime guest room phones or for the manager, that may work, but remember that guests choose inns to feel like a person, not a room number. Be cautious in your installation of this feature.

Be cautious, too, with call-waiting. Many people find this inexpensive telephone service galling. Instead, consider installing a second line that rolls over to an answering machine that says, "We are on another line and will return your call as soon as we hang up"—plus your usual great message. If your inn is small, this second line might be your personal line. It is also possible that a busy signal tells callers that you are popular, so they'll try again, just so long as the primary line doesn't get tied up with long phone calls.

When speaking with a prospective guest, it's essential to articulate a sense of your place in a simple, appealing way. Have ready a few adjective-laden sentences that capture just what it is that makes your inn rare and wonderful. Develop a script and keep it by the phone for you or your reservation people to use.

Base it on a guest's-eye view of the experience of your inn, emphasizing the things you've picked out to highlight in your brochure: architecture, setting, sounds, scents, and activities. Use vivid adjectives to construct the most poetic description possible for your surroundings. You're not the last building on the right at the end of the road; you're at the end of a wooded canyon, where the main sounds are singing birds and the running river. You're not on the left side of the highway; you're on a magnificent promontory jutting out over the Atlantic Ocean. You're not five miles from town; you're high in the hills with a sweeping view of the bay.

Extract the essence into two or three sentences that can be spoken comfortably, without sounding "canned." Rather than responding to the question "What's your inn like?" with a strictly factual account of how many rooms you have and whether there are private baths, have those few lines ready to spark the interest of the caller.

But don't get so involved in what you want to say that you forget to listen. Find out as much as you can about your callers' needs. For example, are they looking for a secluded place or for one within walking distance to shops and restaurants? Point out the ways your place matches what they're seeking.

If you do have a room, your script can make your callers feel lucky to get it. If your inn sounds irresistible, callers will shop no further and are unlikely to cancel a reservation later.

If you don't have a room this Saturday night, get in your two-liner anyway, and volunteer information about when you do have an opening. Mention that weekends book up eight weeks (or whatever) in advance, but during the week they'll have the place pretty much to themselves. Mention how wonderful it is to walk along the beach on a Tuesday morning without running into another soul or to go bicycling along a country road with no weekend traffic. Also, don't hesitate to refer the caller to an inn in your area that has openings; next time the callers will remember your helpfulness and generosity.

If they can't come midweek but sound interested in your inn, encourage them to book the next available weekend, reminding them that most of the inns in your area fill up at least that far in advance. You might also mention something that's going to be of special interest even two or three months ahead, like whale watching or spring blossoms, and suggest they make plans now for the next outing.

If they decide to come to your area on a weekend when you are already booked, invite them to tour your inn. Seeing your place will give them a solid image to store for future vacation plans and a sample of the charm they can expect when they come back to stay.

If you can't get a booking, ask if you can send a brochure if they don't already have one. Add callers to your mailing list, too. Remember, you paid for this inquiry, so use it. At the very least, find out how they heard about your inn so that you can keep track of the ads or sources that are working.

The telephone is a tool to help you make the most of all your other promotional techniques. Use it creatively, with a warm and light touch. Joke around a little; it's fun for you, and people respond to it.

MISCELLANEOUS MARKETING

✳ Cooperative marketing with other inns can increase your visibility and multiply your promotional dollar—besides, it may be fun. Initiate it yourself if a society or club hasn't already been started.

✳ Open houses are a standard for new inns and new owners, but an annual one for the locals has been especially well received when hosted by the owners of the very upscale Inn on Mount Ada, the former Wrigley Mansion on Catalina Island in California.

✳ Tours of inns, whether during the first week in December for the National Bed and Breakfast Open House or as a fund-raiser for a local charity, give you local exposure that is invaluable.

✳ Familiarization tours for travel writers and travel agents are best coordinated with a group of inns and/or with your convention and visitors bureau.

✳ Hiring a public relations agency is like hiring staff; they should have a great deal of experience in the area where you need help. Interview and research carefully.

* Radio advertising can be costly, especially if you don't understand the lingo and best hours, but maybe someone will trade you room nights for air time while you learn.

* TV advertising is expensive; try promotion via a nonprofit fundraiser program. Some television programs featuring a very few inns are being produced. Approach the producers with your press kit.

* International travelers are best reached by coordinating with the state tourism office's overseas visits; you'll need a color brochure.

* Outdoor advertising, such as scenic byway signage, billboards, or freeway Adopt-a-Highway signs, requires research in your particular state and community. Think twice about the message a billboard conveys; be sure it fits with your image.

* Environmental marketing is more than conscience easing; many people will choose your inn if they see the recycled logo on your brochure and learn of your sincere efforts to preserve the earth.

* Niche markets, such as bicyclists, hikers, gays and lesbians, African Americans, business travelers, and so on, are all there for the plucking. Get to know their publications and needs and promote to them.

* Cookbooks are a way into another section of the newspaper. Use them as gifts your guests will use to pass around your name and a statement on how fine your food is.

Most important of all, remember to have fun at marketing. Let your creative juices flow, but promote with a plan and within a budget.

UP AND
RUNNING

✱ PROFESSIONALISM

A variety of things will bring guests to your inn; professionalism will bring them back. Innkeepers must combine skill with flexibility, the warmth and intimacy of Grandma's with the perfection of Buckingham Palace.

Guests are usually understanding and helpful in the face of emergencies at the inn, but they expect peace and comfort. If you accompany mopping up the water from a broken commode with a litany of how tough your day has been, you are breaking the spell.

Professionalism is obvious in numerous small things. At check-in time, for example, the mood of an entire stay is established. It's an insecure time for guests, who bring high hopes along with uncertainty about what to expect; if you're scrambling around to get organized, you add to that insecurity.

Even if you spent the last four hours cleaning rooms, comforting your sick child, and installing a new sink, and even though the groceries you raced out to purchase are still spread all over the kitchen table, what really matters is how your guest feels when you open the door and say, "Hi! Welcome to . . . !"

Among prospective and operating innkeepers, there are a few who want to escape the rat race and "lay back." Nothing, however, will more quickly destroy your efforts to relax in your new career than a double booking, and that's just what you'll get if you refuse to run your inn in a professional way.

Do you want to be casual about innkeeping? Before you begin, take a moment to imagine what it's like to tell a young honeymoon couple that the room they booked and paid for has been given away because you forgot to note their reservation in the calendar book. This is nightmare stuff! Or how about failing to notice that the Smiths never sent their deposit for Saturday night, leaving you with an empty room on one of the few nights you can count on full occupancy? Emotionally and economically, you can't afford a lot of errors like these.

Whether evidenced by cold coffee, grungy sheets, or rude telephone manners, a too-casual approach to innkeeping can ruin you. A professional always tries harder.

⟐⟐⟐⟐⟐

Hospitality Balance
According to innkeeper Susan Sinclair of Maples Inn, Bar Harbor, Maine, "What I call 'hospitality balance' is probably the most important aspect of innkeeping. Not every guest that walks through the door wants to spend lots of time with an innkeeper, but there are many that do. You have to try to understand

the guests' needs and react accordingly. Nothing is worse than an innkeeper that won't leave guests alone, yet to give too little attention to someone who obviously wants it would be awful, too. Since no two people are alike, this gives innkeepers a daily challenge."

SERVICE

Service has become the byword in the hospitality industry, but few segments of the industry are as able to pull it off effectively as the bed-and-breakfast and country-inn business. If you are to succeed in today's competitive market, it will be because of your service mentality.

Because guests expect more of inns, the possibility of disappointment is greater. When you are expected to be both the ideal mom and the world's greatest flight attendant, living up to guest expectations can be tough.

Service has three components: anticipating guest needs, responding cheerfully to guest needs and more than meeting them, and viewing problems as opportunities to serve.

Innkeepers anticipate guest needs by paying attention. When you design your inn, choose the amenities and features you will offer by visiting other inns. Good inns provide what the innkeepers have learned their guests want. Pay close attention to guest requests. If they want a place to put their dinner leftovers, perhaps you might add a guest refrigerator. Do guests rearrange their rooms? If they move a lamp closer to the reading chair, another lamp may be needed. Listening to prospective guests' questions about the availability of private baths, fireplaces, or queen-size beds has caused many an innkeeper to add them.

Anticipating guest needs is more than responding to specific requests; it's also figuring out how to go beyond what a guest might expect or demand. Ask them if they are celebrating a special occasion: you may get the opportunity to present a birthday cake or anniversary champagne when they arrive. If you hear them exclaim over the lilacs as they walk up the front path, put a vase of them in their room. Surprising guests with that unanticipated extra is inn-style service today.

Responding cheerfully to guest needs is not always easy, but it's the basis of good service. The guest who doesn't like your house-special hazelnut coffee is not insulting you, but rather making a request. Everyone who pays you money will not necessarily like everything they have bought. Your challenge is to be thankful that they told you their opinion and to respond cheerfully by not only meeting the request but also double-checking later that your response satisfied their needs. It's strange but true that responding well to a request may please the guest even more than if everything had been perfect for him or her at the outset!

240

Once in a while a guest will complain about something more than your coffee. The toilet is overflowing, there are fleas in the carpet, the bed collapses. These are problems. The secret to handling them is not only to fix the fixable immediately but also to look for an opportunity to extend yourself. While you bomb the fleas, fix the bed, or repair the toilet, offer a picnic basket and a map to a secret spot for a romantic afternoon. Or simply present a bottle of champagne with a note thanking your guests for their patience.

Please Complain!

According to innkeeping *newsletter, the Technical Assistance Research Program's research on unhappy customers shows that you want them to complain to you before they leave, to give you a chance to fix the problem. Ninety-six percent of customers with complaints will never tell you them. Of those who complain, if the complaint is not resolved, only 46 percent will return. Seventy percent of those whose complaints are resolved will return, and 95 percent of the complainers whose problem is resolved quickly and well are likely to return. Interestingly, of guests who do not complain, only 37 percent return. So problems are opportunities to guarantee return guests!*

GUEST-FRIENDLY POLICIES AND PROCEDURES

Inns are as individual as innkeepers, and one inn's set of policies is unlikely to be perfect for any other. Nevertheless, other innkeepers may have solutions you haven't thought of in problem areas like children and pets. There's also a feeling of safety in numbers: an industry standard is easier to assert. Unfortunately, there are not really very many industry standards in policies and procedures among bed-and-breakfast and country inns.

Developing clear policies and putting them in writing is good for your guests as well as for you. Guests to whom you have sent a brochure or letter of confirmation describing your no-pets policy, for example, aren't as likely to muster up much righteous indignation when you stop them at the front door with Fido. But don't let clarity overwhelm hospitality. Some people just don't read anything you send them; it's not their way. If you care about maintaining goodwill—and the studies that show that a dissatisfied guest will tell more people about your inn than an ecstatic guest will—be as flexible as you can comfortably be. Some issues are clear and firm; some you'll evaluate over and over. Here are some specifics.

SMOKING

Stale cigarette odors in a guest room can take days to disperse. Not only that, fires caused by cigarettes kill more people than any other kind of fire. This is due chiefly to smoking in bed, but another common cause is cigarettes that fall into sofas and smolder until finally the upholstery ignites in the wee hours of the night. The combination of cigarettes and alcohol is especially deadly, because people become more careless when they drink.

On the other hand, some potential guests will undoubtedly decide against your inn if they're not permitted to smoke there. You may establish a middle ground by permitting smoking in some limited area of the inn, where it will be least hazardous and least offensive. You may also want to limit *what* can be smoked: cigars are unwelcome at most inns; pipes can smell cozy or lousy. Quite a few inns simply do not permit smoking inside.

Some inns have both smoking and no-smoking guest rooms. This works especially well if you have a separate cottage or a separate floor for the purpose. With wood-burning fireplaces or wood stoves in some rooms, it may be difficult and also less important to enforce a policy against cigarettes there.

So what do you do when there's a problem and your clear policy is being ignored? Often a nice note by the pillow is enough to stop the smoke in a no-smoking guest room. Because it avoids face-to-face interaction, embarrassment on both sides is reduced. If your guest is staying one night, you may prefer simply to console yourself by remembering that they'll be gone in the morning. Some inns charge a cleaning fee (the guest is sent the credit card slip along with a note explaining the circumstances) if a guest violates their no-smoking policy. In most instances where the innkeeper already has the guest's credit card on file and the guest has been informed, both verbally and in writing, of the no-smoking policy, the innkeeper is not challenged with a credit card charge-back by the guest who chose to smoke anyway.

If you encounter a smoking guest in a no-smoking area, a nice line to use is, "Are you going to have trouble with our no-smoking policy?" Take it from there.

CHILDREN AND PETS

In some states it's illegal to refuse to accommodate children; proceed carefully. In addition, it may be determined at a national level that not accepting children is age discrimination. It is true that children may be a problem to guests who are taking breaks from their own progeny, and children may create noise problems. Increasingly, innkeepers are setting up a special cottage or room with an outside entrance to accommodate their former yuppie guest who now has children.

Pets are generally not accepted at inns; however, there are two inn guidebooks written especially for properties that welcome pets. Cat allergies are common among travelers, and sometimes the little critters do bring fleas. But many innkeepers can regale you with stories about the letters and gifts their pets receive from guests, who miss the pets more than they do the innkeepers.

Please keep in mind the same considerations regarding the innkeeper's children and pets. Guests taking a breather from their own children may not enjoy having to converse with the innkeeper's little ones. Likewise, they may be allergic to cats and afraid of large dogs; they may not view your large, oh-so-friendly, bouncing-up-the-driveway German shepherd as a treat. Be sure to mention any in-residence animals in your written materials as well as when taking a telephone reservation.

If you choose to restrict children, setting an age limit is one way to tailor your policy. Just decide at what age the average child will behave the way you prefer your guests to behave. State this policy positively. Here's an example: "Children over ten are warmly welcomed." If you believe that no children can be welcomed as guests at your inn, try this positive approach: "Because of the physical nature of our inn and our concern for your child's safety, we will be glad to refer you to another inn in the area where your family will be welcome." The whole point is to come across as guest-friendly and helpful.

Because many potential guests who want to come with children feel inns are inhospitable to families, the words "children welcome" is not enough to entice or reassure them. Instead, try: "We truly welcome children. We'll help you plan special events for their enjoyment during your stay." "Our cottage is perfect for families . . . come visit us and we'll all have a great time." "You and your children will find our inn a home away from home, from a special kids' welcoming kit to a well-stocked toy box."

Whatever your policy regarding children and pets, it should reflect a sense of the character of the inn and the innkeeper and a sensitive attitude toward your potential guests.

⸻

The Jakobstettel Guest House in St. Jacobs, Ontario, encourages children age six and older to visit. Innkeeper Ellen Brubaker welcomes them with a tour that features the location of the cookie jar! "Kids are great! We just involve them!" says Ellen. "We post their drawings on the refrigerator and let them 'help' make muffins." Families generally do a good job of supervising their own children, she says.

The inn uses pullout sofas in guest rooms for one or two children; they put a mattress on the floor for more, and parents bring sleeping bags.

"Do you accept cash?" As incredible as it sounds, guests ask it. Here's an outline of the advantages and disadvantages of various forms of payment.

CASH
Advantages
* No bank charges
* Almost always "good"

Disadvantages
* Some risk of theft
* Need to make change
* Need to receipt payments

CHECKS
Advantages
* No bank charges
* No change to make
* Good for mail-in deposits
* Automatic receipt of payment

Disadvantages
* Some risk of bouncing
* Risk of theft
* Can't guarantee last-minute booking

TRAVELER'S CHECKS
Advantages
* As good as cash
* Minimal fear of counterfeit

Disadvantages
* Some risk of theft
* Need to make change
* Need to receipt payments

CREDIT CARDS
Advantages
* Can confirm last-minute reservation
* Convenient for guest
* More impulse sales; more expensive rooms sold
* Automatic receipt of payment
* No need for change

Disadvantages
* Bank charges (2 to 4 percent)

* Authorizations take time
* Disputed charges may be difficult to collect (protection varies)

The Old Monterey Inn, Monterey, California, never had much trouble with cancellations, so they didn't take credit cards —until the 1990s recession. Now they find guests book more readily using credit cards for more expensive rooms, and the innkeeper has less bookkeeping related to waiting for checks to arrive.

DEPOSITS

A deposit is the seal on a two-way commitment: the innkeeper commits that the room will be ready and waiting for the guests to arrive, the guests commit to coming. Most inns require a deposit within a week or ten days of the date the reservation is made. For reservations made months in advance, you may wish to allow more time, but it's to your advantage in every way to get the money in hand. Deposits can be the price of one night's stay, half the price of the total stay, the price of the first and last nights' stay, or the total amount. Base your choice on how much commitment you want.

A related procedural issue involves last-minute reservations, made too late to be guaranteed with deposits (except by credit card). Take the call, make the reservation, and guarantee the stay with a credit card. Be sure to state your cancellation policy clearly so that the guests understand their part of the bargain. Say, for example, "Since the reservation is for tonight, it is too late for you to mail us a check. Since we will be holding a room for you and turning others away, we'll have to charge your credit card for one night's stay, even if you fail to come."

It's a tough one, warning callers they'll be billed if they don't show for a last-minute reservation. You want to be guest-friendly, and at the same time you want to reiterate that this is a two-way commitment. You can ask them to take the Girl Scout oath, or intimate that your people will be watching them. Whatever friendly persuasion you use, remember that establishing a personal connection with these callers makes it harder for them to disappoint you while you are guaranteeing not to disappoint them.

CANCELLATIONS

How much notice of cancellation should you require to return a deposit? This philosophical argument is endless. Innkeepers do not want to lose money on a guest who does not come and a room that is not filled, and guests do not want to lose money on a room they aren't going to occupy.

Cancellation policies range from twenty-four hours to seven or more days. Options on this theme include:

✳ Refunding all the money if the room is rebooked, except, perhaps, for a cancellation fee—generally $5 to $10. (AAA-rated properties are not permitted to charge a cancellation fee.)

✳ Refunding no money or only part of the money if the room is not rebooked.

✳ Refunding no money, but giving a gift certificate for the cost of the room.

In the past, innkeepers were quite rigid about cancellations. If the cancellation period required seven days' notice, then a guest who wanted to cancel had better call seven days ahead. Times have changed; travelers are now much less tolerant of what they perceive as inflexible and inhospitable cancellation policies. Smart innkeepers have changed, too. Even though it may be difficult for them to fill a room canceled at the last minute, innkeepers who respond with generosity and grace find it pays off with satisfied repeat guests.

The keys to handling cancellation issues successfully, from the innkeeper and the guest perspective, are clarity and, even more important, flexibility. Be sure guests understand your cancellation policy when you take the reservation and when you confirm it. Some, accustomed to the 6 P.M. cancellation policy of big hotels, will be surprised, but it's usually easy to explain the reason behind your policies: Unlike big hotels, you don't over-book based on a factor for cancellations; you absolutely guarantee a room, and you need your guests to guarantee they'll arrive. Inn guests generally book for special occasions, not last-minute impulses. An innkeeper who has turned away twenty callers for a weekend room may be unable to fill that room if the reservation is canceled on the preceding Tuesday.

Still, things can go wrong for people, so keep it in mind when someone has to make a last-minute change. Nice innkeepers do not finish last. In the short haul, when your room sits empty and the income is gone, it may seem so. But the day will come when the phone rings, and a caller says, "Michael Scott told me that I just have to come and stay at your inn. Do you remember Michael? He had to cancel a reservation and was unable to come, but you were so gracious in working with him that he says this just has to be a great place. My wife's birthday is coming up . . ." That conversation will make your day!

And besides, the longer you're an innkeeper, the more you'll realize that a hundred bucks or two isn't worth even an hour of your anger or unhappiness.

How do you decide what's the best check-in time or period for your inn? In an inn with round-the-clock staff, you might base it solely on the time it takes you to get your rooms ready for the next guests. But if yours is a small operation and the only desk staff is you, limiting check-in to give yourself some time away from the inn to shop, do promotion, or play a game of tennis is also important.

On the other hand, you are in business to accommodate guests. How can you meet both sets of needs? In most cases, reasonable check-in hours can be established, say 2 to 7 P.M. If most of your guests arrive from nearby cities after a day's work, a shorter time, say 4 to 7 P.M., may be adequate. If they are chiefly vacationers, midafternoon hours may work better.

There will always be some people who arrive early either without reservations or hoping to check-in. If they see a sign indicating check-in time is hours away, those without reservations will look elsewhere; those with reservations may get irritated, no matter how clearly you have communicated your check-in hours and the reasons for them. Guests are rightly concerned about beginning their inn experience, not about your needs.

How can you accommodate them? Be creative. Some inns arrange to leave keys or door-lock combinations along with special notes for guests with reservations who must arrive early or late. Some innkeepers arrange special telephone lines at the inn's front door that connect to a neighbor who comes when called to take care of early arrivals. Perhaps that same phone rings in your quarters, where you are having lunch, or the inn doorbell rings where cleaning staff can hear it. You then have a great opportunity to say, "I'm glad you're here. You're welcome to sit in the parlor and enjoy a glass of lemonade or a cup of tea until your room is ready."

You'll be tempted to add, "And please forgive my not being terribly attentive right at this moment, but I want to finish all of the inn's preparation for our guests arriving today," but your guests won't really understand that either. Most of them won't even feel you've done anything extraordinary by greeting them so warmly when they're there early. Call on every emotional reserve to assist your guests right then in whatever way they require; don't let on that their behavior is in any way unusual.

Checkout time at most inns is eleven or noon. Few guests fail to leave on time, but it's often possible to accommodate a requested late checkout time by leaving the room until last for cleaning.

Occasionally, you'll have to knock on a door in order to encourage a guest's departure. You might use a line like this: "I'm sorry to bother you, but did you realize checkout time was noon? I just want to let you know that we'll be cleaning your room in about ten minutes. You're welcome to

leave your bags in the office if you like and feel free to enjoy the garden."
You'll be tempted to speak with just a hint of reprimand in your tone; resist.

BREAKFAST HOURS

If it's 10:30 A.M. and nobody has shown up for breakfast, you'd better
try to remember whether you told them when breakfast is served, and
where. You want your guests to be comfortable, and that involves clear
communication.

If you serve breakfast in bed, ask your guests the night before what time
they'd like it. If you serve everybody promptly at 8:30 in the dining room,
talk it up during check-in time when you show them the inn and their
room. Some inns serve over a range of time, from 8 to 10, for example.

Many inns offer early breakfasts to business travelers. Some also provide
early coffee service in guest rooms or in the common area, where guests can
help themselves. This needs to be communicated to guests. If guests come
down to your 8:30 breakfast and you hear someone say, "Gee, I didn't know
I could get coffee at 6:30," you've got a communication problem.

Flexibility and communication are the keys to guest-friendly policies.
Every bottom line probably has its own bottom line. Mull your system over,
try out variations. Policies can always be changed.

HANDLING RESERVATIONS

Just because you don't have fifty rooms to book doesn't mean you can
afford to be casual about maintaining a proper reservations system.

THE RESERVATION FORM

A well-organized reservation form is the primary source of information
that performs a variety of important functions, including the following:

✳ Ensures that all essential information is taken at one time, when the
guest calls to make the reservation, so it's on the guest's dime.

✳ Ensures that all policies and procedures are described to the guest,
even when you take the call at the busiest moment of the day.

✳ Provides a convenient and time-saving space to make calculations.

✳ Provides marketing data for future advertising and promotional
planning.

✳ Provides the basis for a mailing list.

✳ Allows easy filing and retrieval of reservations.

✳ Becomes an all-in-one innsitter's resource, allowing innsitters to read or quote information accurately without hours of training.

✳ Helps eliminate double bookings, cancellations, misunderstandings, and unhappy guests.

✳ Provides easy retrieval of information on repeat guests. Happy is the guest greeted with warm words of personal recognition based on the previous stay.

Professional inns keep useful, accurate, retrievable information. Here are the basics of how it's done.

Though specific information needs vary from inn to inn, reservation forms can follow some basic rules. Most inns devise their own forms; some use standard 8½-by-11-inch paper, others use 4-by-6-inch cards. Some innkeepers fill blank pages with information in each of several categories they keep in their heads; others use preprinted cards. Some include a lot of information; others include very little. The basic information necessary to ensure a pleasant stay for your guest and a smooth transaction for you is:

NAME It's important to know who called to make the reservation as well as the names and the number of persons in the party.

ADDRESS This should be the preferred mailing address, whether home, work, or elsewhere.

PHONE Try to get business and home phones. Calling home numbers on evenings and weekends when rates are low will save you money.

DATE(S) AND DAY(S) OF RESERVATION Potential mistakes usually show up here, when callers request a day and date that do not occur simultaneously. Ask for both to improve your chance of catching the error. This information can also assist you in tracking business patterns, especially midweek and weekend variations.

ROOM Inngoers often book a specific room and expect to have it.

ROOM PRICE, DEPOSIT, WHEN DUE You'll probably request a deposit equivalent to a night's lodging price, half the total, full prepayment, or some other formula. Record clearly the total price quoted for the stay, the amount requested in deposit, and the date by which the deposit must arrive.

METHOD OF PAYMENT Leave room for credit card number, cardholder name, and expiration date.

POLICIES   You will no doubt have a separate rate and policy sheet to which you refer when there are questions, but it's also a big help to have policies written out on the reservation form in a conversational style that you can actually read over the phone. There should also be a space to check off when the policy is read or described to the caller.

CHECK-IN TIME   Although the only way to make sure guests arrive during a specific check-in time is to ferry them in to an island inn, the odds of their showing up on time improve if you are clear about your check-in time. You may want to work out special arrangements with guests for whom your regular check-in hours are inconvenient.

HOW THEY FOUND OUT ABOUT YOUR INN   This information, which guests are happy to share, is essential for evaluating your advertising and promotional program.

WHO TOOK THE RESERVATION   If more than one person takes reservations at your inn, note who took the booking in case questions arise later.

DATE RESERVATION MADE   If you require prepayment within a certain period, the date of the booking is very important. It may also prove useful or interesting to see how far in advance most reservations are made.

SPECIAL OCCASION AND OTHER NOTES   Important information could be that they're coming to celebrate an anniversary or honeymoon, or are driving up in one day from New York, or that they once lived in your area, hate carrots, or want dinner reservations.

BOOKKEEPING   Save space on the reservation form to record when payment arrives, the date you send confirmation, and the balance due.

THE FINE PRINT

RATES   include breakfast, hot tub use, evening beverage in the parlor; rates subject to change without notice; rates do not include applicable taxes; all rooms are designed for two persons (additional persons may use the sofa beds in the suites at $10 per person extra); singles subtract $5 from listed price.

RESERVATIONS   held pending receipt of one-night deposit; two-night minimum stay on weekends; MasterCard and VISA accepted.

CANCELLATIONS   *require seventy-two hours notice prior to date of arrival for refund.*

FOR THE COMFORT OF OTHERS   *there is no smoking in the main house; courteous smokers accepted in the cottage; no pets.*

CHECK-IN TIME: *3 to 8 P.M. Please call to make the special arrangements that must be made if you plan to arrive later than 8 P.M. If you desire an earlier check-in, please call on the morning of your arrival about the possibilities.*

CHECKOUT TIME: *11 A.M.*

RATE INFORMATION

The lodging industry is notorious for complicated rate structure. Books may come in one basic hardback format at one regular price, but rooms vary in price from Monday to Saturday, from February to June, and for one person, two people, and three people. And you may get a different price if you're a corporate traveler or a tourist.

The reason inns get into the same complexities of rates, amenities, and package deals as the big hotels is because our objective is the same: a full house. Whatever rate variations you work with at your inn, be sure the people who take reservations can find the appropriate rates quickly and communicate them accurately to callers. Whether the rate card is taped to the reservations book, the refrigerator, or the telephone desk, it must be handy, readable, and complete.

GIVING INFORMATION

After you've collected all the information *you* need from your callers, consciously take a moment to inquire about their needs. Perhaps they would like further information about their room, the inn, or the town. Offer to send additional tourist information on what to do and see in the area or about special events during their stay. Ask if they'd like directions to the inn, especially if you've become aware through experience that the map or directions on your brochure are inadequate.

Describe the parking situation or any other important procedural matter. Some innkeepers have devised ingenious ways of dealing with late arrivals: staying up to greet them, even at 3:00 A.M.; specially coding lock boxes for keys; leaving notes with maps and keys; installing intercoms to rouse the innkeepers; or maintaining a firm policy that no one is admitted after midnight. Whatever the late-arrival policy, it shouldn't be a surprise to an expectant guest.

THE CALENDAR

You've just gotten a four-day midweek reservation! Don't get so excited that you forget the crucial step: recording the information on your calendar. Whether you use a special form that lists rooms, dates, and so on, or simply a standard daily/weekly/monthly appointment book, post the name and the specific room on the appropriate dates immediately.

At day's end, most inns apply some form of a checks-and-balances system. Check all reservations taken that day against your calendar. If there are discrepancies, correct them as soon as possible.

Reservation book

Michael Diaz, Ken Armstrong, and Steve Ryan of the Glenborough Inn in Santa Barbara, California, have found a reservation book for innkeepers who are on the go. The loose-leaf, Goretex-covered notebook, available at Staples or K-Mart, has pockets for blank reservation cards, pencil and pen, calculator, portable telephone, extra paper, post-its, and, of course, the reservation calendar pages. It's virtually a desk you can carry upstairs when you clean rooms or outside when you garden.

FILING RESERVATION FORMS

Most inns file individual reservation forms chronologically for easy retrieval if there's a question or problem, to record payment received, or to prepare a weekly schedule of arriving guests.

ONCE PAYMENT HAS BEEN RECEIVED

When the money is in hand, first pull the form and verify that the date, the room, and the amount received are correct. Note on the form the amount paid, the date the confirmation is being sent, and the balance due, if any.

Next, note on the master calendar that payment has been received and send a confirmation or receipt. Finally, refile the form and go to the bank!

MODIFICATIONS AND CANCELLATIONS

While some inns use a separate form for recording this information, most inns put it on the reservation form. The essential points to note are:
* Previous arrival and departure dates.
* New arrival and departure dates.
* Name.

✳ Who is making the change, their address, phone number, position, or relationship to the guest.

✳ What monetary differences are created by the change. Who owes what to whom.

✳ Today's date.

✳ The reason for the change.

When a change is made by phone, ask the previous arrival date and name, then retrieve the reservation form from the file, so you have the guest's history in front of you before you proceed. Be sure to erase the booking on your calendar immediately so that the room will show as vacant and can be rebooked. If you use a separate form for modifications and cancellations, clip it to the top of the reservation form, along with any other correspondence; the cancellation form is now the most critical information in that particular batch.

ORGANIZING FOR GUEST ARRIVALS

There should be a regular point when you prepare for the next day, week, or some definite period of time. Inns do this in a variety of ways. One pulls reservation cards weekly and pins them to the kitchen wall, ready for guest arrivals. Another keeps arriving guests' cards in a desk drawer. Still another makes a weekly chart listing dates, rooms with guest names, and, in a different color ink, notes estimated arrival times, money owed, repeat guests, special occasions, and so on. This sheet is taped to the back of the kitchen door, next to the room keys.

Each of these very different systems appears to work well for each specific inn. Each is a way of streamlining the usefulness of the information collected at reservation time, so it can be used at check-in time. At check-in, ask your guests to register in some way; either a big book or registration cards is a good choice. Do not leave your guests waiting more than half a minute while you get their room key. Guests should feel welcome and expected.

ORGANIZING FOR THE FUTURE

The guest has come and gone. Retrieve the reservation forms from the kitchen wall, the desk drawer, or wherever you keep them to streamline your welcoming routine. These cards are filled with information about people you hope to see again. What do you do with them now? Here are several options for retrievable storage.

✳ A simple filing system includes one expandable date file with numbers one through thirty-one on the tabs, plus twelve file folders, one for each month. The expandable file is used for the current month's reservation forms. All other months are filed chronologically in the monthly file folders, kept in a file drawer. Reservations can be filed by arrival date, then within that date section by name.

✳ File cards alphabetically on a Rolodex. They can be flipped through quickly and pulled out. Keep a separate Rolodex for each year.

✳ Computerize. Standard inexpensive software, available for most home systems, allows you to enter a number of different fields for each file record. You can enter not only names and addresses for future mailings but also other demographics, such as reservation date, room selected, special occasion, and advertising source. This will allow you to print lists by categories, such as referral source, effectiveness of specific ad, length of stay, where guests come from, special-occasion business, and business travelers.

In addition, over the years, a number of small companies have developed reservations software specifically for inns. No one package is perfect for every inn, but most developers will work with you on modifications unique to your inn.

Reservations software should enable you to

✳ Take guest information once to make reservations, print confirmations, and create guest histories.

✳ Produce reports and letters.

✳ Check room availability by calendar page and by reservation.

✳ Sort information by date, name, and many other categories.

✳ Create mailing labels.

✳ Modify screens and reports as much as possible.

✳ Track travel agent commissions, referral sources, special needs of guests, deposits.

✳ Accommodate multiple tax structures, multiple rate structures, and seasonal variations.

✳ Print daily, weekly, monthly reservation reports.

✳ Print room occupancy report by day, week, month, year, by room, and/or by income per room.

✳ Print housekeeping and other reports.

✳ Maintain guest information in query file when canceling a reservation.

Helpful features include

✳ on-line help,

✳ pop-up menus,

✳ pop-up calendar.

There are more than twenty companies marketing reservations software to the industry. If you want to computerize, contact the ones that seem as though they produce what you need. Get a demonstration copy and put it through its paces on your own computer. Make notes about what works for you and what doesn't, and talk to the sales people.

When you purchase a package, get a thirty-day money-back guarantee. Also think about buying a maintenance contract.

Is it essential to computerize? Of course not. But consider it if

∗ You have more than ten rooms.

∗ You're serious about marketing and don't want to sit up at night hand-addressing inn promotional pieces.

∗ You like computers.

STAFFING

"What! You want to come in here and mess up my clean inn?" When you answer the doorbell feeling like that, it's time to think about getting help.

Many innkeepers start out doing everything themselves, often thinking they'll continue this way forever. They usually are concerned about the expense, paperwork, and loss of autonomy that hiring staff means. And there's no question that the intimate, homey feeling of an inn changes when hired help takes over the jobs previous performed by the owners. Innkeepers often fear the public reaction to this and, in addition, feel that "no one else does things the way I want them done."

When innkeepers do hire staff, it's often to make time for the things only they can do or things they can do better than anyone else, like some kinds of promotion, planning, and financial projections. Staff can also free owners to do the things they enjoy most, such as gardening, perhaps, or spending extra time with guests. In some cases, staffers provide expertise owners don't have. But most importantly, owners hire staff to give themselves time off and to avoid jobs they dislike.

A good way to decide what staff to hire is to make a list of all the tasks done in the inn. Here's a start:

Cook and serve breakfast
Clean rooms
Clean common areas and kitchen
Take phone reservations
Confirm reservations
Bookkeeping
Promotion
Flower arranging

Now put four columns next to your list, for things you like to do, things you don't like to do, things someone else can do, and things only you can do. Review your list and put check marks in the appropriate columns; ask the other partners to do so as well. This process will make clear to you which tasks you might hire someone for. And it's also a beginning on writing a job description.

The job description should include each task to be done, the number of hours and days of the week required, the pay scale, and the experience and education required. Under the Americans with Disabilities Act (ADA), you must also list the physical requirements and limitations of the job. In conjunction with other hospitality industry associations, PAII has compiled position descriptions that meet ADA requirements. When calculating hours and wages, be careful to consider seasonal variations, so you don't give applicants unrealistic expectations. Type the job description and keep it on file. It should be the first thing you give an applicant to review.

Where do you find applicants? Word of mouth works well for some owners as a method of recruitment, but this varies within each community. Asking present staff for recommendations also helps to screen potential recruits, since your staff are frequently protective of "their inn." One innkeeper uses a networking technique, calling ten people and describing his staff needs; the word spreads from there.

The success of local classified ads depends on the community's available workforce. In many small towns it becomes necessary to recruit outside the area for good employees—or any employees! Try advertising, stating clearly the nature of the position, both positive and negative, and see what happens. Different times of year may yield differing levels of success, depending on the school year or military base transfer patterns. December is generally a difficult month to find new employees.

Local schools sometimes have internship programs that are ideal sources for specialized food service, promotional, or hotel management positions. Posting notices in high school and college employment offices can reap valuable staff.

If your town has a small workforce to draw upon, be creative. Would you like someone with great handwriting to address envelopes or an experienced breakfast cook? Contact a local senior-citizen group. Try local churches, women's groups, service clubs, or nonprofit agencies.

Different kinds of people get along well with different innkeepers. Some inns prefer to hire people who are a bit older, then give them more responsibility; other inns hire young people to do jobs like housekeeping and dishwashing. High school and college students need to schedule their work around school, which often fits in with your busy-season needs, but requires flexibility in scheduling.

If there are few suitable applicants, consider offering benefits that are especially appealing or valuable in your area. These might include the opportunity to bring children to the job, avoiding the expense and uncertainty of childcare. Some inns can develop a small apartment for a staffer or provide meals for students. Inns also offer other pluses for staff, including varied tasks and flexible scheduling, a chance to interact with guests, and often an opportunity to become an integral part of the business. Don't hesitate to mention these.

THE HIRING PROCESS

Your task is to find a good employee as directly and efficiently as possible. You do yourself and your applicants no favors by spending time with people you know instantly you will never hire. How do you work smart here?

A clear ad, posted position-available announcement, or telephone conversation with someone who has been recommended to you allows applicants to screen themselves right at the beginning, saving them and you time. Before you accept an application, confirm that the person understands the position and meets its requirements. Manager, public relations, or chef applicants will probably have résumés, which are unnecessary for housekeepers, wait staff, or dishwashers. Handwritten application forms (available from office supply stores if you don't have your own) will give you, in addition to important information, an idea of the applicant's handwriting for reservation cards or mail.

Once you have gathered all the applications or résumés, review them to select the top applicants using consistent criteria, such as direct experience that relates to the job or a good understanding of local tourist activities. Further screen them by telephone. In an inn, every position is a public contact position; if they don't speak well or clearly to you, how will they represent your inn? Then schedule and perform personal interviews.

For the interview, dress and act like an employer, not a harried innkeeper, to establish a tone of professionalism. If you have several people to see, schedule them consecutively, about thirty minutes apart. Be sure someone else will handle phones while you interview, and find a quiet, private part of the inn away from guests and other staffers.

Indicate clearly to the prospective employees what the position is; don't glamorize it. Ask questions that help you assess each applicant's commitment to the area, future plans, attitude toward work, background, and present situation. Do *not* ask questions about marital status, age, race, or pregnancy. It's illegal to consider these issues when hiring. If you're concerned about age or pregnancy because it might affect a candidate's strength for certain tasks, ask about strength.

Follow a consistent format during the interviews. It will help you compare candidates more effectively. Here are sample interview questions to ask after you've introduced yourself, toured some or all of the inn, and described the job.

* Why do you think you could do this job?
* What are your strengths and weaknesses?
* How would you describe yourself?
* Why do you want this job? What circumstances bring you to apply for it?
* What was your favorite previous job, and why? What other jobs have you had, and why did you leave them?
* What other jobs are you applying for?
* What things do you think would be problems with this job?
* How long a time commitment can you make to this job?
* What are your plans for the future? What do you hope or expect to be doing in five years?

You may want to send your best candidates directly to a second interview, ideally with someone else who'll supervise the new employee. After you've interviewed all candidates, check references on your best prospect(s). Get the names and phone numbers of a previous and a present employer, if possible. Here's a format for a reference check.

* Describe your job opening, and ask about X's suitability for it.
* Ask what kind of work X did for the reference, for how long, and why X left.
* Ask whether the reference would hire X again.
* Ask about X as an employee. Listen carefully for key words and write them down.
* Ask what was the major problem with X. If the problem sounds like it could also be troublesome to you, ask how it was worked out in the previous position.
* Ask about X's strengths and weaknesses and for any other information that the reference believes would be helpful.

Once you've made your choice, take a night to think about the decision, then call and offer the job. Be very specific: Reconfirm the job title, salary or hourly rate, and hours. Suggest a specific time on a specific day to begin work, suggest appropriate attire, and describe what will happen on the first day and how much time it will take.

Ann and Gene Swett of the Old Monterey Inn in Monterey, California, hire a variety of people for their bed-and-breakfast inn. "Younger people are here to learn things and often do not stay more than a couple of years," Ann says. "I don't want anyone to feel obligated to stay here. We had a woman with a master's degree who really needed to move on to other things, and I encouraged her to do just that. On the other hand, our manager has been with us for ten years as well as a housekeeper who we encouraged to speak English; she's been here for six years. We care for staff as well as we care for our guests. We are like a supportive family. For example, a student who worked for us until he graduated now works at a local bank, but when we have an emergency, he pitches in on his time off. His family is in Chicago; we're his other family. We find out what an individual's strengths are and change the job to use them. Still, it is a fine line to be nurturing and to be in charge."

HIRING MANAGERS

Salaries for managers of bed-and-breakfast and country inns range from $1,000 to $3,000 a month, not including room, board, and benefits. Salaries increase with responsibility. So an assistant to an on-site manager-owner is likely to receive less than a fully in-charge manager hired by a rarely present owner.

It's probably not wise to include the value of a room at the inn as compensation for a manager, since with the room comes a high level of stress.

In many cases owners expect managers to be exact replicas of themselves, even expecting them to work long hours without additional pay (which, of course, owners do). If the extra hours worked are not agreed to by contract or paid for in overtime, you could be liable for extra pay for hours worked over forty hours a week should the employee go to the labor board in your area.

It's your job to provide time off, reasonable pay, encouragement, and moral support on the job. Without this you will eventually lose a valuable investment; you may discover other surprises after your employee leaves, such as cash embezzlement, unhappy staff, tasks half done, and disappointed guests. For up-to-date details on your legal requirements regarding staff, contact your local labor board.

TRAINING

Be prepared for your new employee on the first day. Have a training plan and a time card ready. It's obvious to most innkeepers that detail is necessary to task training, but don't overlook the importance of values training. Equipping your staff to understand what the inn is about will contribute immensely to their ability to convey the spirit of the inn and to meet your expectations. Consider spending an hour to cover the areas outlined here.

HISTORY

✳ Why and how you got into innkeeping. This will tell them a lot about your expectations for innkeepers and the inn. And besides, guests will ask staff for the story.

✳ Why you chose the area and the structure you did. Much of your own image of the inn will be revealed in this.

✳ The personal values involved in your decision to open an inn. This can be especially revealing if you left another career or saw innkeeping as a way to earn a living and still spend time with your young children.

OBJECTIVES

✳ Complete this sentence: I will feel successful when _____. You may define success in terms of money, smooth operation, free time, or fame. Your definition makes a big difference in how you run your inn and what your staff people understand to be important.

✳ Set specific goals if you can, such as a regular 10 percent increase in occupancy year to year or getting paperwork and cleaning out of the way by 1:00 P.M. Make charts that convey your objectives visually and help you and your staff evaluate your achievements.

ORGANIZATION

✳ Are you the head honcho in every area and are your staff people the assistants? Or do you see your organization as a team with different people responsible for specific areas like maintenance, food preparation, and paperwork? Assistants behave differently from "division managers." Staff people like and need to know not only their own roles but also the roles of their coworkers and how they fit together into a total structure.

✳ What about the future staff structure you envision? Is there room for advancement? Will a good housekeeper ever get a chance to be a weekend innkeeper or manage the office?

MANAGEMENT PRACTICES

✳ If you encourage staff ideas and suggestions, make it known. Act on them when they come!

✳ Is there a regular period, perhaps six months or a year, after which you review performances and consider giving raises? Is there a standard increase staff people can expect?

✳ Describe the criteria you use for determining whether and how large a raise to give. It will probably be helpful to you and to your staff to have a formal list of standards; it gives them something to work for, as well as a very tangible demonstration of your work values, and helps you maintain consistency and fairness in decisions about pay levels.

Then describe your method for task training. List the skills to be learned and the criteria for success. For example, the goal for a cleaning person might be to change a bed, arrange the flowers, and dust and vacuum a room in thirty minutes. You might use a checklist that shows every task involved in getting a room ready for the next guests. Be sure to plan enough time in your own schedule to explain things, demonstrate, check progress, give feedback, and correct errors. Let your new staff people know what standards must be met before they are on their own in the job.

As you go through this training process, developing a notebook will make subsequent training much easier. It also provides a reminder and refresher to staff and reduces the need for repeating details. A loose-leaf notebook indexed for various subjects is perfect; include breakfast, room cleaning, reservations policy, and cancellation procedures.

KEEPING GOOD STAFF

The best way to keep good staff is to pay them such a good salary that no other job is tempting. Think you can't afford it? Don't forget how expensive it is in time, energy, and wages to find and train new staff over and over again.

Split tips fairly. Housekeepers, wait staff, and innkeepers are all likely to receive tips. Be sure everyone understands how they are to be handled. For example, if guests tip housekeepers at checkout, the tip should be split among all housekeepers who worked during the guests' stay.

Making your staff people feel part of the inn team is important in keeping them. Inns usually can't offer large salaries, so you need to make other job benefits clear. Be a caring, fair employer, respecting the ideas and feelings of your staff. Reward good performance, and be sure everyone knows what you consider that to be. Everybody likes to be appreciated, and encouraging and rewarding good work pays off in the spirit as well as the economics of your inn. Here are some ideas.

CONTESTS   Start a competition among staff members who handle the telephones and reservations. Give the one who gets the most midweek bookings during a specific period a night's stay at another inn. You can probably arrange a trade, so the room won't cost you anything. A bonus for you—in addition to increased midweek bookings—may be that your staff will see the inn in a new light as they look for the words to bring in the business.

AWARDS   Corporations reward employees who come up with cost-saving and money-making ideas. Why not do this at your inn? At Ten Inverness Way a staff member came up with an idea for saving $300 a year in the cost of dairy products by dealing directly with the local delivery company. Shopping time was reduced as well. Mary and her partner were so impressed with the idea that they instituted a standing incentive award: Any idea that produces continuing, quantifiable savings or earnings is rewarded with a check in the amount of 50 percent of the first year's cash benefits.

GRATITUDE   It is surprising how important it is to thank staff. And it's equally surprising how often we forget to do it. Look for and mention things your staff members do especially well. It could be the smooth handling of a difficult phone call. It could be a creative touch with making bouquets out of next to nothing from your frostbitten garden. It could be handling a complex agenda item particularly well. You will almost certainly be amazed at how many people you will please by noticing their good work.

PROMOTION AND RAISES

Base employee rewards on the value of staff people to your business. Take care that the more responsible jobs command the higher pay and that pay scales also reward length of employment at the inn. Don't raise pay prematurely or capriciously. Pay increases should be based on regular individual evaluations of established criteria. If you're not entirely satisfied with a job, say, "I'd like to raise your pay to X dollars, but I need to feel confident you'll _____. When I see that this is happening regularly for a month, I'll give you the raise."

When you promote someone, they're often taking on a whole new job. Just because they've been on staff in another capacity doesn't mean they don't need thorough training in the new slot.

Don't promote and give raises just before your slow season unless you're sure you can afford it.

BENEFITS

Paying a competitive salary is the best way to keep good staff, but a benefits package certainly sweetens the pot. If you see yourself and your staff in this for the long haul, health insurance, bonus plans, and retirement savings plans should be in your budget and staffing plan.

Health insurance may be more reasonably priced through local or state associations, either chambers of commerce or lodging groups. To find the best rate for a plan in your area that meets your insurance needs, call Quotesmith Corporation at (800) 556-9393. Their service is free.

Bonus plans vary in design, depending on the nature of the business. Sometimes innkeepers give a bonus to staff who complete the full season. Others base it on profit in relation to the individual's wages. Still others merely provide a holiday bonus. As the boss, you will want to find a system that both reflects your cash flow needs and motivates staff.

Retirement plans do not necessarily require a financial output from you. In the United States you can arrange with an investment counselor to set up a plan (SAR/SEP) where your employees choose to deduct from their paychecks, prior to taxes (except social security), a set monthly amount to be deposited in a retirement fund. The employees can save for retirement on their own, often with very little decrease in their take-home pay, because of the reduction of taxable income and thus of taxes, and you end up being the good guy for setting it up.

A Staff Bonus Program that Works

Susan Zolla, owner of the fourteen-room Channel Road Inn in Santa Monica, California, has a staff bonus program that has reduced waste, improved morale, and reduced turnover.

"I instituted this program because I wanted the employees to take home a decent salary, especially during our good months," says Susan. Although she has a six-month employee performance review and usually gives a raise at that time, Susan was concerned that if raises were high, she would be locked into higher wages during bad months. "With a bonus, everyone shares in our extra income during busy months, when they work extra hard."

In addition, the bonus involves sharing the responsibility of expenses, including utility bills and food waste. This particular system has given Susan's eight staff members an idea of the costs of running an inn and the power to control those costs. The repeated repairs on an overloaded washer have stopped. Staff now do not hesitate to pull hair from drains, because they know plumbing costs. Personal telephone calls are reduced. Keeping the clothes dryer filter cleaned and taking care of the computer and copy machine have become everyone's responsibility.

How It Works

The bonus is derived from a combination of net revenue (income after expenses, also called profit) and the savings from original budgeted costs. The bonus pool is 3.5 percent of the monthly profit and 10 percent of the difference between budgeted costs and actual expenses. Ideal expenditures are 70 percent of income. Bonuses are distributed monthly among employees on the basis of hours worked during the month.

Additional details increase fairness. As much as 5 percent can be added to reward individual performance. Vacation hours are not included in monthly hours, encouraging staff to take vacations during slow seasons rather than when they could get the largest bonus. First- and last-month employees are not given bonuses. Annual expenses (taxes, insurance) are spread out over the entire year rather than deducted in the month paid.

THE BOOKWORK

When you hire employees, you become responsible for maintaining records for unemployment insurance, disability insurance, workers' compensation insurance, state and federal income taxes, and social security. Your state employment service office should be able to give you current information about your legal responsibilities as an employer.

Sometimes innkeepers think they can just pay housekeepers "under the table" or as independent contractors, avoiding all the paperwork and taxes. However, the penalties for this are twofold. First, if they catch you, the government holds you responsible for all the back taxes and penalties and flags your income tax records, making an audit likely. Second, if the employee is injured, you are liable for all medical bills and may be sued. Furthermore, a disgruntled employee may report you to the labor board,

IRS, or other government entity. In an inn, it is unlikely that you will use independent contractors except for outside or temporary help, such as gardeners or plumbers. And even then, you need proof that they have covered themselves for workers' compensation. The IRS can provide a very clear twenty-step pamphlet that will help you to clarify whether you are stepping over a dangerous line.

For your own purposes, you'll probably want to keep a personnel file for employees, including their applications, up-to-date addresses, reference information, and work history. You'll also want to create a payroll file; records should be kept current and retained for several years. Stationery stores can provide time cards and payroll systems that help you create records for yourself and your staff people. Here's what to include.

* time cards
* W-4 and W-2 tax forms
* I-9 Immigration and Naturalization Service forms
* payroll cards
* quarterly tax records
* time sheets
* communication with employees:
    performance reviews
    letters of reprimand or commendation
    contracts
    the employee's initial application materials and job description

Also nice to have in each person's file are the following:
* emergency contact person
* family member names
* birthdays, anniversary
* samples of good work

These are the forms and the information to gather prior to hiring staff.

* * Federal identification number from the Internal Revenue Service. They will issue a number and will then begin forwarding forms, to be completed quarterly. The employers' guide will be sent for figuring federal income tax to be withheld and forwarded to the IRS as well as the percentage rate for FICA (social security) for you and the employee to pay.*

* * State income tax withholding (if your state has it) from your closest state employment office. They will issue a number and will then begin forwarding forms, to be completed quarterly. Some states also require a disability tax.*

* * W-4 forms from IRS or office supply stores.*

* * W-2 forms from IRS or office supply stores.*

* *I-9 Immigration and Naturalization Service forms.*
* *Workers' compensation insurance from private insurance carriers or through state association plans.*
* *Health insurance from private insurance carriers.*
* *Consider a dishonesty bond from private insurance carriers, which covers all employees up to a certain amount, protecting you from potential losses due to employee embezzlement.*

FIRING EMPLOYEES

Firing employees doesn't have to be that awful if you've clearly communicated your expectations and standards all along. For example, staffers need to understand the job description and duties and your expectations about hours, dress, and pace. If attitude is an issue, describe it in concrete terms. For example, courtesy to guests and staff is concretely exhibited in saying "please" and "thank you."

Put in writing any warning or ultimatum that could result in dismissal. When you fire someone, explain your reasons for it. In many states, dismissal for incompetence does not preclude former employees from collecting unemployment compensation; as an employer, you're responsible for screening out the incompetents before you hire them.

Laying off employees for lack of work is a different matter completely. Be sure to discuss the situation and the possibility of rehiring when conditions change. Sometimes you can negotiate a reduced-hours arrangement with an employee you want to keep but can't presently afford.

INDEPENDENT CONTRACTORS

Independent contractors can sometimes perform necessary services, but they will not be employees. They have their own businesses, provide their own tools, and establish their own work parameters. For example, it's not up to you to set a contractor's hours; they are arrived at by mutual agreement. Independent contractors pay their own social security, taxes, and unemployment and disability insurance. If your contractors have not covered their employees for workers' compensation, you're responsible if they're hurt.

At year end, you need to fill out an IRS form 1099 for each contractor to whom you have paid $600 or more. Copies must be sent to the IRS, the state income tax agency, and the contractor. The rules defining independent contractors are specific; when in doubt, check with your accountant on whether your planned arrangement applies. Always sign a contract, such as the one in Appendix 5, page 303.

In some work areas, innkeepers can choose whether to hire an employee or work with a contractor. Gardening services are a perfect example. If you're not already an employer, it would probably be wisest to work with an independent gardening service rather than to set up the necessary structure and paperwork systems to hire a gardener as an inn employee.

The Americans with Disabilities Act and Employees

If you have fifteen or more employees, you must reasonably accommodate the disabilities of qualified applicants and employees, including modifying applications, the interviewing process, and workstations and equipment, unless undue hardship would result.

Review Job Descriptions

Job descriptions should not be worded in such a way that they would discourage applicants with disabilities. People with disabilities are deemed to be qualified for a position if they are able to perform its "essential functions." Essential functions are those the individual must perform unaided or with the assistance of reasonable accommodation. The definition does not include marginal functions of a position. For example, bookkeepers cannot perform the job without mathematical skills. However, it is not necessary, even if it would be more helpful, for them to be able to lift boxes or even walk. When designing descriptions, break a job down into its four basic elements:

* Purpose (the reason for the job),
* Major tasks (those *essential* to accomplish the purpose),
* Job setting (the workstation and conditions),
* Worker qualifications (minimum requirements a worker must meet to perform the major tasks).

Restructure Jobs

To assure that you can accommodate individuals with disabilities, consider restructuring the job in several ways. Restructuring schedules may mean dividing a job into two positions to accommodate someone who can work a half but not a whole day. Some disabilities occasionally necessitate brief periods of hospitalization (kidney diseases, hemophilia) or weekly therapy sessions (substance abuse recovery, cancer, mental disorders). Appropriate time off must be granted.

Flex time may solve disability-related punctuality problems when morning personal preparations may not always last a predictable amount of time. Implementing "core hours" allowing an employee to work an eight-hour shift sometime between 6:00 A.M. and 6:00 P.M. may be desirable.

Reassigning incidental duties should also be considered. You have an assistant chef with a bad back. She receives and inventories provisions. Lifting fifty-pound boxes is not a necessary part of the job. With someone else to help, she can perform the essential inventory-taking part of her job.

JOB INTERVIEWS

You can ask questions that determine the applicant's ability to perform the functions of the job, but you *cannot* ask an interviewee to list the answers to or verbally respond to the following questions:

✳ Are there any conditions or diseases for which you have been treated?

✳ Have you ever been hospitalized?

✳ Have you ever been treated for any mental condition?

✳ Do you have a history of alcohol or drug abuse?

✳ Do you have any disabilities or impairments that may affect your performance in this position?

✳ Have you ever filed for workers' compensation insurance?

✳ What's the prognosis or expectation regarding your condition or disability?

✳ Will you need treatment or special leave because of the disability?

An alternative to a question like, "How many days were you absent from work last year?" might be to communicate to the prospective employee that employment at your inn requires a specific number of days of attendance per year. Then ask whether or not the applicant can meet this particular requirement. Avoid direct inquiries such as, "What disabilities do you have that would keep you from performing this job?" This does not mean you cannot ask an applicant whether or not he or she has the ability to perform a specific job, however.

You may seek information regarding a person's ability to perform the essential functions of a job with questions like these.

✳ Based on this job description, are you able to perform these tasks with or without accommodation?

✳ How would you perform the tasks and with what accommodation?

✳ Based on what you have been told regarding our work hours and leave policies, are you able to meet these requirements?

Avoid unrelated subjects. An applicant could complain that the real reason he or she was denied a position is that the employer knew the applicant had a child with Down's Syndrome and assumed the applicant would continually be called away from work to care for the child. To preclude such charges, stay away from discussing friends and family during the application process.

Finally,

* Don't make medical judgments. Don't reject an applicant with a readily apparent disability. The applicant should be permitted to demonstrate or explain how he or she would perform the essential functions of the job.

* Be accessible. Individuals with disabilities need access to the employment process. Use your TDD telephone number in classified ads. Make it possible for employees to work at your inn. You are required to make alterations to your work spaces when employees' disabilities demand it.

* Ask about cash incentives. A company that works with a local vocational-rehabilitation agency can receive partial reimbursement for the wages of disabled employees. For more information, contact your local agency. Under the Job Training Partnership Act an employer can set up on-the-job training and be reimbursed for half of the first six months' wages of an eligible disabled person. Contact your chamber of commerce.

THE IRS AND YOU

The Internal Revenue Service has been taking a serious look at bed-and-breakfast operations, even creating a special publication for agents on how to examine them. One thing is clear: The more you treat your inn like a business, the more the IRS will. If you run a ten- or twenty-room inn with completely self-contained owner quarters, a full-time staff, and year-round demand, the IRS is less likely to question your business status. If, however, you prepare your own dinner in the same kitchen where guest breakfasts are cooked, do all the work yourself, and store your Aunt Agatha's furs in the back closet of the Rose Room, you're in the gray area of the home-based business.

In 1988 the IRS tightened home-based business rules to prevent, for example, attorneys who write briefs at home a couple of times a week from writing off their home office/guest bedroom. According to IRS Publication #587, *Business Use of Your Home*, you must meet specific tests in order to take a deduction for the business use of your home. The IRS rule is, "Generally you cannot deduct expenses for business use of your home. But, you can take a limited deduction for its business use if you meet the following tests: exclusive use, regular use, principal place of business, place to meet customers." How do these criteria apply to inns?

* "Exclusive use" means use only for business. If a particular part of your home is used for personal purposes, it does not meet the exclusive use test. So even though you had to completely renovate your kitchen to meet health department requirements, you cannot deduct or depreciate that expense, unless you can show that the kitchen is for guest meal preparation only.

Solution: Use a separate kitchen and dining area for yourself or develop a kitchen area in your quarters. You can get an apartment-type sink-stove-refrigerator combination cupboard that will fit in a small space. Exclusive use also means that friends and family cannot sleep in guest rooms for free or the deduction is lost. (Those of you who plan to sleep from vacant guest room to vacant guest room, take note!) So create a place where family and friends can stay—a futon on the floor perhaps. Or establish a payment policy for these visitors.

✳ "Regular use" does not mean welcoming occasional paying guests or guests only during season or weekend business only, even if that part of your home is used for no other purpose. It is not deductible.

Solution: Keep good occupancy records to show you are regularly doing business. If in fact you do not regularly receive guests because your business is still new, show your intentions by saving promotional and advertising materials. In your start-up years, you might keep track of tours given prospective guests by saving names, addresses, and dates in the guest book. If your occupancy is low, you may need to prove you are a business and not a hobby.

✳ "Principal place of business" is easy to justify for most inns, because you do business nowhere else. Factors to consider are the total time you regularly spend doing work there, facilities you need to complete the work, and relative amount of income you get from doing business at home.

✳ "Place to meet customers" deals primarily with doctors who have offices elsewhere. If you have customers on a regular basis in your home, you can deduct expenses for that area used exclusively for such use.

Hobby or Business? How the IRS Decides

IRS regulations list nine factors relevant to innkeepers among those considered when determining whether a taxpayer entered into or continued an activity with the objective of making a profit.

✳ *The manner in which the taxpayer carries on the activity. The fact that the taxpayer operates in a businesslike manner and maintains complete and accurate records may indicate that the activity is engaged in for profit.*

✳ *The expertise of the taxpayer or his advisors.*

✳ *The time and effort expended by the taxpayer in carrying on the activity.*

✳ *Whether there is expectation that the assets used in the activity may appreciate in value.*

✳ *The success of the taxpayer in carrying on similar or dissimilar activities.*

✳ *The taxpayer's history of income or losses with respect to the activity.*

✳ *The amount of occasional profits, if any, that are earned from the activity.*

✳ *The financial status of the taxpayer. The fact that the taxpayer does not have substantial income or capital from sources other than the activity may indicate that an activity is engaged in for profit.*

✳ Elements of personal pleasure or recreation. The presence of personal motives in the carrying on of an activity may indicate that the activity is not engaged in for profit, especially where there are recreational or personal elements involved. However, the fact that the taxpayer derives personal pleasure from engaging in the activity is not sufficient to cause the activity to be classified as not engaged in for profit, if the activity is engaged in for profit as evidenced by other factors.

LOOKING LIKE A BUSINESS TO THE IRS

In case you're focused more on the pancakes than on the profit and loss statements, here are some reminders about businesslike operations.

✳ Keep your personal checkbook separate from your inn checkbook. This seems logical to some folks, but seems like extra work to others. Just do it.

✳ Keep separate records and receipts of all expenditures for the inn and for your personal life. For items such as food and utilities, this is crucial.

✳ Keep clean income records. Faithfully record receipts and deposits of cash, checks, and credit cards. The IRS has several key ratios they use to flag the possibility that cash is being skimmed. If the IRS doesn't catch it, your staff will, and they might first help themselves to the cash and then, if disgruntled, report you to the IRS.

✳ Allocate appropriately in your tax records the fringe benefits like food, health insurance, and living quarters that you receive as an innkeeper.

✳ Keep tidy petty cash accounts. Establish a standard balance, $50 or $100, diligently keeping receipts as money is spent. When it's almost gone, write a check in the exact amount of the receipts, allocating those figures directly to the proper accounts, such as food and postage. When the check is cashed, the petty cash account returns to the initial balance. This system also keeps you in control of cash handling by staff: no receipts, no reimbursement.

✳ Use professional business materials. Letterhead stationery, brochures, business cards, registration cards, and guest registries all indicate that you are doing innkeeping for real.

✳ Pay local, state, and payroll taxes. Susan Hill, CPA, says state and federal agencies work together. If a state examiner picks up discrepancies during a review, the information will likely be sent to other governmental bodies. Also, if a state employment office review results in a reclassification of contract labor to employee status, it's an automatic ticket for IRS attention.

✳ Have at least two telephone numbers. One is automatically considered your personal phone: no deduction. List the inn phone in the phone book. Tax preparer Jim Carney observes that if you receive business only through a reservation service and do not advertise publicly through the phone book, you are likely to lose any claim that you are running a business.

✳ Show your professional status by joining associations and attending seminars, thus demonstrating that you are developing skills and knowledge in your field. Add "conferences and seminars" to your chart of accounts.

✳ Keep an automobile log. Innkeepers typically use their cars for more than business. You can keep a record of business trips on your calendar and use it as the formal tally or keep track of mileage in a log kept in the car. The exact format of this log is open, but how much you use the vehicle must be very clear.

MINIMIZE YOUR CHANCES OF BEING AUDITED

The IRS has developed mathematical formulas that prompt their computers to spew out returns for possible audits. For example:

✳ Huge losses "walk and talk" like tax shelters and are often flagged. These may be unusually high losses from a natural disaster or from extensive renovation. The IRS is especially watching those B&B owners that renovate in a nice retirement area, deduct their expenses for a couple of years, and then retire—from the B&B business.

✳ High repair and maintenance costs, says CPA Susan Hill, are often shown on a tax return when actually the taxpayer should have capitalized them over a number of years.

✳ Skimming cash is detectable. According to Hill, if credit card charges in proportion to income and linen expenses in proportion to number of rooms sold are above a certain percentage, the IRS will look for unaccounted-for cash.

✳ Sole proprietorships making over $100,000 are ten times more likely to be audited than corporations earning the same amount, says Hill. If this is your situation, consider incorporating.

✳ Another red flag: basis too low for declared expenses. You must have invested more money in the corporation (basis) than you claim as losses. Hill recommends handling this by taking out a personal loan and investing it in, or lending it to, the corporation rather than having the corporation borrow the money from the bank.

✳ The longer you record losses, the greater the risk of audit. If you lose money more than three out of five years, you can only deduct the loss to the level of your gross income.

So what if the worst happens and you're audited? Get Frederick W. Daily's book *Stand Up to the IRS* (Nolo Press) and relax. You've done everything right.

Case Study: Rosewood Inn

Winnie and Dick Peer of the six-room Rosewood Inn in Corning, New York, had, since opening in 1980, taken lodging as serious business. Dick speaks with awe of Winnie's bookkeeping prowess. In 1989 the Rosewood, among numerous other inns in the Finger Lakes area, became a target for an IRS focus on the "business use of your home."

Tax advisor and former innkeeper Jim Carney, who represented not only the Rosewood Inn but also several other Finger Lakes inns, is convinced that Winnie's organization and consistently businesslike practices won their appeal. (Carney stepped in when the couple's original tax preparer panicked at the thought of an audit.)

When the IRS questioned exclusive use of the dining room and parlor, Carney showed that for 80 percent of the days of the year, a paying guest was staying in the house, thus making this area not available for personal use. He won this point.

When the IRS questioned their business to personal utility ratio, Carney used Winnie's guest records, showing not only rooms rented but also the number of people using each room, to justify an 88 percent deduction of utilities.

Although the IRS did not allow the kitchen to be deducted, the 80 percent deduction claimed for expenses and depreciation of the building held on appeal—even though it was originally disallowed by the auditor.

When asked about their contribution to the local museum, Winnie explained that the museum is a source of business. She also demonstrated how her church donations were recorded as a personal expense. The appeal officer said Winnie should put the museum contribution under "promotion" and let it stand.

When questioned about flowering plants purchased for the front garden, tax preparer Carney asked if the officer had ever seen Carney's former inn (located on a major highway). When the officer replied affirmatively, Carney pointed out that flowers had drawn attention to the property and that this kind of positive notice brings business to the Rosewood. The flower expense was completely allowed.

Many more items were questioned, but all were allowed, even the World Book volumes. Carney explained that Dick's background as a journalist and Winnie's as a teacher brought people looking for the kind of conversations that often ended in a need for reference material!

INSURANCE

An elderly guest has a heart attack and tumbles down three flights of polished stairs in your vintage Victorian. Are you liable?

It's an hour past checkout time, and your cleaning staff gets no response
from repeated knocks at the door of a guest room. They open it
and find the bed occupied. Is this invasion of privacy?

A staffer, straightening the kitchen, slashes his hand on your bread
knife. Do they apply for workers' compensation?

Mrs. Arnold in the Camellia Room chokes on your magnificent eggs
Benedict, permanently injuring her voice. Was this a case of products hazard?

A guest leaves your dining room and on the way down the front steps
slips and falls on an ice patch. Are you liable?

According to an attorney who works with innkeepers, "The question
isn't *whether* you'll be sued, it's *when.*" People with small businesses are
among the most vulnerable. No longer a Jane or John Q. Citizen, innkeepers are viewed by juries as business owners with marketable assets. On the
other hand, inns aren't big enough to have the protection of a corporate
legal department or rich enough to keep an outside attorney on retainer. If
you need to hire an attorney to defend you in a lawsuit—even just to have a
"nuisance" lawsuit dismissed—you can plan on spending at least $10,000.

Dreary, isn't it? Fortunately, hospitality insurance has been designed to
package appropriate protection for the contingencies faced by inns and
innkeepers. Shop carefully. The inn packages are likely to get you the right
coverage at a lower price than if you buy it in pieces. Whether packaged or
not, policy prices vary widely. Ask for detailed comparisons of proposals and
ask about special payment plans.

Whoever insures you, you will need to prepare a complete inventory of
your possessions, not only to determine how much insurance you need but
also to substantiate subsequent claims. It's wise to supplement a written
inventory with color photographs or videotape records, separately held in a
safe-deposit box.

If you lease your inn property, the building should be insured by its
owner. Be sure that it is. And whether the building belongs to you or to
someone else, be sure your insurance protection begins right away. You'll
need to be covered during remodeling, but you probably won't need all the
coverages of an operating inn.

QUESTIONS INNKEEPERS ASK ABOUT INSURANCE

"I know what it says, but what does it mean?"
Let's start with a few terms and definitions, which may clarify the insurance language used in policies.

✳ *Property and Casualty.* The standard insurance policy is divided into two sections: property and casualty (also called liability). When the policy is divided into two or more sections, it is referred to as a package. Property refers to the building(s), the equipment used to maintain them, and all the items contained within. Casualty refers to liability—any accidental injury or damage to someone other than an employee or relative who lives with you.

Property coverage types. *Special causes of loss* is the most comprehensive coverage form available, protecting your property against every peril unless the peril is specifically excluded. *Broad form* covers about eighteen perils, and *named peril*, the most limited, covers approximately six perils. In the last two coverage types, perils covered must be specifically named in the policy.

Casualty (liability) coverage. Commercial general liability is comprehensive, including overall limits and per-occurrence limits for products and completed operations, personal and advertising injury, and medical payments.

✳ *Actual cash value or replacement cost value.* Property value is determined on the basis of one of these two concepts. Actual cash value takes depreciation into consideration; replacement cost coverage replaces something without depreciating its value. Take a roof, for example. Let's say it cost you $8,000 to have it installed nine years ago, but it would cost $14,000 today. Supposing it were smashed by a tree. With replacement cost coverage, you would be paid $14,000. With actual cash value coverage, however, you would receive $14,000, less the cost of nine years of depreciation.

Replacement cost coverage is not more expensive than actual cash value, but you insure for a higher limit, which increases the premium. Under most circumstances, you will want to repair damages or replace objects, so replacement cost is the way to go. If you are not interested in rebuilding your inn on its present site in case of a loss, actual cash value may be most cost-effective coverage.

✳ *Coinsurance clause or agreed amount/stipulated amount.* An insurance policy is a legal contract between two parties. Each has a role and, legally, they are considered coinsurers. The insurance company agrees to pay for covered losses, less a deductible. The insured agrees, in turn, to pay the premium, disclose necessary information to the insurance company, and insure to the full value of the property.

The coinsurance clause requires you to carry a specified amount of insurance based on the cost to rebuild the insured property; if you fail to comply with the clause, you will suffer a penalty in the event of a partial loss. Let's say your building has a value of $100,000 and an 80 percent coinsurance clause (80 percent being the most common). If you insure the building for less than $80,000, the amount you will receive in case of a loss will be the ratio of the amount of insurance carried to the amount required. For example:

$$\frac{\text{amount carried} \quad (\$50,000)}{\text{amount required} \quad (\$80,000)}$$

So, if the insurance company finds that the building is insured for $50,000, they will only pay you five-eighths of the value of the claim, regardless of its total size. In no case will you receive more than the value of the insurance you bought, in this case, $50,000.

✳ *Ordinance replacement coverage.* This is insurance for what it would cost to reconstruct your building according to current ordinances. Inn-business insurance experts say it's one of the most important and most overlooked coverages. If you have to rebuild after a loss, code changes may require you to install sprinklers, fire walls, upgraded electrical service, and so on. Ask your contractor to give you a figure on what it would cost to replace your structure today; that is the amount of insurance you need to buy. For example, let's say that 60 percent of your building is damaged in a fire. Your town or county may require demolition of the undamaged part of your building and require replacement with fire-resistant construction, sprinklers, fire walls, and Americans with Disabilities Act compliance—all of which would substantially increase the cost of preparing your building for reuse.

The extra cost to you is not covered by your policy unless specifically added by an endorsement. If you have a *replacement cost* endorsement, the company will pay you for replacing with like kind and quality, but not for the legally required improvements.

✳ *Products coverage.* Products liability is designed to protect you from claims occurring as a result of injuries to your guests other than those caused by property. For example, products coverage would protect you from a suit by a guest who became ill upon finding half a worm in your baked apple.

✳ *Guest coverage. Guest injury* (liability) coverage is for medical payments. Most general liability policies have $5,000 medical payments coverage automatically built in to pay for doctor and hospital fees, regardless of your negligence. This is "goodwill" coverage, designed to relieve your guests of immediate payment responsibility for minor accidents on your property. *Guest property* coverage may need to be added by specific endorsement; check with your insurer.

✳ *Personal liability.* This term is a perfect example of the insurance industry's unique interpretation of the language. Personal liability does not cover injuries like broken feet, but does cover hurt feelings. The perils covered include libel, slander, invasion of privacy, and unlawful entry, for example. This is extremely important coverage for anyone dealing with the general public, especially in a business where it's possible to walk in accidentally on someone taking a bath.

* *Spoilage coverage.* Restaurateurs, take note.
* *Umbrella/excess coverage.* This type of policy increases your total liability coverage. It is written as a separate policy that comes into force when your liability policy has been exhausted.

"How much liability coverage do I need?"

Whatever allows you to sleep well at night. Even small properties worth less than a million dollars can be sued for tens of millions. If you are held liable in such a suit, underinsurance could result in the loss of your business, and even your personal assets. Worse still, most banks won't lend you the money you may need for legal costs if you're being sued for more than the amount of your insurance coverage.

Your liability limit should equal at least the value of your property. As a general rule, a liability policy should never be written for anything less than $1 million, and it is frequently recommended that an additional $5-million umbrella policy accompany it. Higher limits protect you in court. As long as the award sought in the suit is within your liability limit, the insurance company will have to pay all attorney and court costs even if, in total, award and costs exceed your limits.

Talk with your agent about your possible risks and the cost of liability insurance to protect against them. You need to reach a compromise between affordability and peace of mind.

Also, because you can be held liable for the acts of outside contractors who perform work on your property, be sure your policy covers you for this and that the contractors you hire have adequate coverage themselves.

"As an innkeeper, should I have commercial coverage or homeowner's?"

If you have a standard homeowner's policy, which does not have a specific bed-and-breakfast or country-inn endorsement, you could have serious problems in the event of a loss. A homeowner's policy will not cover bodily injury to guests or damage to their property. This means you are responsible for any medical bills, physical therapy, disability, and the like incurred by a guest because of an injury sustained on your property. In addition, you cannot insure for loss of income. You will not have any guest liability coverage and will be personally responsible for providing your own lawyer and paying for your own defense costs in the event of a lawsuit. Be aware that when selling rooms and food, your home becomes commercial property. If an insurance person promises that your homeowner's policy will suffice, request that assurance in writing from the carrier, not the insurance agent.

"What about punitive damages? Am I covered?"

Many states do not permit insurers to cover the costs of punitive damages, the award given the plaintiff to punish the defendant for gross negligence. Punitive damages can be awarded if the court decides there has been gross negligence in something like knowing your wiring is substandard or defective and nevertheless inviting the public onto your premises. You may not be able to insure for this peril, but you need to be aware of it.

"Is my garage covered?"

Under most business policies, appurtenant structures—garages and such—are covered. However, fences, signs, and windows, are usually not covered unless they are specifically listed. Ask your agent to do so.

"How do I figure out how much contents coverage I need?"

Most people underestimate the value of their furniture and other household contents. The best way to determine the value is to list your property room by room.

Here's an experiment that may help you judge whether your contents coverage is adequate. Sit at the kitchen table and make a list of the contents in some other room of the inn. Then put a value on each item; replacement value is best for this. Now go into the room you inventoried mentally and check your list. Most people find their original estimate low—as low as 50 percent.

If the contents of your inn are insured for only half their value, you've got a major problem on your hands in case of a loss. Have you priced sheets, mattresses, dishes, and glasses, lately?

An itemized list of all your contents will not only establish the proper level of coverage, it will also make the claim process a lot easier for you and your insurer. Trying to remember everything in a room and establish values for it is difficult enough on a tranquil afternoon. Imagine what it's like after a major fire.

"So if my contents limit matches my inventory, I'm okay, right?"

Wrong. Furs, jewelry, coin collections, silver, china, crystal, paintings, and things like camera equipment, musical instruments, or other tools that you use professionally are subject to specified limits in normal policies. Ask your agent to schedule such items if you wish to cover them.

"Am I financially responsible for guests' jewelry?"

Individual states have passed laws limiting your liability to a set dollar amount for property left in the guests' rooms. These laws are for your protection. If guests give you property for safekeeping, and you accept it for safekeeping, inventory it and take special care of it until they want it back.

Innkeepers legal liability insurance covers this exposure only while the property is in your care, custody, and control.

"Is there insurance that would protect our guests from neighborhood crime and catastrophe?"

No. Even if you have innkeepers legal liability coverage, damage or loss to your guests' property will be covered only when you are legally responsible for the damage or loss. The key phrase here is "legally responsible," which means that the law would find you responsible. Where neighborhood kids do damage, where contents are stolen from a guest car parked in your lot or in front of the inn, or where a guest is mugged two doors down the street, the law would most likely not hold you responsible, and therefore the insurance company won't pay for such losses.

There are nevertheless plenty of situations where innkeeper's legal liability coverage is very beneficial. If, for example, your child broke a car antenna, the damage would be covered. If faulty wiring caused a fire in one of your rooms, any loss of guest property would be covered.

The bright side of this question, from the guest perspective, is that most guests would find that such situations are covered under their own homeowner or automobile policies.

"If we serve wine at our inn, do we need special liability coverage?"

If your guest consumes alcoholic beverages at your inn, leaves, and is involved in an auto accident causing serious injury to a third party, can the injured party sue you? Of course. Will your insurance provide your defense and pay a judgment? Not likely, unless you have purchased liquor legal liability coverage. "Liquor legal" provides liability coverage to you for the negligent acts of others arising from their consumption of alcohol provided by you.

If you charge a fee for alcohol, you must have a separate liquor liability policy. However, the issue is clouded when you provide complimentary alcoholic beverages. Are you in the business of "serving or furnishing"? Some insurance companies says yes, some say no. Find out the position your company takes and get it in writing from the carrier (not the agent). All innkeepers need to be completely sure there is no gap or question in coverage. The innkeeper who has wine or other beverages available for guests at a charge or not, with a license or not, is likely to be considered "furnishing and serving" alcoholic beverages to guests.

"Do I really need to have workers' compensation insurance?"

Better to be safe than sorry. Even in those states where workers' compensation insurance is not required, it is not worth the potential financial risk of exposure.

Workers' compensation provides coverage for an employee injured on the job. The policy provides medical expense coverage, disability payments, life insurance, and unlimited rehabilitation. It entitles individuals to receive benefits for all job-related injuries, regardless of who is at fault (the employee or the employer). In many states you have to reach a certain threshold number of employees before the law applies to you; regardless of state requirements for insurance, if an employee is injured, you are responsible. You, as owner, have the option of excluding yourself from coverage.

Workers' compensation protects the employer as well as the employee. It is an "exclusive remedy," which means if employees are injured on the job, their only means of compensation is the workers' comp policy. In other words, employees cannot sue you for further damages. (In rare cases where there is extreme negligence on the part of the employer, the "exclusive remedy" clause is waived and the employer can be sued.) If a business is without workers' compensation insurance, employees are entitled to three times the amount they would have been awarded under a workers' comp policy, and they may sue the employer for damages.

Benefits are calculated on preinjury, preillness, or predeath wages. The amount of benefits or fixed weekly dollar amount that an individual might receive from a claim also varies according to a number of factors, including the degree of impairment resulting from the injury.

Premium rates vary from state to state. Some states allow the insurance companies to establish their own rates; in these states the rates are usually lower because of competition. Other states require the insurance companies to use an established rate set by a ratings bureau that fixes rates at a cost per hundred dollars of gross payroll. In most of these states, many insurance companies will not offer workers' compensation insurance, so the employer must purchase a policy from a state agency or an assigned risk pool. If insurance companies do offer workers' comp policies in these states with an established rate, the only competition among insurance companies is in the area of service. A ratings bureau will also assign a percentage figure to your total premium based on your history of injuries and losses. This *experience-modification* rating, determined by a complicated mathematical formula, is intended to penalize businesses with high-loss records and to reward employers with good safety records.

The *correct classification* for inns is a complicated issue. Many states lump bed-and-breakfast and country inns into a "hotel" category that covers a variety of tasks. However, if you have employees who do nothing except clerical work, they can be classified "clerical." This may substantially reduce your premium. Do not cheat; your clerical person may not carry bags or help with breakfast, even occasionally. The state does audit workers' compensation.

"What about 'loss of income' and 'extra expense' insurance?"

As a business owner, you need both. If you experience a loss that is covered by your insurance policy, loss of income insurance will reimburse you during repair or rebuilding. For example, if an oak tree falls through the roof of the inn, you'll need to close for repairs. It is designed to provide a reimbursement to you for continuing fixed expenses as well as the loss of income you suffer if no guests are able to come to the inn.

Be careful with this coverage, as it is written in various ways. The best form is *unlimited loss sustained*. "Extra expense" is an additional coverage.

"How high a deductible should I take?"

Insurance should be considered protection against a catastrophe, not just an everyday problem. Use deductibles wisely to lower or raise the cost of your insurance. For a commercial policy in most states, a $1,000 per loss deductible on a commercial policy could result in an 18 percent lower premium in property rates as compared to the standard $250 deductible. A larger deductible is more attractive to your insurance company, assuring them that they will not be paying maintenance claims; they're willing to give a substantial credit for that.

GENERAL INSURANCE TIPS

✳ Ask questions. If you feel uncertain about any of the issues raised here, make an appointment with your agent. Insurance is supposed to give you security; think how secure you'll feel when you're sure you're covered.

✳ Report all losses. Insurance is confusing and there are unquestionably occasions when it isn't clear what is covered and what is not. Wind-driven rain damage, for example, is not normally covered. Rain damage because shingles blew off a roof during a storm and then rain caused further damage is probably covered.

Since these issues aren't clear-cut, it's a good plan always to call your agent and report any loss. Any question you ask helps you make better decisions about limits, perils, and coverages.

✳ Keep records. Pieces of paper with numbers on them are very impressive to insurance claims people. Remember that they run into a lot of crooks, so they're probably as suspicious of you as you are of them. Keeping good records of contents, appraisals, and receipts makes things easier for everyone concerned.

✳ Risk management. Insurance is just one aspect of a complete program to protect you, your guests, and your inn property. Another element is risk management. Many insurance companies provide risk management information and consulting, even for small businesses. Something as simple as putting nonslip pads under the oriental runners can avoid a multimillion dollar lawsuit, and providing staff with instructions on the proper way to lift can avoid workers' compensation claims. Ask your insurance agent about information and assistance in this area.

Note: This short introduction to insurance issues does not provide all the answers. Many variations exist, and you need to be aware of the options to make an informed purchase decision. Your insurance agent is your best source of information. Ask questions and fully disclose your activities and operations. The Professional Association of Innkeepers International's special report "Insurance: That Nine-Letter Word" is a great reference tool. Get it; use the insurance checklist, and then approach your insurance person to purchase the most cost-effective coverage for your bed-and-breakfast or country inn.

Special thanks to Christy Wolf (see Resources, page 307) for her invaluable assistance on this section.

▨ SETTING RATES

Setting your room rates is anything but an absolute science. How do you decide how much to charge your guests or when to make a change in the fees? For most innkeepers rates are determined through trial and error at best. Now, you can profit from their experience. Read on!

STEP ONE: SELF-EXAMINATION

If the Consumer Price Index is any indication, other businesses raise rates regularly, generally from 2 to 10 percent annually. So you might simply keep up with your area CPI.

However, innkeepers tend to complicate things. As Hugh Daniels from the Old Miners Lodge in Park City, Utah, wrote shortly after his inn opened, "We went from comfortable upper-middle class to abject poverty just by opening our inn." A personal economic plunge can prevent innkeepers from really believing that anyone would pay $150 or more for a room. But just because you, the innkeeper, cannot afford to pay such a price for a room does not mean an average two-income couple cannot. Hey, these folks are desperate to drive their Porsche to a romantic weekend hideaway with a fireplace and Jacuzzi!

Even if you believe there are clients that can afford these rates, chances are your innkeeping partner won't. Often, one partner begins to lobby for an increase long before the other is ready to countenance it. "We just raised prices when Junior left for college." Your reply may be, "But he graduates in June!"

These difficulties shouldn't surprise you. Simply acknowledging that you are in business to make money (among many other more altruistic reasons) is a big step for many innkeepers. Does it seem morally wrong to charge even more than you do now to people you feel you would invite into your home? But wait! Guests are used to paying for good value. The experience in your inn is no doubt the best around, right? Why sell it short by undercharging? Usually, inns compare favorably with the finest lodging in town, offering at no charge services and amenities that others charge for, like all-day coffee and tea, homemade cookies, and complimentary sherry and hors d'oeuvres.

Innkeepers also tend to put off raising rates in anticipation of the terror they'll feel when quoting the new prices on the phone. You are convinced that the caller will screech obscenities and hang up as soon as you mumble the new rates. That just doesn't happen. (But if it does, the caller was looking for the YMCA and misdialed or has a six-year-old guidebook—relax!) Remember, rarely will you speak to someone who makes less money today than he or she did two or three years ago—unless it is an innkeeper who hasn't raised room rates in years!

So, you're still not psychologically prepared? You're ready for . . .

STEP TWO: LOGIC

Ask yourself these questions, using your occupancy records, other relevant materials, and a pad and pencil. Use your calculator.

✳ How do your rates compare with those of other inns you have visited? Are the room features similar?

✳ When do you turn guests away? If you have a regular season when you could fill twice as many rooms, you have twice the chance of finding people who will pay a higher price. Does it really make a difference if you fill up eight weeks in advance, or two weeks, or even two days? As long as you are full, anyway, why not make a little more money when your rooms are at a premium? The old law of supply and demand keeps small entrepreneurs alive, just as it does corporations. Bill Oates, New England inn business consultant, believes that if you're selling your rooms to the first person who calls, you can raise rates.

✳ What is your most popular, first-booked room? Raising rates does not need to be across the board. Your price range can be fairly wide. To assuage your guilt, have from low to high prices, so both the economy- *and* luxury-minded clients will be pleased.

✳ Does a room's popularity vary with the season? In summer a fireplace suite doesn't have the same appeal as in the dead of winter. Reducing the rate may be necessary. On the other hand, by adding a day bed or a futon during the summer months, you might increase a room's value by opening it up to families.

✳ Do you have one room that is the least popular? Probably you apologize for it and keep the rate low. But what is the problem? Perhaps adding a Jacuzzi, fireplace, queen-size bed, or canopy would solve it. Sometimes just paint and a quilt can spruce up a room. Don't keep prices low because of a problem you can fix.

✳ Are your prices so low that commissioning travel agents is painful and you resent discounting a room? Offering reductions to former guests during slow times or participating in a well-publicized discount program are good for business. However, if you feel that your already-slim profit margin has been annihilated every time someone takes advantage of one of these deals, you will not be a gracious innkeeper.

✳ Do you like working harder for less money? Innkeepers often say, "But if my prices are higher, my occupancy will go down." Maybe. But even if it does, you will make—worst case—the same amount of money while working less.

Rates are a marketing tool, a reflection of your quality. If they are too low, potential guests may wonder what's wrong with the inn. If you frequently advertise $39 specials, for example, it will cheapen the inn's image. But if your room prices are high, guests will have high expectations, possibly higher than you're prepared to meet. Fortunately, once you've mastered the psychological hurdles, there's a sort of science to the setting of rates.

STEP THREE: RESEARCH

The biennial *Bed and Breakfast/Country Inn Industry Survey and Analysis* tracks inn prices and price increases. It has found, unsurprisingly, that guests expect to pay more for a room with a view, fireplace, Jacuzzi, or even extra space or privacy. As you evaluate the changes you want to make to your new or existing inn, look at what will bring you more income. A private bath can increase the room's value by $12 to $40, with $22 the average, according to the 1994 study. A whirlpool tub in a room with its own bath will probably be worth an extra $15 to $55, and a fireplace is worth an extra $15 to $59 depending on the season and the area.

Adding special features to a room not only increases the income per night but also increases its rentability, further increasing income.

If your most popular room has a fireplace, can you add more, perhaps even simple free-standing zero-clearance woodstoves or direct-vented gas fireplaces? If you invest $3,000 in a fireplace in a room with 50 percent occupancy, raising the room price a conservative $30 realizes a first-year increase of $5,475—enough to pay off your investment and go on vacation! And that's not counting the likely increased occupancy!

1994 AVERAGE RATE BY ROOM FEATURE			
	Low	High	Average
Whirlpool, Spa	$74	$227	$133
Cottages, Separate Building	66	220	129
Balcony, Patio, Garden	66	163	129
Suite	65	275	128
Fireplace, Stove	53	200	117
Audio/Video Equipment	60	185	107
Kitchen, Wet Bar	78	230	n/a
View/Window Seat	45	178	99
Basic Room/Private Bath	43	175	88
Corporate Rate	45	148	75
Basic Room Shared Bath	37	130	66

THE SKY IS NOT THE LIMIT

Why are some of the least responsible innkeepers the most enthusiastic about raising rates? Before you raise yours, take a close look at your property and services. If your rooms need paint and share baths, if your breakfast is no more than breads and fruit, if you offer no special amenities like bikes or cookies, think twice before you hike the rates. Guests buy value for their dollar. Long-term success requires that you provide it.

WHERE HAS ALL THE MONEY GONE? CASH FLOW MANAGEMENT

Almost every inn has busy seasons, months when income is high, and slower periods when income is low. Many expenses, however, remain more or less constant. Cash flow management is the art of staying solvent year-round. Planning is key. Here are some solvency strategies that work for existing inns.

* Establish a reserve account for large annual payments, such as property tax and liability insurance.
* Establish a credit line with your bank.
* Take out credit cards and use as necessary.
* Prioritize the order of bill paying. Take into consideration the cost of interest charged for late payment versus the cost of borrowing to pay now. Communicate with those who you must pay later to maintain your good name.
* Take advantage of cash discounts for immediate payment in fat times to establish credibility for negotiating late or partial payment in lean times.
* Plan major purchases for the high season.
* Put money away regularly for big-ticket items such as washing machines that will eventually have to be replaced.
* Plan special events or a gift certificate push to bring money in during slow periods.
* Plan staffing with seasonal variations in mind; be realistic when expressing expectations to your staff about hours.
* Consider taking a part-time job.
* Sell products at the inn—your homemade jam, note cards, or potpourri—or have a holiday bazaar.
* Barter for services such as printing, carpet cleaning, or legal advice.
* Collect deposits early for the fall foliage season or summer at the shore.
* Close off-season or midweek to cut expenses.
* Market harder.

THE INN GROUP: INNKEEPER ASSOCIATIONS

The existing inns in your area, your state, and your region can be great resources. In many places, innkeepers have banded together on a variety of fronts for their mutual benefit.

* Group marketing, including advertising, brochures, media campaigns, and special events.
* A single referral or reservation number for area inns.
* Setting standards and administering inspection programs.
* Political clout.
* Group membership in high-cost visitor bureaus or chambers of commerce.
* Sounding board, professional support system, communications network.
* Establishing an image.
* Fun.

If you join an association that is already doing many of these things, expect to pay yearly dues. In addition, depending upon the association, you may pay extra fees for brochure printing and distribution, site inspections, special-event marketing, and public relations campaigns.

There is a lot of strength in innkeeper associations, evident, for example, in states where positive legislative changes for the industry were influenced by innkeepers. Problems do occur occasionally; like marriage, associations are no cinch. On the other hand, like marriage, they have benefits you can't easily get elsewhere: common concerns, someone to share expenses, and complementary interests and talents.

When problems surface, apply some marriage strategies. Consider these options.

✳ One of the biggest hurdles in marriages is making peace with the realization that, despite your expectations, your partner isn't responsible for your happiness or success. By the same token, no association can improve your occupancy rate or fix cash flow problems. This doesn't mean that either the marriage or the association is a worthless relationship.

✳ When people in your group seem unreasonable, try really seeing them as the whole individuals they are, not just as sources of support or frustration for your purposes. They too have goals and disappointments and babies that keep them up all night.

✳ If you feel you're doing more than your share in terms of time or money, either accept it or change it, but don't be a martyr. Being unhappy is dull, and it will cause you to create sideshow problems that will hamper the effectiveness of the group.

✳ Make it a policy never to talk about anyone. If people are behaving in ways you don't like, handle it with *them*. What's more destructive than the unbridled tongue?

✳ As to who's getting the glory, it's a waste of time to be jealous of anyone else's success. You do the best you can.

✳ Spend fun time together. Smiles do good things for the face. And as Sophia Loren reputedly said, "By the time you're forty, you'll have the face you deserve."

Lake to Lake Bed and Breakfast, Michigan: Eight years ago, a small group of innkeepers from the southern Lower Peninsula banded together for promotional purposes. Since then, Lake to Lake has grown to become a professionally staffed, statewide innkeeper association. Their scope today covers not only promotion but also education, legislation, insurance, and other member services, including design input and participation in industry studies in cooperation with Michigan State University.

They worked on the enactment of state legislation to define bed-and-breakfast. Their Lake to Lake members' directory has been published annually since 1985 and is now distributed by the State Travel Bureau at highway welcome centers and via a toll-free number.

In recent years they have hired an executive director and inspect every member to check that they meet the standards set by the organization.

<hr>

The Seattle Bed and Breakfast Association has a central phone number for thirteen inns with a total of sixty rooms. The phone number appears in the joint brochure that goes to state convention centers and car rental agencies. To be included, the inns must be members of the association, inspected by two officers, and licensed by the city. The group line operates year-round, rotating answering duties among themselves every three days using call-forwarding. They started out using an answering service, but that was too costly. A central fax line keeps room availability information current.

TAKING CARE OF YOURSELF

Burnout in the early years is one of the primary reasons innkeepers quit. Although every innkeeper experiences burnout sooner or later, and to a greater or lesser degree, there are several ways to recognize the danger signals and minimize the burnout.

The first step is to believe it can happen to you. Discuss with your partner the way you react to fatigue, and talk about how you would like to be treated when you're suffering. Maybe you want permission and encouragement to take time off. Maybe you prefer a nudge out the door. Make specific plans about how you can care for each other.

Unfortunately, instead of detecting and defusing each other's burnout, partners often feed it. One demands an impossible performance of the other or feels guilty when a partner outperforms him or her. Couples frequently run into problems when one partner works outside the inn. The innkeeping partner often wants more help in the inn while the outside partner feels that he or she is doing plenty by working to cover the income deficit. Perhaps the outside partner doesn't know the inn procedures well enough to help out satisfactorily, but may feel guilty about relaxing when the innkeeping partner is still folding laundry at 9 P.M.

Don't buy into these guilt trips. It's important for each partner to encourage and celebrate the care and concern from the other partner.

Burnout is cumulative and progressive. It is a depletion of personal energy that affects jobs and relationships. You cannot think it away, but you can take steps to avoid or reduce it.

SPACE

No matter how well you plan your living quarters, space may still be a factor in burnout, so hold out for the best living situation you can manage. Remember that if you share space with guests, you can't consider it inn footage for IRS purposes. Consider the following matters when you make your plans:

✳ Can you live with just a bedroom, or will you need larger private quarters at the inn? Innkeepers who do not have their own space soon become impatient with the guests. When you are making a decision about living space, err on the side of generosity to yourself.

✳ Do you want a separate sitting area or living room, or don't you mind being asked what's for breakfast when you're nine pages from the end of a Robert Ludlum novel?

✳ If you have an open kitchen where guests can freely come and go, be aware that you may be sharing your peanut butter and onion sandwiches at midnight with some well-meaning guest who just meandered in looking for a doggie bag.

✳ Discuss how you will accommodate other family members who live at the inn or come home for vacations. Also take a look at where friends will stay. Will they always need to rent a room?

✳ Do you prefer to do paperwork uninterrupted, or will you be comfortable having your office desk in the kitchen available to staff? Keep your inn records out of guest hands, not only because it takes away from their fantasy but also because you don't want your blank checks or guest credit card information available to just anyone who walks in. Be careful, too, about having your desk in your private space; it is too easy to bring your work into the bedroom.

Discuss these issues together before making space decisions. Respect everyone's need for space; frequently, one person will need more distance or privacy, or need it in a different way. Acknowledge and appreciate these differences.

The less you accommodate your space needs initially, the more important the issue of space will become. Even if you can't provide yourselves with the quarters you want and need at the outset, at least develop a plan for them and a timetable, so you will see a light at the end of the tunnel.

WORK SCHEDULES

Work patterns and responsibilities should be divided so that partners can truly spell each other. If one partner prepares breakfast and rooms, greets guests, and supervises staff, he or she will get little time off, unless partners alternate being fully in charge from day to day. Another approach is to share the tasks, so one handles breakfast, then breaks for the afternoon while the other supervises staff or cleans rooms, then comes back on duty at three to greet guests.

No matter how you divide up the jobs, there is always more to do, so get a work schedule down on paper, *including breaks*. The work will get done; the breaks are what tend to be forgotten.

INN STYLE AND BURNOUT

Burnout prevention strategies are often reflected in inn policies and procedures. Many innkeepers plan check-in and checkout times to meet their needs to take a breather, to leave the afternoon free for a concert or the evening for a dinner date instead of waiting around for a single late arrival.

Be cautious here. Although it is true that integrating innkeeping and your personal life is crucial for success, remember that guest needs are paramount. You cannot manage your inn just to meet your needs. Sound contradictory? In fact, it's not, but it may require hiring help with flexible hours to welcome guests while you take a break.

Extra services such as providing afternoon refreshments and making dinner reservations take extra time. But they are wonderful touches and guests appreciate them. Try to evaluate whether the lack of any particular service will be a disappointment to guests, or whether providing it will really help to bring them back again.

Some of the services you provide do not have to affect your personal time during the day. Be creative about the way you provide services. For example, self-serve hot beverages can be available all the time if you provide an instant hot-water faucet or insulated hot pots. You might develop materials for guests that will augment your presence. Instead of describing to every individual guest the process of renovating the inn, provide a scrapbook of before and after photographs. Make a folder of information about what there is to do in your area. Fill a basket with collected restaurant menus, and let guests fill a blank book with their own reviews. Maintain a scrapbook of articles about the inn and the innkeepers. All these are ways to meet guest needs for information without the every-moment personal involvement of the innkeeper.

Listen to what your guests tell you and respond accordingly. That's the key to success. When do your guests most need you? When they are planning their activities for the day or selecting an evening activity or restaurant?

Perhaps they want an afternoon debriefing after their hike? Set your personal time priorities accordingly.

Plan a reasonable way for guests to reach you or the innkeeper on duty. You shouldn't have to leap up every time someone appears in the parlor, and guests shouldn't have to wander around calling your name. A bell on the door to your quarters or a specific phone extension will show guests that you are available, while preserving your privacy and theirs.

PLAN FOR PRODUCTIVITY

Since burnout occurs when you're busy but don't feel productive, make long- and short-range plans that will help you minimize worry and let you see results. For example, if you want to increase occupancy this year by 5 percent overall, figure out what that means in terms of a daily or weekly increase in business. How many more rooms must you rent this week to accomplish your goal? Or say you want to replace all the drapes in the guest rooms this year. Plan a monthly schedule for redecorating room by room, or for ordering fabric one month, purchasing hardware the next, and so on. Seeing the day's work in relation to a grander scheme makes the little jobs seem more meaningful and less routine.

STRESS PREVENTION

Plan ahead to design your innkeeping lifestyle for stress prevention.

✳ When will you get regular exercise? At least three days a week of twenty to thirty minutes of heart-pumping, heavy-breathing exercise will give you stamina, and you'll need it.

✳ How will you arrange time off for each working partner? Begin that pattern early, so it will feel like a right—which it is!

✳ How can you arrange unhurried, balanced meals? Plan for good nutrition and meals that are events: a late breakfast in the kitchen, a sandwich in the park, a family supper around the fire when the inn is empty. This sounds easy now, but just wait!

✳ Don't finish off the breakfast coffee, the cocktail sherry, and the cheese and crackers without thinking. Moderation is healthy.

✳ Find an escape location outside the inn, perhaps a membership club, a gym, the woods, or the beach. You need a place where you can rejuvenate.

✳ Stimulate your brain as well as your body. Take a class or volunteer at your church, the local library, or the child abuse center. You need to feel good about yourself apart from the inn.

✳ Analyze the ways you become focused and centered; develop and make room for them. If attending church, writing, or getting a massage are important to you, don't let innkeeping push them out of your life. Because it will — if you let it!

✳ Know your limitations and honor them. If you don't want to host weddings and meetings or accommodate groups at your inn, don't.

✳ If you're an innkeeping couple, work to maintain and enjoy closeness. Plan ways to nurture your relationship. Some innkeepers kidnap one another for a special day or night every month. Others play guest in various rooms of the inn on low-occupancy nights.

Sure, burnout is a problem. But you have solutions.

Confessions of a Former Innkeeper:

I know that taking care of myself is my weakest skill, so every summer I would sit down and plan two days off every week, so I would not end up relieved that high season was over and hoping never to see another guest.

The first week, I would get away, but I'd do inn errands for a day and a half — stopping in the big-city yardage store for curtain material and delivering brochures to the visitor center. Since these weren't my usual errands (I usually got the grocery store, the bank, and maybe — if I was lucky — the dog groomer), I told myself I did have a break from my routine.

Week Two: I decide to take my time off at the inn. Sure. Every time the phone rings, I jump. I go outside to read in the garden, and guests come and ask questions. Since I'm on my day off, I'm all theirs.

Back inside (it's just too difficult sitting outside with a box over my head trying to look like I'm not there), I go through the kitchen and automatically start folding towels. I don't mind folding towels, except that now the staff want to ask me questions.

So, the third week I leave the inn and wander around town. I feel homeless and incapable of deciding what to do with this free time. I end up falling asleep in my car in the parking lot of the botanical garden. Then I go to the library and fall asleep in their chairs. Then I go to the movies and eat out alone because I don't even have enough energy to see friends. What fun!

The next morning I'm relaxed enough to stay in bed and read. Then I start writing a news release for the upcoming town gala — there it is again: work!

Week Four: I resolve to leave town for two days. Trying desperately to be spontaneous, I drive off in search of adventure. I decide to go bodysurfing and discover I've forgotten my bathing suit. I drive to Los Angeles to surprise my mom, but spend an hour talking about inn problems on the phone. The next morning I vow to find an adventure: I do stop for a short hike on my drive back.

Week Five: By the time my days off come, I'm just getting up to full steam. Somehow, if I'm not desperate to leave, I don't think I need to do so.

And so it went. Unless I had something actually scheduled with someone or an appointment, I could not count on actually taking time off. I sabotaged my best intentions. I don't get a lot of satisfaction from physical activity; I just get tired and sore, but still I feel unproductive or unhealthy when I just read. That's my idea of a day off, but how do you make an appointment to read? I've been known to spend the night at friends' homes when they are away or at a local inn or camping, just so I can read without interruption.

Probably the greatest truth I've learned about taking time off is that you have to schedule it so that it will happen. If you don't, it won't.

Marriage and Innkeeping

John and Maureen Magee, Rabbit Hill Inn, Lower Waterford, Vermont: "Every day we experience the challenge of balancing a business partnership in our inn/home with our love relationship. We had wanted the inn so much, and yet watched it begin to take priority over our marriage. We wouldn't accept this. We made a plan to restore the balance.

"Together we identified the recurring pitfalls that heightened stress. We now plan ahead for these situations as much as possible. We took back control by creating and maintaining systems to handle them.

"We discovered that as long as we don't hear the ring of our business phone when someone else is scheduled to answer, we can separate emotionally from the job. We acknowledged our need for more staff, taking a financial risk to hire the right people. But it has paid benefits to our business and our love relationship many times over.

"Our next step required the most discipline. We recommitted ourselves to emotional intimacy. We discovered simple techniques for initiating personal conversations and closeness that preclude innkeeping talk. We went back to doing simple things for each other. Now we prayerfully begin each day with a commitment to each other."

IF I HAD KNOWN THEN . . .

If I had known then what I know now, I would:
Pat and Jo Ann's list:

✳ Replace every window that was even a little bit difficult to open or close.

✳ Use only one brand of one color of white paint and enamel paint on the doors.

✳ Have more money and brutally realistic financial projections.

✳ Plan 150 percent for renovation projections.

✳ Install all private baths right from the beginning.

✳ Apprentice at an inn.

✳ Put in twice the number of electrical outlets and be sure there's one on each wall. The plugs were never in the right place for clocks, lights, hair dryers, shavers, curling irons, heaters, and so on. And add another electrical panel to accommodate the outlets.

* Install three times the outlets I thought possible to use in the kitchen.
* Hire staff sooner.
* Cooperate with others sooner.
* Ask for more help from those who had already done it.
* Assure my private quarters were soundproof from inn activity.
* Heavily soundproof all guest rooms.
* Plan for and take vacations with my children, even in the middle of our season.
* Put a refrigerator with an ice maker in an area where guests can help themselves.
* Buy a commercial dishwasher and save myself time.
* Install an instant hot-water spigot in my kitchen and in a marble-topped buffet in the dining room for guests to make instant beverages or soups.

Susan's list:
* Hire an architect and work out an overall plan for what my property could look like ten years from now, with maximum expansion.
* Prepare in advance a complete media package, so I wouldn't be running around getting pictures printed the night before a media representative is due.
* Be careful with initial room pricing. It's better to start high and discount than to try to inch your prices up from $50 to $120 a night.
* Develop a theme or gimmick early in the game so that my inn would stand out more from the competition.

Mary's list:
* Furnish guest rooms with dressers with pull-out writing surfaces, to double as desks.
* Ask my assistant innkeepers to bring me breakfast in bed on my days off, and do the same for them on their days off (for live-in staff, of course).
* Buy a larger property where I could build a separate cottage for myself and family.
* Only hire staff I really like, even if the ones I like less look better on paper.
* Even if I did nothing else different, my innkeeping life would be changed because my sister Marty finally said to me, "Righty tighty, lefty Lucy." Invaluable advice for innkeeper handyperson jobs.

APPENDICES

Appendix 1

WORKSHEET: FINDING THE RIGHT LOCATION FOR YOUR INN

Property Address: _____

A. General Area
___ Proximity to large metropolitan area (within three hours)
___ Convenient public transportation to area, airport, train, bus
___ Close to major highways or interstates
___ Tourist attraction, good restaurants, entertainment, shopping
___ Good climate and environment
___ Businesses, manufacturers, government offices, retailers
      (commercial businesses)
___ Meets your family's environmental needs (weather, ocean, desert, mountain)
___ Meets your family's educational and employment needs
___ Cost of utilities, possibility for solar

B. Neighborhood
___ Close to, but not too close to, restaurants, retailers, tourist attractions
___ Low crime rate and safe environment
___ Convenient to freeways
___ Within service area for fire, police, medical, utilities
___ Resale value
___ Zoned for B&B, dinner service, alcoholic beverage sale

C. Specific Structure—House, Barn, Inn to Be   *(comments)*
___ Zoning, master plan _____
___ Structurally sound foundation_____
___ Curb appeal, charm, character, historical significance _____
___ Room for expansion _____
___ Adjoining property, dogs barking, types of neighbors _____
___ Outdoor area, patio, garden, spa, croquet, barbecue _____
___ Innkeeper's quarters, privacy, storage_____
___ Garage, parking for guests' and innkeepers' cars _____
___ Adequate heating, air-conditioning (if needed)_____
___ Plumbing, septic tank or sewer, water heater, potable water _____
_____

___ Electricity, age, type, 220 available _____

___ Landscaping, big trees, sound insulation for traffic _____

___ Laundry facilities or in area_____

___ Storage facilities for linens, roll-away bed, cleaning equipment _____

_____

D. Rooms—Size, Ventilation, Sun and Wind Exposure, Traffic and
    Neighborhood Noise, Entry and Exit

___ Living room or parlor _____

___ Space for dinner service, if you need it _____

___ Kitchen, including equipment_____

___ Other common areas _____

___ Guest rooms and bathrooms or space or closets to create bathrooms _____

_____

___	Room 1 _____	Room 5	_____
___	Room 2 _____	Room 6	_____
___	Room 3 _____	Room 7	_____
___	Room 4 _____	Room 8	_____

Sketch the basic floor plan while it is fresh in your memory.

Appendix 2

PERSONAL FINANCIAL STATEMENT: AN INVENTORY

ASSETS

Liquid Assets
(Cash is readily obtainable from these.)

Cash on hand	$_____
Checking account(s)	
(banks and amounts)	_____
Savings account(s)	
(passbook, money market, etc.,	
banks and amounts)	_____
Stocks (companies and cash values)	_____
Bonds (companies and cash values)	_____
Insurance (whole life—companies	
and cash values)	_____
Other (autos, jewelry, silver,	
gold, coins)	_____
TOTAL LIQUID ASSETS	$_____

Nonliquid Assets (These take
time to tap, due to roll-over
dates, the need to sell, etc.
Can be used as collateral.)

Property/real estate (market value)	_____
Location	_____
Location	_____
Time certificates of deposit	_____
Location	_____
Pension fund	_____
Name	_____
Other	_____
TOTAL NONLIQUID ASSETS	$_____

Other Assets (Assets that are
not necessarily liquid or useful
as collateral, but show wealth.)

Personal property (china, silver,	
furs, art, clothing)	_____
Furnishings	_____
Livestock, pedigreed animals	_____
Subchapter S or privately held stock	_____
TOTAL OTHER ASSETS	$_____
TOTAL ASSETS	$_____

LIABILITIES

Property mortgages	
(current balances, banks, and	
expiration dates)	$_____
Loans	_____
Auto	_____
Other	_____
Credit accounts	
(banks and department store	
names and current balances)	_____
Other	_____
TOTAL LIABILITIES	$_____

NET WORTH
Total assets less total liabilities	$_____

ANNUAL INCOME
Employment (salary)	_____
Business operations	
(your own business)	_____
Spousal/child support	_____
Interest	_____
Rentals	_____
Dividends	_____
Other	_____
TOTAL ANNUAL INCOME	$_____

ANNUAL EXPENSES
Property taxes/assessments	_____
Income and other taxes	_____
Mortgage payments and interest	_____
Other contract payments	_____
Insurance	_____
Living expense	_____
Spousal/child support	_____
Auto payments	_____
Children's education	_____
Rent	_____
Other	_____
TOTAL ANNUAL EXPENSES	$_____

CREDIT AVAILABILITY
(Itemize and state limits for each.)
Bank credit line	_____
Bank credit cards	_____
Department store credit cards	_____

Appendix 3

WORKSHEET: PROPERTY EVALUATION

Address: _____
_____
Area occupancy rate: _____%

All amounts and percentages are estimates.
Number of guest rooms:
    original house: _____
    proposed addition: _____

Area room rate:
    private bath: $_____
    shared bath: $_____

Number of guest bathrooms:
    original house: _____
    proposed addition: _____

A. Financial Needs: Purchase/Renovation Phase

			GUIDE
Purchase:	Total price:	_____	1st, 10% fixed, 25 years
	Mortgage(s):	_____	$15,000–50,000 per guest room
		_____	
Down payment		_____	Usual is 20–30% of price
Closing costs, loan fees, etc.		_____	Get realtor or banker estimate
Moving costs		_____	
Working capital		_____	Expenses from purchase period (_____-month renovation)
Renovation and furnishings: including bathrooms		_____	Estimate $20,000 (good condition) to $40,000 per guest room in original house
Additional guest rooms: construction		_____	Estimate new construction at $90–$200 per sq. ft. (room with bath—250 sq. ft.)
Additional bathrooms: construction		_____	Estimate $5,000–10,000 each
Additional guest rooms: furnishings		_____	Estimate $7,000 per room
Other _____		_____	
Total		$_____	

B. Income

__ rooms × 365 days × average room rate $_____ = income @ 100% occupancy $_____

1ST YEAR PROJECTION:
    50% of area rate _____% = _____% × 100% occupancy = $_____
2ND YEAR PROJECTION:
    1st year _____% + 10% = _____% × 100% occupancy = $_____
3RD YEAR PROJECTION:
    2nd year _____% + 10% = _____% × 100% occupancy = $_____

C. Per Room Expenses—PAII *Industry Study*

5 rooms	$7,674	7 rooms	$6,801	9 rooms	$8,166

Survey Expenses (No. of rooms _____ × $_____[survey]) = $_____
Mortgage, lease payment =   _____
Adjustment for reality (See E—Detailed Exp., Col. 2) =   _____
Owner's salary/draw =   _____
                                             TOTAL $_____

D. Cash Flow Projection / Break-even Analysis

	1st Year	2nd Year	3rd Year
Income (B)	$_____	_____	_____
Per room expenses (C)	_____	_____	_____
+ or − Cash flow	_____	_____	_____

To break even:

Expenses / Income @ 100% = $_____ = _____% occupancy needed

$_____

E. Detailed Expenses

Standard Percent of Income	Expense Category	Annual Expenses Using Standard Percentages	Adjustments For Reality	Comments
7	Food & nonfood hourly employees	_____	_____	
3	Food & nonfood salaried employees	_____	_____	
1	Auto expense	_____	_____	
2	Bank fees	_____	_____	
4	Business taxes and fees	_____	_____	
1	Commissions	_____	_____	
1	Dues and subscriptions	_____	_____	
8	Food and beverages	_____	_____	
3	Insurance	_____	_____	
1	Legal and accounting fees	_____	_____	
6	Maintenance, repairs, and fixtures	_____	_____	
8	Marketing, advertising, and promotion	_____	_____	
1	Office supplies and postage	_____	_____	
2	Outside services	_____	_____	
3	Room and housekeeping supplies	_____	_____	
2	Telephone	_____	_____	
1	Towels and linens	_____	_____	
1	Training	_____	_____	
1	Travel and entertainment	_____	_____	
6	Utilities	_____	_____	
62%	Total operating and labor expenses not including owner's salary/draw or interest expenses	_____ (T)	_____	
38%	Mortgage	_____	_____	
	Salary	_____	_____	
100%	GRAND TOTAL operating and labor expenses, including owner's salary/draw and interest/lease expenses	_____ (GT)	_____	

To find TOTAL EXPENSES as percentage of income

STEP 1: _____ × _____ = $_____(T)
      # of rooms   (C) from Worksheet
(Expenses per room for labor and operations)
Insert (1) in column 1 Total above.

STEP 2: (T) _____ divided by .62 = _____(GT)
Insert in Column 1 Grand Total expenses including mortgage, owner draw, and adjustment for reality (Col. 2).

STEP 3: Take each individual percentage and multiply by (GT) to figure Column 1 percentages of income.

STEP 4: Reality Test: Correct the individual expense items to reflect your situation.

STEP 5: Subtract Col. 1 (T) from Col. 2 (T); enter difference in C. Adjustment for reality.

Appendix 4

CASH FLOW PROJECTION — MONTH BY MONTH

	Jan.	Feb.	Mar.	Apr.	May	June	July	Aug.	Sep.	Oct.	Nov.	Dec.
Projected Occupancy %												
INCOME												
Room rental revenues												
Product sales												
Total Income												
EXPENSES												
Food and beverages												
Room and housekeeping supplies												
Hourly/part-time employees and payroll taxes												
Utilities												
Towels and linens												
Marketing, advertising, promotion												
Travel commissions and bank charges												
Office supplies and postage												
Telephone												
Travel and entertainment												
Dues and subscriptions												
Auto expenses												
Maintenance, repairs, and fixtures												
Outside services												
Insurance												
Legal and accounting fees												
Business and property taxes and fees												
Interest and/or lease expenses												
Salaried or permanent employees												
Total expenses												
CASH FLOW												

Appendix 5: State of California Form 55-037

PROPOSAL AND CONTRACT

Date_____, 19____

To _____
    _____

Dear Client:

_____ propose to furnish all materials and perform all labor necessary to complete the following:

_____
_____
_____
_____
_____
_____
_____
_____
_____
_____
_____

All of the above work to be completed in a substantial and workmanlike manner according to standard practices for the sum of _____ Dollars ($_____)

Progress payments to be made _____

_____ as the work progresses to the value of _____ percent (___%) of all work completed. The entire amount of contract to be paid within _____ days after completion.

Any alteration or deviation from the above specifications involving extra cost of material or labor will only be executed upon written orders for same, and will become an extra charge over the sum mentioned in this contract. All agreements must be made in writing.

Name and Registration Number of any salesperson who solicited or negotiated this contract:

Respectfully submitted,

By_____
_____
Address
_____
Telephone

Name_____No._____

Contractors are required by law to be licensed and regulated by the Contractor's State License Board. Any questions concerning a contractor may be referred to the registrar of the board whose address is:

Contractor's State License No. _____

You, the buyer, may cancel this transaction at any time prior to midnight of the third business day after the date of this transaction.

Contractor's State License Board
1020 N Street
Sacramento, California 95814

ACCEPTANCE

You are hereby authorized to furnish all materials and labor required to complete the work mentioned in the above proposal, for which _____ agree to pay the amount mentioned in said proposal, and according to the terms thereof.

ACCEPTED _____ Date_____, 19____

Appendix 6

ROOM PLANNING WORKSHEET

Room name (or location): _____

Type of room: _____

Atmosphere desired: _____

Natural light: _____

Colors: _____

ITEMS TO BE PURCHASED OR INSTALLED	Budgeted	Spent	Ordered	Installed
Bed				
Headboard				
Mattress/springs				
Dining Table				
Light				
Chairs				
1				
2				
3				
Nightstands				
Table for lamps				
Bed lights				
Dresser				
Firewood container				
Armoire				
Desk/dressing table				
Mirrors				
Makeup				
Dressing				
Heating/air-conditioning				
Wall treatment				
Window treatment				
Floor treatment				
Bed covering				
Fireplace tools				
Linens				
Accessories				

In the format above, make a master list of items needed in more than one room, such as beds, linens, carpeting, draperies, and accessories, which you may be able to purchase in quantity.

▓ RESOURCES

BUSINESS

B&B/Country Inn Industry Study. In-depth biennial study of occupancy, amenities, marketing sources, prices, employees, revenue and expenses, rate of return on investment, and break-even. Broken out by geography, size, location (urban, rural, destination), and age of the inn. Santa Barbara, CA: Professional Association of Innkeepers International.

Daily, Frederick W., *Tax Savvy for Small Business.* Berkeley, CA: Nolo Press, 1995. Available through PAII.

McKeever, Mike, *How to Write a Business Plan.* Berkeley, CA: Nolo Press, 1995. Available through PAII.

Phillips, Michael, and Rasberry, Salli. *Honest Business.* New York: Random House, 1981. A good general introduction to doing any kind of business of your own.

Small Business Administration. Ask for the current catalog and send for the titles that look relevant, such as "Planning and Goal Setting for Small Business," "Learning about Your Market," "Marketing for Small Business," "Selecting the Legal Structure for Your Firm," "Checklist for Going into Business," and "The ABC's of Borrowing."

RENOVATION AND DECORATION

Earth Works Project. *Fifty Simple Things You Can Do to Save the Earth.* Berkeley, CA: Greenleaf Publications, 1990.

Greco, Gail. *The Romance of Country Inns.* Nashville: Rutledge Hill Press, 1994. More than 300 full-color photographs illustrate this 256-page art piece. From cooking to entertaining, the author has gleaned the best ideas from innkeepers. Available through PAII.

Home Decorators Collection Catalog. 2025 Concourse Drive, St. Louis, MO 63146.

Kemp George Catalog. 2515 East 43rd Street, Chattanooga, TN 37422.

National Trust for Historic Preservation, 1785 Massachusetts Avenue NW, Washington, D.C. 20036. Ask for a copy of their most current historic preservation information booklets. Two of interest are *A Guide to Tax-Advantaged Rehabilitation*, booklet #2189, and *Buyer's Guide to Older and Historic Houses*, booklet #2174.

Old House Interiors. Boulder, CO. 800-462-0211. Classic approach to decorating and remodeling homes both old and new.

The Old House Journal. Boulder, CO. 800-234-3797. Magazine on home restoration.

Victorian Warehouse Catalog. 190 Grace Street, Auburn, CA 95603.

Vintage Woodworks Catalog. 513 South Adams, Fredericksburg, TX 28624.

COMPUTERS

Listed below are six reservations software packages. This is just a sampling of available products. For a complete listing, contact PAII for their *World of Computers* special report.

Innkeeper. InnSoft, 3421 23rd Avenue South, Minneapolis, MN 55407. 800-288-2773. (MS/DOS and Windows)

Innkeeper/InnManager. CAPA Holdings, 23151 Verdugo Drive, #101, Laguna Hills, CA 92653. 714-859-3711. (MS/DOS)

InnManager. JK Software Systems, 1030 South Street, Portsmouth, NH 03801. 603-433-3252. (Macintosh and Windows)

InnPAL. PAL Computer Systems, P.O. Box 790, Manchester Center, VT 05255. 800-334-PALS. (MS/DOS, Macintosh, Windows)

KozyWare. Forster & Associates, P.O. Box 551, Springville, NY 14141. 716-592-2397. (MS/DOS)

RESERVE/5. Sunbelt Century Systems, 3623 Latrobe, #115, Charlotte, NC 282T1. 704-364-3222. (MS/DOS and Windows)

MARKETING AND PROMOTION

Guide to the Inn Guidebooks. An annotated bibliography of the printed books, CD-ROMs, and electronic on-line services published as guides for inn travelers, where you'd like your inn listed. Published annually by PAII, P.O. Box 90710, Santa Barbara, CA 93190. Call 805-569-1853 or fax 805-682-1016.

Inn Marketing Newsletter. 98 South Fletcher Avenue, Amelia Island, Fl 32034. 904-321-2720. Marketing and promotion ideas for innkeepers.

Marketing Handbook. From the basics of writing a news release to writing brochure copy, this compilation of over 140 pages of promotional ideas keeps your inn in the media's eye. Compiled from back issues of *innkeeping* newsletter. Santa Barbara, CA: Professional Association of Innkeepers International.

Phillips, Michael, and Rasberry, Salli. *Marketing Without Advertising.* Berkeley, CA: Nolo Press, 1987. Good practical ideas. Available through PAII.

FOOD AND RECIPES

Greco, Gail. *Secrets of Entertaining from America's Best Innkeepers.* Old Saybrook, CT: Globe Pequot, 1996. Hints collected from innkeepers. Available through PAII.

Tucker, Mary Lynn. *Heart-Healthy Hospitality.* Manor at Taylor's Store, Rt. 1, Box 533, Wirtz, VA 24184. 703-721-3951. Low-fat breakfast recipes by an innkeeper.

Kirby, John and Carol. *Muffins and Marketing.* Sea Crest by the Sea, NJ. 800-803-9031. Inn recipes laced with 50 secrets of successful innkeeping.

OPERATIONS

George Washington Slept Here and, Boy, Was He Messy. A 28-minute training video along with a training guide and employee checklists, produced by American Hotel & Motel Association's Educational Institute with modifications by PAII. Revised and updated for inns, this is a training tool for new staff and a retraining tool for experienced staff. Available in both English and Spanish. Available only through Professional Association of Innkeepers International.

Insurance: That Nine-Letter Word. This 25-page report demystifies insurance while providing concrete information on why you need it, how much you need, the latest insurance trends, choosing an agent, and shopping for price. Santa Barbara, CA: Professional Association of Innkeepers International, 1996.

Staff Manual. Federal Labor regulations, finding and selecting great staff, how to keep good staff, rightful termination, and more, all specifically written for bed-and-breakfast/country innkeepers. Santa Barbara, CA: Professional Association of Innkeepers International, 1994.

World of Computers. Developers of inn-specific reservations software packages present their products. Also includes an overview of basic computer operating systems; choosing a computer, upgrading, or buying new; basic types of applications. Santa Barbara, CA: Professional Association of Innkeepers International, 1995.

Inn Marketing Yellow Pages. 98 South Fletcher Avenue, Amelia Island, Fl 32034. 904-321-2720. "The complete Yellow Pages for bed-and-breakfasts, country inns."

POLITICS

Anderson, Kare. *Cutting Deals with Unlikely Allies, An Unorthodox Approach to Playing the Political Game.* Anderson Negotiations/Communications, Inc., Tiburon, CA. If you get into political trouble, this is the practical guide to getting out. A step-by-step approach to influencing decision-makers. Available through PAII.

AMERICANS WITH DISABILITIES

Employer Incentives. President's Committee on Employment of People with Disabilities, 1331 F Street NW, Washington, D.C. 20004-1107. 202-376-6200. Free booklet.

Accommodating All Guests. American Hotel & Motel Association, 1201 New York Avenue, NW, Washington, D.C. 20005. 202-289-3100.

Americans with Disabilities Act Handbook. Equal Employment Opportunity Commission (EEOC) and Department of Justice, Office on the Americans with Disabilities Act. 202-514-0301.

Equal Employment Opportunity Commission
    1801 L Street NW, Washington, D.C. 20507
    800-669-EEOC or 800-800-3302 (TDD)

Office on the Americans with Disabilities Act
    Civil Rights Division/Department of Justice
    P.O. Box 66118, Washington, D.C. 20035-6118
    202-514-0301 Information line
    202-514-0383 (TDD)
    202-514-6193 (electronic bulletin board)

Architectural and Transportation Barriers Compliance Board (Access Board)
    1331 F Street, NW, #1000, Washington, D.C. 20004-1111
    800-USA-ABLE (voice and TDD)
    202-653-7863 FAX

National Council on Independent Living
    4th and Broadway, Troy Atrium, Troy, NY 12180
    518-274-1979

Independent Living Research Utilization
    2323 S. Shepherd, #1000, Houston, TX 77019
    713-520-5138

TDD/ Teleconsumer Hotline for information on free relay service between TDD and voice phones, Washington, D.C. 800-332-1124.
    Also contact your local building department and state architectural or building commission.

EXPERT COUNSEL

INN VALUATION AND APPRAISAL

Michael Yovino-Young and Alison Teeman, Yovino-Young Associates, 2716 Telegraph Avenue, Berkeley, CA 94705. 510-548-1210.

William A. Oates, Oates & Bredfeldt, P.O. Box 1162, Brattleboro, VT 05301. 802-254-5931. Publisher of *Innquest newsletter*, written for people interested in buying existing inns.

INSURANCE

These companies offer national programs written specifically for bed-and-breakfast and country inns. All programs may not be available in all states. Call for information.

Arndt-McBee Insurance, Doug or Gerry Arndt, P.O. Box 1106, Martinsburg, WV 25401. 800-825-4667.

B&B Insurance Specialist, Mitch Seaman, 1140 E. Brickyard Road #76, Salt Lake City, UT 84106. 800-356-6517.

James W. Wolf Insurance, Jim or Christy Wolf, P.O. Box 510, Ellicott City, MD 21041. 800-488-1135.

Potter, Leonard, and Cahan Insurance, Michael Dunkin, P.O. Box 82840, Kenmore, WA 98028. 800-548-8857.

INN TRAVELER PUBLICATIONS
Country Inns/Bed & Breakfast. P.O. Box 182, S. Orange, NJ 07079.
Discerning Traveler newsletter. 504 West Mermaid Lane, Philadelphia, PA 19118.
Inn Marketing newsletter. 98 South Fletcher Avenue, Amelia Island, Fl 32034. 904-321-2720.
Yellow Brick Road newsletter. 2445 Northcreek Lane, Fullerton, CA 92631.

SERVING DINNER
Kazarian, Edward A. *Foodservice Facilities Planning*, 3rd edition. New York: Van Nostrand-Reinhold, 1989.
Birchfield, John C. *Design and Layout of Foodservice Facilities.* New York: Van Nostrand-Reinhold, 1988.
National Sanitary Foundation Testing Laboratory Inc. P.O. Box 1468, Ann Arbor, MI 48106. Contact in writing only for questions concerning food service equipment and an approved list of manufacturers.

HOMESTAY HOW-TO'S
Notarius, Barbara. *Open Your Own Bed and Breakfast.* New York: John Wiley & Sons.
Stankus, Jan. *How to Open and Operate a Bed and Breakfast Home.* Old Saybrook, CT: Globe Pequot Press, 1995.

OTHER BED-AND-BREAKFAST AND COUNTRY INN HOW-TO'S
Hotch, Ripley, and Carl A. Glassman. *How to Start and Run Your Own Bed-and-Breakfast Inn.* Harrisburg, PA: Stackpole Books, 1992.
Shortt, C. Vincent. *How to Open and Successfully Operate a Country Inn.* Stockbridge, MA: Berkshire House Publishers, 1993.

SO YOU THINK YOU WANT TO BE AN INNKEEPER? WORKSHOP
The pioneer (1981) in aspiring innkeeper workshops, this semiannual workshop is still being held in Santa Barbara, California. Students are guided through three in-depth days of the delights and headaches of opening an inn.

Conducted by veteran owner-innkeepers and PAII co-executive directors (and former innkeepers Pat Hardy and Jo Ann Bell), this foursome has a collective total of over sixty years in the business. These leaders have also had careers that range from professional educator, chef, and personnel manager to psychiatric social worker and executive director of a nonprofit agency. The greatest advantages of this training are the national breadth of expertise and the twenty-four-hour availability of these experts to answer questions and give a glimpse into the lifestyle of an innkeeper.

Much of the content of this book grew out of the original framework of these workshops, although more detailed examples, personal attention to individual questions during nonclass time, and more depth in numerous areas typify the on-site workshop.

For a descriptive brochure and/or reservations, contact PAII at P.O. Box 90710, Santa Barbara, CA 93190. Call 805-569-1853 or send faxes to 805-682-1016.

PROFESSIONAL ASSOCIATION OF INNKEEPERS INTERNATIONAL (PAII)
This is the trade association of the bed-and-breakfast and country inn industry, providing services and information to innkeepers, aspiring innkeepers, and innkeeper organizations. For

information, contact PAII, P.O. Box 90710, Santa Barbara, CA 93190. Call 805-569-1853 or send faxes to 805-682-1016.

"There is really only one resource to consult when it comes to innkeeping technical assistance—PAII."

Maye and Robert H. Bachofen, The Reluctant Panther, Vermont

innkeeping NEWSLETTER

Coauthors Pat Hardy and Jo Ann M. Bell are the editor and publisher of *innkeeping*, the national monthly newsletter for people who own and run bed-and-breakfast and country inns. Because it's written and published by former innkeepers, the information relates to the real world—you can put it right to work in your own inn. Published monthly since 1982; $75/year, included in PAII membership. Contact PAII, P.O. Box 90710, Santa Barbara, CA 93190. Ask for the index to back issues. Don't open an inn without it!

Here's a sample of subscriber comments:

"Your newsletter is the only one I keep, read, highlight, etc. Thank you a thousand times for being there!"

Jean Wu, Prescott Pines, Arizona

"Of the fifty or so business and trade magazines we receive each month, *innkeeping* is one of the few publications read (and enjoyed!) by everyone in our office. The best ideas come from operators themselves rather than from those in ivory towers."

William J. Hoffman, President, Trigild Corporation, California

"We have really gained a lot from *innkeeping* over the past eight years. We really need you."

Shirley Dittloff, Barrow House, Louisiana

"*innkeeping* is an excellent monthly newsletter that keeps its finger firmly and capably on the pulse of the B&B and country inn industry and often publishes items that inspire articles seen here."

Successful Hotel Marketer

"Articles are germane and to the point, tips are useful. Yours is one of the best trade newsletters I've seen."

Joan and Dane Wells, The Queen Victoria, New Jersey

THINKING OF OPENING AN INN?
This resource is a must

To receive a FREE Aspiring Innkeeper packet, which includes "Ten Questions to Ask Yourself before Buying an Inn" and "List of the Ten Best Resources to Guide You to Success," tear out this page and:

Fast: Mail to PAII, P.O. Box 90710, Santa Barbara, CA 93190
Faster: Call 805-569-1853
Fastest: Fax 805-682-1016 or Internet email jmb@paii.org

 **INDEX**

A

Accountants, 42, 59–60, 89
Accounting:
    computers, 143–6, 253–4;
    need for CPA, 59–60, 67;
    sample accounts, 74–7;
    task distribution, 60
Acquisition costs, 69, 71–2,
    83–8, 100
ADA. *See* Americans with
    Disabilities Act
Advertising, 225–7; outdoor,
    236; radio, 236. *See also*
    Marketing
Alcohol, 52, 173, 183, 279;
    liability 250–1
Ambience, 117–9, 201–2; first
    impression of, 167–8
Amenities, 8, 10, 171–6
American plan, 180; modified,
    5, 180–1
Americans with Disabilities
    Act (ADA), 307; building
    access, 137–41; choosing a
    consultant, 140, 229; em-
    ployees, 256; marketing
    your accessibility, 228–30
Answering machines, 233
Appraisal terms, 101–2
Appraisers, 100–2, 307
Apprenticeships, 29, 108
Architects, 55, 67, 122–3, 124
Arrivals, 247–53; late 247
Artists, 214, 227
Associations, innkeeper, 12,
    286. *See also* Professional
    Association of Innkeepers
    International

Attorneys, 28, 42, 60, 67

B

Balance sheets, 88–9
Bankers, 61, 65, 69, 82, 90–1,
    92–3. *See also* Business plan
Bathrooms, 54, 72, 119,
    122–3, 130–1, 134–5, 140;
    "green," 119; private, 7–8,
    125
Bed-and-breakfast: confusion
    about term, 3; homes, 3;
    hotels, 5
Bed-and-breakfast inns,
    definition of, 4
Beds, 133, 164–5
Bids, obtaining, 122–5, 215
Bookkeeping, 25, 27–8, 59–60;
    for an IRS audit, 270–2; for
    insurance purposes, 281–2;
    on staff, 264–6. *See also*
    Accounting
Breakfast service, 152–60;
    hours, 154, 248; practical
    considerations, 150–2, 154;
    recipes, 155, 157–9;
    settings, 152–60; special
    diets, 155–6, 159
Brochures, 207–17; checklist,
    218; color, 208–10;
    content, 210–13; format,
    212–20; printing, 215;
    using consultants, 206–9,
    214; using your computer
    to design, 215
Brokers, choosing, 110

Budgets, 77–88; development
of, 74; for dinner service,
192–5; reality adjustment,
79, 81. *See also* Chart of
accounts *or* Expenses
Building codes, 52, 122, 123,
124, 126; ADA access,
137–41. *See also* Zoning
Burnout prevention, vii–viii,
13–22, 30–1, 288–94
Business licenses, 52, 54,
99–100
Business plan:
need for, 65–6;
resources for creating, 305;
structure of, 66–71;
uses of, 65–6, 305.
See also Bankers
Business structure of inns,
42–50
Business travelers, 6–8, 32
Buying an inn, 97–110;
disclosures at time of sale,
105–6; finding, 99–100;
increasing income, 103;
negotiation, 104; transition
between owners, 106–8;
valuation, 100–4

C

Cancellations, 245–6, 252
Capital, 69, 73. *See also*
Bankers
Capitalization rate, 101
Cash flow:
analysis, 82, 84, 85, 87, 88;
management of, 285–6;
projection worksheet, 93–4,
300–1, 302
Chart of accounts, 74–7

Check-in/checkout policies,
247–8, 250–3
Checklists:
brochure hints, 208–9;
build your model inn,
99–100;
consider before renovating
your kitchen, 150–2;
disclosures upon sale of an
inn, 105–6;
evaluating existing inns,
35–6;
factors in inn location,
36–7;
federal, state, and local
regulators, 51–4;
forms of payment—
advantages and
disadvantages, 244;
glossary of appraisal terms,
101–3;
guidelines for dealing with
travel writers, 222–3;
guidelines to help you make
wise advertising
decisions, 225–7;
functions of a reservation
form, 248–51;
if I had known then . . . ,
293;
loan proposal ingredients,
91–2;
physical features of your
inn to consider for
renovation, 124;
possible amenities, 10,
171–6;
possible zoning regulations,
38–40;
requirements of reservation
software, 254–5;

researching your market, 30;

resources for acquiring skills, 27–9;

resources for researching your specific location, 34;

shopping list for decorating your inn, 131–7;

skills checklist, 25–7;

solvency strategies that work to manage cash flow, 285–6;

supplies for a kitchen prepared for special diets 156–60;

three steps to setting rates, 282–5;

types of dinner service, 180–1;

ways to increase income, 103–4;

what goes into a business plan?, 65–71;

what makes a "green" room?, 119–21;

what to consider in initial renovation, 129–31;

what to include in your promotion file, 217–20;

why join a group?, 286;

will you make a good innkeeper?, 15–22

Children:
policies concerning, 242–3;
raising at the inn, iv

Chefs:
hiring, 188–92;
job description, 190–1

Color, use of, 170–1

Computer, 3; accounting, 143–6, 253–4; brochure development, 215; marketing, 207, 224–5, 231–2; reservation software selection, 143–6, 254–5, 305; uses, 144. *See also* On-line marketing

Conditional use permit, 40, 97

Consultants, 34, 307;
accessibility (ADA), 140;
brochure, 206–9, 214;
choosing, 28, 58–9;
innkeepers as, 35–6

Contractors, 124–5, 307;
brochure, 206–9, 214;
choosing, 123–4; general, 124–6; independent, 127–8, 266–7; laundry, 161; lien release, 124–5; printing, 215; working with, 126–8

Cookbooks, 236

Corporate travelers, 6–8

Corporation, 45–61;
subchapter S, 46

Costs:
acquisition, per guest room, 72, 81;
before opening, 73, 82, 83, 84, 85, 87, 88;
computer, 144–5;
decorating, 72–3;
renovation, 72, 83, 84, 85, 87, 88;
start-up, 69, 71–4.
See also Renovation

Country inn:
buying an existing, 180;
definition, 4–5

D

Decorating, 117–8, 160, 162–71; costs, 72–3; planning, 162–71, 304; sources and suppliers for, 175–6, 305
Decorators, 171
Definitions of bed-and-breakfast/country inns, 3–5
Deposits, 245
Depreciation, 89
Dietary restrictions, 155–6, 159; kitchen supplies, 156–60
Dinner service, 177–96; equipment, 184–5; financial feasibility, 192–5; kitchen and building readiness, 182–4; menu planning, 184; personal involvement of owner, 182; pros and cons, 179–80; staffing, 185–92; type of service, 180–1
Direct mail, 230–1; computer database, 254–5
Disabled guests. *See* Americans with Disabilities Act

E

Employees. *See* Staff
Environment: effect on, 40–1; "green" rooms, 119–21, 305
Equipment: "green" room, 119–21; kitchen, 151, 184–5; laundry, 161–2
Existing inns: benefits, 97–9;

evaluation, 35; valuing, 100–3. *See also* Buying an inn
Expansion, 4, 6, 11–12, 32, 88
Expenses: 5-room inn, 79–83, 89; 7-room inn, 79, 84–6, 89; 9-room inn, 79, 87–8, 89; chart of accounts, 74–7; dinner service, 193–5; operating, 101; projected, 79–89. *See also* Business Plan *and* Chart of Accounts

F

Federal regulations, 51
Fictitious business names, 52
Financial feasibility: dinner service, 192–5. *See also* Expenses
Financial publications, 305
Financial statements, 88–91; balance sheets, 88–9; developing budget, 74–7; personal, 13, 49, 70; projecting income, 77–9
Financing, 90–5; business plan, 65–71. *See also* Bankers
Finding construction workers, 123–4
Fire, 53
Fireplaces, 144–6
Floor plan, 160–1, 171, 304
Floors, 166, 168, 169, 170. *See also* Decorating
Food services: restrictions, 39, 54–5, 56; skills needed, 182
Furnishing. *See* Decorating

Furniture. *See* Decorating

G

Gift certificates, 228
Goodwill, 102
Government regulations, 3–5, 50–4; alcoholic beverage, 52; building, 24–6, 52, 122–3; fire, 53; health, 54–5; lobbying to change, 56–9, 306; planning, 37–8, 53, 55–6; review boards, 53; taxes, 51–2, 54. *See also* Zoning
Grandfathered conditions, 40, 97
"Green" rooms, 119–21, 305
Guests:
    arrival of, 247, 253;
    expectations of, 8;
    profile of, 31–3, 40;
    repeat visits, 230–1;
    spending in community, 40;
    types of, 31–3
Guidebooks, inn, 220

H

Health department, 39, 54–5
Historical preservation, 3–5, 41, 71, 123, 305. *See also* Renovation
Hotels vs. inns, 3, 9–11, 40–1

I

Income and expense statement, 88–9

Income:
    dinner service, 192–3;
    personal benefit, 70;
    projection of, 77–9
Influencing governing bodies, 37–42, 55–8, 306
Innkeeper associations, 286–8, 308
Innkeepers:
    as good neighbors, 40–1;
    burnout, 288–94;
    desirable traits of, 12–22;
    how to talk to, 35–6;
    lifestyle adjustments, 9, 13, 30–1;
    living on site, 3–4, 9;
    professionalism of, 15, 239;
    single, 14;
    skills checklist for, 25–27;
    workshops for prospective, 308–9
Innkeeping:
    competition in, 8–9;
    support services, 12, 58;
    trends in, 9–12
Innkeeping newsletter, 12, 309
Innsitting, 108. *See also* Apprenticeships
Inspections, 3, 11, 39, 54–5, 98
Insurance, 12, 61, 273–82; choosing an agent, 306, 307–8; definitions of coverage, 274–7; during renovation, 124, 127–8, 279–80; fireplaces, 143; information from agent, 281–2; questions about, 274, 277–80, 306; workers' compensation, 279–80
Interior design. *See* Decorating
International guests, 236

Internet. *See* On-line
marketing
Interviewing, 191–2, 257–8,
268–9
Investment analysis, 88
IRS, 269–73; looking like a
business, 271–2; minimizing
audit, 272

J
Job descriptions, 189, 190,
256, 267

K
Keys, 174
Kitchens:
furnishing, 184–5;
health codes, 45, 154;
licensing standards, 40,
183;
organization of, 150–2,
183–4

L
Laundry, 161; saving time and
water with "green" rooms,
120
Leasing inns, 111–14
Legal structure of inn business,
42–50
Liability, 45–50, 276–7. *See
also* Insurance
Licenses, 97–8, 105; business,
52, 54; liquor, 52
Lien release, 162, 163, 165,
166, 170, 174
Lifestyle changes, 3–5, 13,
30–1, 49, 288–93

Lighting, 167
Limited liability company,
46–7
Linens, 3, 6, 162, 165, 170,
174
Liquor:
considerations for serving,
183;
evening beverage service,
173;
insurance, 279;
license, 52, 97
Loans:
sources of, 90–3.
See also Bankers
Location, researching a, 29.
See also Site selection
Logo:
designing, 205–6;
using a computer, 226.
See also Name

M
Maintenance, skills needed, 16,
20, 26, 28
Manager, 257, 259
MAP, 5, 180, 181, 185
Marketing, 306; business plan,
67; computer use, 215,
224–5; creating an image,
201–2; direct mail, 230–1;
materials needed, 217–20;
niche, 201–2; ongoing,
216–36; research, 30, 40;
skills needed, 25–6;
telephone, 232–5;
through travel agents, 232;
to disabled guests, 228;
urban inns, 6–8; use of
brochure, 207; use of

special events, 223–4. *See also* Advertising
Meals, planning. *See* Breakfast service *and* Dinner service
Mechanics lien, 124
Media, 221–3; kit, 217–20, 221–3
Menu planning:
    as it affects dinner-serving style, 180–1, 184;
    breakfast, 152–9

N
Name selection, 202–5
Negotiating, 104
Newsletter:
    direct mail, 230–1;
    industry, 308;
    Innkeeping, 309
Niche, 201–2

O
Occupancy rates, projection of, 78–9
On-line marketing, 224–5
Operating expenses, 101
Organizing, 239, 248, 253;
    computer use, 254–5;
    marketing, 216–17;
    operating expenses, 101;
    reservations, 252–3

P
PAII. *See* Professional Association of Innkeepers International
Painting, 161, 168, 169, 171
Parking, 38–9

Partnership, 43–5, 49–50
Payment:
    forms of, 244–5;
    policies concerning, 245–6, 249;
    received, 252, 253
Permits, 40, 73; building, 52; business license, 54; health, 54; sales tax, 51
Personal benefit income, 70
Personnel. *See* Staff
Pets, policies concerning, 242–3
Photographs, 208–9, 216, 217–8, 219, 230
Planning department 37–8, 53, 55–6
Policies, 211, 241–8; cancellation, 245–6, 251, 252–3; check–in/checkout, 247–8; children and pets, 242–3; deposit, 245; hiring and staff, 260; payment, 244–6, 249; smoking, 242, 251
PR agency, 235
Press:
    kit, 217–20;
    travel writers, 221–23
Printer selection, 215
Professional Association of Innkeepers International (PAII), 108, 308–9
Professionalism, 14, 15–22, 239–40
Profit and loss statement, 88–9
Promotions, 216–36, 306. *See also* Advertising, Marketing, Press
Properties:
    adjoining, 36;

comparison of, 35–7, 83–7, 300–1

Property evaluation forms, 300–1; 5–room inns, 83; 7–room inns, 85; 9–room inns, 87

Publications, 305–9. *See also* Newsletter

R

Rates, 77, 81–2; setting, 251, 282–5

Realtors, 58–9; working with, 99–100, 104, 110

Recipes for breakfast, 152–9, 306

References on job applicants, 258

Remodeling. *See* Renovation

Renovation, 72, 122–5, 129–31, 232, 305; accommodations for disabled guests, 137–41; bids on, 122–5; costs, 129; fireplaces, 141–3; "green" rooms, 119–21; kitchen, 150–2; site selection, 29–37; working with subcontractors, 126–8

Research: PAII B&B/Country Inn Industry Study, 10, 74, 77, 305; Yellow Brick Road Guest Survey, 40

Reservations, 232–5, 248–51; cancellations of, 245–6, 252; form used for, 252, 254; use of calendar, 252

Reservations service organization (RSO), 3

Return-on-investment calculation, 88

Room rates, calculation of, 77, 282–5

S

Safety, 52, 163; fireplaces, 142–3; for disabled guests, 139–40, 273–4, 281–2

SCORE, 34, 92

Service: definition of, 240–1; dining room, 186–7, 196; mise en place, 195; trends in, 9–12. *See also* Amenities

Shopping: for furnishings, 131–7; for kitchen and dining room supplies, 184–5

Signs, 38, 54

Single innkeepers, 14, 43

Site selection, 6–8, 29–37

Skills, 12, 15–22; checklist, 25–9; methods of acquiring, 27–9

Small Business Administration (SBA), 34, 92

Smoking, policies concerning, 242, 251

Software, innkeeping, 254–5

Sole proprietorship, 43

Soundproofing 125

Special events, 223–4

Staff, 27, 303; dinner service, 185–92; employer responsibility, 264–6; finding, 108, 256–7; firing, 266; handling tips, 261; hiring, 257–9; independent contractors, 127–8, 266–7; record-keeping, 51, 264–6; retaining and promoting, 261–4; training, 27, 28, 29, 69–72, 259–60, 306; transition between owners, 99, 107–8

Start–up costs, 69, 71–4; projected financial needs, 69, 82–3, 84, 85–8; working capital, 69, 73–4. *See also* Renovation *and* Decorating

Stress. *See* Burnout prevention

Success, 6

T

Tax:
credits, 89;
identification numbers for, 51;
implications, 47–8;
IRS, 269–73;
local, 54;
sales permits, 51;
self-employment, 51;
understanding, 47

Telephones, 146–9, 173; answering machines, 149–50; answering services, 150; cellular phones, 149; computer aided, 148; in-room, 147–8; systems, 147–8; use in marketing, 232–5, 243, 251

Tips, housekeeping, 261

Tourist, definition of, 32

Training, 187–8, 259–60, 261; video, 306. *See also* Apprenticeships

Travel agents, 232

Travel writers. *See* Press

Trends, 5–12; "Green" rooms, 119–21

Typesetting, 213, 214–15

Turndown service, 172–3

U

Urban inns, 6–8

V

Vacancy sign, 202

Valuation of existing inn, 100–3; appraisers, 100–2; assessors, 54, 89; goodwill, 102

Voice mail, 234

W

Wait staff, 185–92. *See also* Dinner service

Wall treatments, 168–9. *See also* Decorating

Wholesale, 176

Windows, coverings for, 169–70. *See also* Decorating

Workers' compensation, 266, 271, 279–80

Working capital, 69, 73–4, 82–3, 84, 85–8

Worksheets:
cash flow projection, 302;
inn location, 297–8;
personal benefits, 70;

personal financial
statement, 299;
property evaluation, 300–1;
room planning, 304
Workshops for prospective
innkeepers, 309
Writers, travel, 221–3. *See also*
Guidebooks *and* Press

Z

Zoning, 37–42; changing laws,
37–42, 55–9; grandfathered
conditions of, 40; influ-
encing decision makers,
40–2, 55–9; regulations,
38–40